TRANSLATING THE MIDDLE AGES

Translating the Middle Ages

Edited by
KAREN L. FRESCO
University of Illinois at Urbana-Champaign, USA

CHARLES D. WRIGHT
University of Illinois at Urbana-Champaign, USA

LONDON AND NEW YORK

First published 2012 by Ashgate Publishing

Published 2016 by Routledge
2 Park Square, Milton Park, Abingdon, Oxon OX14 4RN
711 Third Avenue, New York, NY 10017, USA

First issued in paperback 2017

Routledge is an imprint of the Taylor & Francis Group, an informa business

British Library Cataloguing in Publication Data
Translating the Middle Ages.
1. Translating and interpreting – History – To 1500. 2. Transmission of texts – History – To 1500. 3. Language and culture.
I. Fresco, Karen Louise, 1947– II. Wright, Charles Darwin, 1954–
418'.02'0902–dc23

Library of Congress Cataloging-in-Publication Data
Translating the Middle Ages / edited by Karen L. Fresco and Charles D. Wright.
p. cm.
Includes bibliographical references and index.
1. Translating and interpreting—History. 2. Literature—Translations—History and criticism. I. Fresco, Karen Louise, 1947– II. Wright, Charles D.

PN886.T75 2012
418'.0209—dc23

2012014717

ISBN 13: 978-1-138-10813-4 (pbk)
ISBN 13: 978-1-4094-4697-2 (hbk)

Contents

List of Figures

List of Contributors

Robert W. Barrett, Jr., is Associate Professor of English, Medieval Studies, and Theatre at the University of Illinois at Urbana-Champaign. His most recent publications include the monograph *Against All England: Regional Identity and Cheshire Writing, 1195–1656* (2009) and an essay on food and ethnicity in the Chester Shepherds' Play for the collection *Mapping the Medieval City: Space, Place, and Identity in Chester c. 1200–1600* (2011). He is currently editing the Chester Whitsun Plays for the TEAMS Middle English Texts Series.

Catherine Batt is Senior Lecturer in Medieval Literature at the School of English, University of Leeds. Her research interests include translation, material culture, gender studies, poetics and the representation of women, Anglo-Norman Literature, Arthurian Literature, early and later Middle English romance, saints' lives, devotional literature, and twentieth-century medievalism. She has published on, inter alia, Clemence of Barking, Caxton, the Gawain-Poet, Thomas Hoccleve (including *Essays on Thomas Hoccleve* [1996]), Thomas Malory (including *Malory's Morte Darthur: Remaking Arthurian Tradition* [New York, 2002]), and Sylvia Townsend Warner. Her translation of Henry, Duke of Lancaster's *Book of Holy Medicines* is forthcoming with the French of England Translation Series, University of Arizona Press.

Jeanette Beer, Emerita Professor of French, Purdue University, is a Senior Member of Lady Margaret Hall and of St. Hilda's College, Oxford. She is the author of *Villehardouin—Epic Historian*, *A Medieval Caesar*, *Narrative Conventions of Truth in the Middle Ages*, *Medieval Fables—Marie de France*, *Master Richard's Bestiary of Love and Response*, *Early Prose in France*, and *Beasts of Love—Richard de Fournival's* Bestiaire d'amour *and a Woman's Response*; the editor of several books on medieval translation; and general editor for many years of *Teaching Language Through Literature*, the *Romance Languages Annual*, and *Purdue Studies in Romance Literatures*. She is the recipient of awards from, among others, the National Endowment for the Humanities, the American Philosophical Society, and the American Council of Learned Societies.

Alison Cornish is Professor of Italian at the University of Michigan, Ann Arbor. She is the author of a book on astronomy in the *Divine Comedy* (*Reading Dante's Stars,* Yale 2000), and of various articles on Dante, Boccaccio, Petrarch, and Elsa Morante. Her most recent book is a study on early translation in Italy (*Vernacular Translation in Dante's Italy: Illiterate Literature*). She has been a fellow at the Harvard University Center for Renaissance Studies, Villa I Tatti, and is currently working on readership in fourteenth- and fifteenth-century Italy.

Réka Forrai earned her PhD degree in medieval studies at the Central European University-Budapest with a dissertation entitled "The Interpreter of the Popes:

The Translation Project of Anastasius Bibliothecarius" (2008). Her research focuses on the history of Greek-Latin translations in the Middle Ages.

Russell Hopley is a Lecturer in Arabic Studies at Bowdoin College in Brunswick, Maine. His research interests focus on Islam in the western Mediterranean during the twelfth and thirteenth centuries. He has published articles on the plague in medieval North Africa and Islamic Spain, the practice of hostage-taking and ransoming in medieval Iberia, and most recently, trade and commerce in the western Mediterranean during the Almoravid and Almohad periods. He is currently preparing a study of the Arabic poetry of Islamic Sicily.

Christopher Kleinhenz is the Carol Mason Kirk Professor Emeritus of Italian at the University of Wisconsin-Madison, where, from 1968 to 2007, he taught medieval Italian literature. Among his numerous publications are *The Early Italian Sonnet* (1986) and *Medieval Italy: An Encyclopedia* (2004). He served as President of the American Association of Teachers of Italian, the American Boccaccio Association, and the Medieval Association of the Midwest, and as Editor of *Dante Studies*. A Fellow of the Medieval Academy of America, he has received the Fiorino d'Oro from the Società Dantesca Italiana, the Chancellor's Award for Excellence in Teaching, the CARA Award for Outstanding Service to Medieval Studies, the AATI Distinguished Service Award, and the ADFL Award for Distinguished Service in the Profession.

Aden Kumler is an Assistant Professor of Art History at the University of Chicago and the author of *Translating Truth: Ambitious Images and Religious Knowledge in Late Medieval France and England* (New Haven, 2011), as well as articles in the journals *Studies in Iconography* and *Res: Anthropology and Aesthetics*.

Brian Merrilees is Professor Emeritus of French at the University of Toronto and a specialist in medieval lexicography and Anglo-Norman language. His early publications included *The Voyage of Saint Brendan* in English (1979) and French (1984, 2006) with Ian Short, and editions for the Anglo-Norman Text Society. In 1994 he and William Edwards published *Le Dictionnaire de Firmin Le Ver* with Brepols, for which he was awarded the Prix Honoré Chavée by the Académie des Inscriptions et Belles Lettres (France); he has since coedited two other Latin-French dictionaries (1998, 2002). Since 2002 he has been a Fellow of the Royal Society of Canada.

Ana Pairet is Associate Professor of French at Rutgers University, New Brunswick. The author of a study of medieval narratives of metamorphosis (Honoré Champion, 2002), she has worked extensively on the transmission of Ovid in the late Middle Ages. Her current book project on the dynamics of translation in early print culture focuses on adaptations of French courtly romances in the Iberian Peninsula.

Russell Stone is a Postdoctoral Fellow in Core Humanities at the University of Nevada. His work on classical histories and medieval romances of Alexander the Great has been recently published in *Viator* and *Medium Aevum*. At present, he is completing *From Tyrant to Philosopher-King: A Literary History of Alexander the*

Great in Medieval and Early Modern England, a survey of the lasting influence of Latin and Greek histories of the conqueror and the creation of his political legacy.

Ryan Szpiech is Assistant Professor of Spanish and Judaic Studies at the University of Michigan. He has recently edited a special issue of the *Journal of Medieval Iberian Studies* 3.2 (2011) on the subject of "Gender and Genre in Later-Medieval Separad: Love, Sex, and Polemics in Hebrew Writing from Christian Iberia" and has also recently contributed a chapter to the *Oxford Handbook of Medieval Latin Literature* (2012). He has edited and translated Arabic and Latin selections from the *Pugio Fidei* of Ramón Martí, and is currently a coeditor of the critical edition of the text, to be published by the Bibliotheca Philosophorum Medii Aevi Cataloniae. He has published articles on the writing of converts Alfonso of Valladolid, Pablo de Santa María, Juan Andrés, and Anselm Turmeda, and has also written a book-length study of conversion narratives in medieval polemical texts entitled *Conversion and Narrative: Reading Authority in Medieval Polemic* (forthcoming from University of Pennsylvania Press).

Boris A. Todorov has been full-time Lecturer at Yonsei University, Seoul, and is presently Advanced Academia Fellow of the Centre for Advanced Studies, Sofia. He obtained his PhD in medieval history from UCLA in 2007. His recent and forthcoming publications include "The Value of Empire: Tenth-Century Bulgaria between Magyars, Pechenegs, and Byzantium" in the *Journal of Medieval History* 36 (2010), and the chapter on "Trnovo" in the two-volume *Europe: A Literary History, 1348–1418*, edited by D. Wallace (forthcoming with Oxford University Press).

Editors' Foreword

Translating the Middle Ages includes 13 contributions originally presented at an international conference held at the University of Illinois at Urbana-Champaign on 28–29 October 2008. From the earliest planning stages our intention was not to limit our theme to the examination of textual translation or to one particular national or linguistic tradition. Rather, we hoped that bringing together medievalists working on translation from different perspectives and within a variety of disciplinary traditions would impart new synergy to a subject already very much in the forefront of current work in medieval studies. This was certainly the case at the conference, and we believe that the essays we have been able to include in the present volume will "translate" that synergy for a much broader audience, not only of medievalists but also of scholars in other periods who can benefit from the diverse methods and approaches to translation exemplified herein.

Another important dimension of "translating the Middle Ages" is the modern translation of medieval texts, which was represented at the conference by American poet-translators W.S. Merwin and Robert Pinsky, who discussed their English translations of Dante's *Divina Commedia* in a "CultureTalk" event moderated by novelist and University of Illinois Swanlund Professor Richard Powers. In a memorable evening at the Krannert Center for the Performing Arts, Merwin (whose papers are held by the University of Illinois Rare Book and Manuscript Library) read from his translation of the *Purgatorio*[1] and Pinsky read from his translation of the *Inferno*.[2] Professor Powers then engaged the two poets in a wide-ranging conversation about how they were drawn to translate Dante, what intellectual and aesthetic challenges they confronted in the process, and why Dante's *Commedia* remains so powerful for modern readers. And in the week preceding the conference, a "Dante marathon" organized by Professor Eleonora Stoppino of the Department of Spanish, Italian, and Portuguese featured readings by volunteer faculty and students of the entire *Commedia* in translation, canto by canto, in nearly a dozen different languages.

The editors wish to express our gratitude to the William and Flora Hewlett International Endowment for providing a generous grant that made the conference possible. We are grateful also to W.S. Merwin and Robert Pinsky for discussing their translations of Dante; to the Steven Barclay Agency (representing both poets); to former University of Illinois Chancellor Richard Hermann and the Center for

---

[1] Dante Alighieri, *Purgatorio: A New Verse Translation*, trans. W.S. Merwin (New York, 2000). Merwin's papers include not only the drafts and materials relating to his translation of the *Purgatorio*, but a nearly complete draft of an unpublished translation of the *Paradiso*.

[2] *The Inferno of Dante: A New Verse Translation*, trans. Robert Pinsky (New York, 1994).

Advanced Study for sponsoring and funding the CultureTalk event; to the Krannert Center for the Performing Arts and its Director Mike Ross for hosting it; and to our colleague Richard Powers for moderating it so superbly. Additional generous financial support for the conference was provided by the Program in Medieval Studies, the College of Liberal Arts and Sciences, the School of Literatures, Cultures, and Linguistics, the Center for Translation Studies, the Center for South Asian and Middle Eastern Studies, the Illinois Program for Research in the Humanities, the Program in Comparative and World Literature, the Departments of English, Germanic Languages and Literatures, History, Spanish, Italian, and Portugese, as well as the Department of French's pluridisciplinary center, French@Illinois, and the World Wide Universities Network. We would also like to thank all of the conference participants, including the members of the Medieval Studies Advisory Committee and its graduate student member, Kimberly Fonzo, who evaluated abstracts submitted for the conference; the speakers, including those who were not able to offer their papers for the present volume; and the audiences who contributed to lively discussions. Special thanks are due to our editorial assistant, Amity Reading, who copyedited and formatted the essays according to the Ashgate stylesheet.

Finally, we are grateful to Catherine Batt, who not only contributed an essay of her own but also very kindly agreed to write the introduction to the volume and to the individual sections, surveying the arguments and highlighting the significance of each of the contributions to *Translating the Middle Ages*.

Urbana, November 2011

Introduction

Catherine Batt

> The practice of translation remains a risky operation which is always in search of its theory.[1]

The medievalist, by virtue of the discipline, continually inhabits, practices, works with, negotiates, evaluates, and interprets translation and its several manifestations. If Paul Ricoeur's remark about translation practice and theory—a remark applicable to all intellectual endeavor, including that of the medievalist as simultaneously investigator and practitioner of translation—is inconclusive about their relation, his term "linguistic hospitality" nevertheless offers an appealing, even seductive, trope for translation as reciprocity and exchange.[2] To think of two languages as host and guest, as of necessity mutually accommodating, gives their relationship a particular dynamism, and opens it up to scrutiny from a new perspective, not least when one considers how the roles of host and guest might themselves be ultimately interchangeable. (Brian Merrilees's essay for this volume features, pertinently, the Old French *hostelables*, a translation of the Latin *hospitabilis*, which is glossed as "one who freely gives hospitality or who is worthy of being received as a guest" [p. 15]).[3] Ricoeur also sees translation as properly defining not only relations between different languages, but between different registers from within "the same linguistic community."[4] Alan Shapiro, writing about his own experience of literary translation, welcomes and elaborates on Ricoeur's image of hospitality as cultural openness and mutual enrichment, both for its acknowledgment that communication is, in fine, based on difference, and for its image of translators

---

1 Paul Ricoeur, *On Translation*, trans. Eileen Brennan, intro. Richard Kearney (London, 2006), p. 33. Ricoeur's *Sur la traduction* (Paris, 2004) was unavailable, though a comparison between it, Kearney's translated excerpts in his introduction, and Brennan's full translation, could prove fruitful. On the dangers and necessity of translating theory, see Sarah Kay, "Translating Theory," *New Medieval Literatures* 9 (2007): 199–202. Kay observes, p. 199, that theory is itself "a tool of translation."

2 Ricoeur, *On Translation*, p. 10 and passim. See also Kearney's discussion in the introduction, pp. xv–xvii.

3 On the permeability of the host-guest relation, see further Jacques Derrida, *On Hospitality*, trans. Rachel Bowlby (Stanford, 2000), pp. 123–5.

4 Ricoeur, *On Translation*, p. 24.

as "both host and guest: we simultaneously inhabit the other's words in their linguistic home even as we receive the other's words into our own."[5]

The hospitality metaphor is saved from sentimentality by the sense of danger an open invitation ushers in; just who might arrive at one's home, and with what consequences? It also has the advantage of providing an arguably more flexible and imaginative way of considering relations between source and target languages than does the timeworn association of translation with the poles of fidelity and betrayal (even though it is in part grounded in it), the culturally compromising nature of which Lori Chamberlain's critique exposes.[6] In response to the trope's assumptions about gender, sex, social organization, hierarchy and power, Chamberlain aims to readdress the question of translation's power relations in more productively fluid terms, even though recourse to Derrida's writing on translation as a "solution" perhaps instead raises further questions about the ingrained quality of certain modes of expression and thought.[7] No one metaphor does adequate service to describe or to facilitate the work of translation, of course, and the host-guest relation is no less culturally revealing than any other formulation. What is important is the nature of the space it sets up for interpretative thinking, and the awareness it requires of the investigator/practitioner about how that space has been established.

The broadening of translation as a category to include all forms of linguistic communication, within, as well as across, languages, together with the self-conscious critical investigation of metaphors for translation, would seem to confirm the trend Eliot Weinberger (perhaps most well known as the translator of Octavio Paz) identifies in a witty and aphoristic lecture on his own work:

> there is, perhaps, no subject in literature more suited for theoretical rumination in its current modes than translation: the authority of the author, the transformation of the sign, the tenuousness of signifier and signified, the politics of what is/isn't translated and how it is translated, the separation of text and author, the crossing (or impossibility of crossing) cultural barriers, the relativism of the translation as discourse, the translator as agent of political/cultural hegemony, and so on. All of which are sometimes interesting in themselves, but generally unhelpful when one actually translates... .With this preoccupation with the translator—and the self-evident and now excessively elaborated corollary that everything is a form of translation—the translator has suddenly become an important person, and explaining translation a minor but comfortable academic career and a source of invitations to conferences in exotic climes.[8]

---

[5] Alan Shapiro, "Translation as 'Linguistic Hospitality,'" *Literary Imagination* 12 (2010): 140–50 at 142.

[6] Lori Chamberlain, "Gender and the Metaphorics of Translation," *Signs* 13.3 (1988): 454–72.

[7] See also Ruth Evans, "Translating Past Cultures?" in Roger Ellis and Ruth Evans (eds), *The Medieval Translator* 4 (Exeter, 1994), pp. 20–45 at p. 42, note 45.

[8] Eliot Weinberger, *Anonymous Sources: A Talk on Translators and Translation*, Encuentros 39 (Washington, DC, 2000), p. 10.

While impressing on his audience the necessity of translation, Weinberger, above all practical and pragmatic, claims a relatively modest role for his profession and at the same time declares a rift between what he terms "so-called theory" and the parameters of his own practice. He also denies that, as a translator, he is best placed to be a literary critic: "my expertise is entirely microscopic," he says of his knowledge of Paz: "I am a tree surgeon rather than an ecologist."[9] However, Weinberger sees a particular function for translation. It is, for example, necessary to any culture's growth: "Translation is not appropriation, as is sometimes claimed; it is a form of listening that then changes how you speak." It is also a question of "invent(ing) a new music for the text in the translation-language" as part of what he calls translation as "advocacy criticism," which brings foreign literature to new audiences. Weinberger is also firm that as a translator he is not himself a writer, but someone writing by proxy, one who is anonymous, although, he acknowledges, the translator may, paradoxically, be held to account for what another has written, or has perceived.[10]

If Weinberger as practitioner can cheerfully dispense with theory, *pace* Ricoeur's pronouncement, where does the medievalist, seeking to recuperate and understand medieval translation across time, and for whom it can be simply a statement of fact that "everything is a form of translation," stand with regard to theory and practice? Weinberger's experience as a modern practitioner usefully begs comparison and contrast with medieval translation practice. A medieval translator—one fictionalized example is Chaucer's narrator in *The Legend of Good Women*, the prologue to which concerns in part the translator's answerability for the works he draws on[11]—might well sympathize with the modern translator's simultaneous attempt to circumscribe the creative reach of his craft, and to recognize the inherent and uncontrollable dangers of making public a work that is and is not his own. A medieval translator would also know the joy of cross-fertilizing languages, and of finding new contexts and audiences for texts through their translation, whether into a vernacular or a learned language. But not all translators, medieval or modern, might share Weinberger's avowed purpose, or identical ideological or political perspectives and aims. At the same time, the situation the modern translator describes (interestingly, as novel), toward the end of his essay, has something in common with the flux of medieval culture and the situation in which medieval writers may find themselves, whereby international cultural traffic is such as to translate the translator, repositioning and refiguring him and his work in unexpected ways.

The medievalist her/himself, meanwhile, a kind of proxy writer by proxy, is involved in many ways with translation; s/he has of practical necessity (through ignorance of a medieval language, for example) to be an audience for others'

---

9 Ibid., pp. 11–12.

10 Ibid., pp. 5, 8, 9, 13.

11 Chaucer, *The Legend of Good Women*, in Larry D. Benson (gen. ed.), *The Riverside Chaucer*, 3rd ed. (Oxford, 2008), pp. 587–630.

translations, one acutely aware of the mediated nature of the texts in question.[12] And the medievalist has to be a translator her/himself, and to justify and interpret the value of the past to present audiences. Furthermore, as the self-conscious tropes for translation perception and practice remind one, and as Ruth Evans's powerful overview of theoretical and practical approaches to translation in the Middle Ages makes clear, "(t)ranslation is itself a metaphor for the kind of negotiation between past and present cultures which medievalists constantly perform."[13]

The terms of that negotiation are themselves continually under revision. The Cardiff Medieval Translator conference, for example, hosted triennially and peripatetically by Western European institutions, and now just one forum among several for continuing debates about medieval translation, has greatly expanded, in terms of practice, range of topic, and theoretical approach, since the first set of conference proceedings, marked by a careful practical and theoretical circumspection of what then seemed largely uncharted territory, appeared in 1989.[14] Projects such as *The Oxford History of Literary Translation in English* not only recognize translation as mainstream, integral to medieval and post-medieval culture, but are also internally in productive debate, and pleasingly inclusive—volume 1 of the Oxford project, for example, both makes possible comparison of medieval and early modern texts, and has room to consider such topics as scientific and medical writing.[15] The Conference on *Translating the Middle Ages*, organized by Karen Fresco and Charles D. Wright, at the University of Illinois at Urbana-Champaign in 2008, under the auspices of the Program in Medieval Studies (in collaboration with the Center for Translation Studies), where versions of the papers in this volume were first presented, proves the continuing value of bringing together scholars from a wide variety of disciplines to share information and ideas. Ruth Evans identifies as "problematic" the relation between "empirically driven scholarship" and "theoretically-informed approaches," though she notes

---

12 On the role of translation in comparative studies, see Michelle R. Warren, "Translating in the Zone," *New Medieval Literatures* 9 (2007): 191–8.

13 Evans, "Translating Past Cultures?" p. 36.

14 Roger Ellis (ed.), assisted by Jocelyn Price [Wogan-Browne], Stephen Medcalf and Peter Meredith, *The Medieval Translator: The Theory and Practice of Translation in the Middle Ages*, papers read at a conference held 20–23 August 1987 at the University of Wales Conference Centre, Gregynog Hall (Cambridge, 1989). The *Medieval Translator* volumes have been published by Brepols, Turnhout, since 1996. Jeanette Beer has also undertaken important editing work in the wake of conferences; see Jeanette Beer (ed.), *Translation Theory and Practice in the Middle Ages* (Kalamazoo, 1997), which arose from sessions at the 1993 Kalamazoo Medieval Congress, on "Theory and Practice of Translation in Middle Ages"; see also her collections with a focus on translation in early France: Jeanette Beer (ed.), *Medieval Translators and their Craft* (Kalamazoo, 1989), and Jeanette Beer and Kenneth Lloyd-Jones (eds), *Translation and the Transmission of Culture between 1300 and 1600* (Kalamazoo, 1995).

15 Roger Ellis (ed.), *The Oxford History of Literary Translation in English*, vol. 1: *To 1550* (Oxford, 2008).

also that these perspectives need not be exclusive.[16] One solution, as Evans herself implies, is to listen carefully to the specificities of medieval cultures themselves, as do these articles. The diversity of approaches and fields of study apparent here emerges as a strength because of the valuable work it performs in gathering insights across a range of complementary subjects and approaches, in a way that is mutually illuminating. As translation both describes and effects relations between languages and cultures, so translation studies have the potential continually to expand the grounds on which one understands not only past cultures, but their relation one to another.

Translation studies are increasingly sensitive to the effects of linguistic diversity and of cultural materialism; examples in late-medieval British studies include the work of such as Mark Ormrod, who stresses the need to take into account a language's diverse registers, as well as oral and written contexts, in considering the interrelation of English, French, and Latin; of Ardis Butterfield, who asks how medieval people experienced their multilingual cultures; and of Jocelyn Wogan-Browne and others at work on the French of England.[17] The essays from the Illinois conference are attuned to the consequences of medieval cultures' own appreciation that translation is more than the simple conversion of data from one language into another—Christopher Kleinhenz is particularly eloquent on this topic in his work on Dante—and that languages do not exist in isolation, either from other languages or from their broader culture. And the horizons of translation and translation study are broadened further by means of the general assumption that language itself demands consideration within the broader contexts of cultural artifacts, of the material and the visual, which gives these essays, collectively, their particular strength.

The essays' organization into sections here indicates how they speak one to another about various aspects of medieval translation practice and its recuperation: lexis; the conceptualizing of spiritual selfhood; literature within, and across, boundaries of nation, space and time, and genre; and translation's implication in ideology, politics, and religion. There are, of course, other conversations to connect with, between, and across the individual essays and their groupings, notably about their shared interests in the diverse ways in which translation has been understood and deployed in the medieval period and beyond, the relation between word and image, the projection, appropriation, and manipulation of authority, and the culturally revealing tropes of translation itself. This arrangement simply offers a means of access for considering how different investigations into medieval translation studies might prove mutually informing.

---

[16] Evans, "Translating Past Cultures?" p. 36.

[17] Mark Ormrod, "The Use of English: Language, Law, and Political Culture in Fourteenth-Century England," *Speculum* 78 (2003): 750–87; Ardis Butterfield, *The Familiar Enemy: Chaucer, Language and Nation in the Hundred Years War* (Oxford, 2009); Jocelyn Wogan-Browne (ed.), with Carolyn Collette, Maryanne Kowaleski, Linne Mooney, Ad Putter, and David Trotter, *Language and Culture in Medieval Britain: The French of England c.1100–c.1500* (Woodbridge, 2009).

These essays all in some way interrogate, and reinvestigate, accepted categories and interpretations, working with the close details of cultural, literary, and linguistic analysis to identify areas for fresh investigation and new forms of engagement, methodologies that recognize, among other things, the cultural embeddedness of linguistic evidence. They belong to the same impulse to cultural reconfiguring as, for example, Butterfield's work, mentioned above, or Denis Renevey and Christiania Whitehead's call for a history of translation that focuses on literature's "points of dissemination" rather than on "national boundaries," the better to appreciate the medieval period's "networks of ideological exchange and cultural influence";[18] or again, as the work of David Wallace and his collaborators, in "Regeneration: A Literary History of Medieval Europe, 1348–1418," with its re-mapping of European literary and cultural interconnections, a project that yields important information about the cultural translation and reinvention of writers, as well as of texts.[19]

Clemence, a learned nun writing at Barking Abbey in England in the late twelfth century, justifies her translation of the *Life of St. Catherine* in her introduction to her work, and outlines her method; an earlier translation of this *Life* exists, she says, but fashions change, and people are more exigent, critical and demanding now than once they were: "E aprés nus serrunt uncore" [and they will be even more so after our time]:[20] Clemence works in both Latin and French, acknowledging her romance pre-text even as she exploits the possibilities her Latin source (and, as becomes evident in the course of her retelling, other Latin texts) offers. Clemence gives a rationale for translation practice as literary creativity that holds good also for translation studies in general; translation is integral to rereading. To return to Ricoeur's aside on the apparent elusiveness of an overarching theory of translation, theory is inherent in translation's continuing practice, as in the critical inquiry that attends it. The primary "risk" of the undertaking is perhaps simply that of not knowing where the attempt to engage with communication may lead. The hospitality metaphor serves translation (and the study of translation practice) well because it accommodates dynamic reciprocity, but also that element of the unexpected.

---

18 Denis Renevey and Christiania Whitehead (eds), *Lost in Translation?*, The Medieval Translator / Traduire au Moyen Âge 12 (Turnhout, 2009), pp. 1–13 at p. 13.

19 For the "Regeneration" project, see David Wallace, "Problematics of European Literary History, 1348–1400," in Indira Ghose and Denis Renevey (eds), *The Construction of Textual Identity in Medieval and Early Modern Literature* (Tübingen, 2009), pp. 38–109; <http://www.english.upenn.edu/~dwallace/regeneration/>. See also such initiatives as the French of England and French of Italy projects at Fordham University: <http://www.fordham.edu /frenchofengland/> and <http://www.fordham.edu/frenchofitaly/>.

20 Clemence of Barking, *The Life of St. Catherine*, ed. William MacBain, Anglo-Norman Text Society 18 (Oxford, 1964), p. 2, v. 40. My translation. For a full translation, see *Virgin Lives and Holy Deaths: Two Exemplary Biographies for Anglo-Norman Women*, ed. and trans. Jocelyn Wogan-Browne and Glyn S. Burgess (London, 1996), pp. 3–43.

As Weinberger says, “Translation is change and motion.”[21] And as these essays show, knowledge of the nature of that change proceeds incrementally, through appreciation of each individual “tree surgeon’s” intervention, which both contributes to and tests a broader appreciation of the culture to which it belongs, but also adds to the critic’s self-conscious awareness of the potential relativism of that appreciation. The medievalist has, above all, to be generously open-minded, critically, culturally, and linguistically; translating the Middle Ages is a continuing conversation, both with and across past cultures and present practices.

---

[21] Weinberger, *Anonymous Sources*, p. 13.

PART 1
What's in a Word?

Dictionaries and wordlists, far from being politically neutral or dustily uninformative, can offer valuable information about language use and relations between languages, as well as about how cultures conceptualize and organize knowledge. Brian Merrilees, a specialist on late-medieval Latin-French dictionaries, and involved in using modern technologies both to disseminate and understand them, concentrates on two groups of dictionaries from the fifteenth century, one apparently produced for the learned, represented by Firmin Le Ver's *Dictionarius* of 1440, the other more evidently an aid to those still learning Latin, of which a *Vocabularius* printed c. 1490 by Guillaume Le Talleur (the earliest version of which may date from nearly 150 years before) is typical.[1] Merrilees shows how definitions can involve a degree of glossing and interpretation, and of creativity and ingenuity in coining new words, although some of these seem not to pass into common use. The study of feminine endings raises the question of to what extent they represent cultural norms—were there indeed women bagpipe players, *cornamusaresses*, Merrilees asks, while noting wryly that, where the medieval dictionary gives *escriveresse* for woman writer, the modern-day *Trésor de la langue française* does not recognize a feminine form for *écrivain*. While dictionaries invite cultural scrutiny, and yet cannot answer all the questions one wants to ask of them, online projects to make these medieval storehouses of knowledge electronically searchable nonetheless make it possible to trace their lines of influence and dissemination, as Merrilees's research demonstrates.

Russell Hopley's essay on "The Translation of Nature: Al-Sharīf al-Idrīsī on the Plant Life of the Western Mediterranean" reconstructs a rich cultural context for appreciating the work of this Moroccan-born scholar, considering in particular the relations between an increasingly beleaguered Andalusian Islamic culture and Sicily, where Idrīsī, himself moving around and across the Mediterranean, between North Africa and Europe, and finally "translated" to Roger II's Norman court of Palermo in 1139, finds the space and resources to write detailed travel books, as well as the botanical work, derived from Greek and Arabic sources, on which Hopley concentrates here. Hopley compares Idrīsī's work to that of the

[1] On these texts, see also, Merrilees's "L'apport des lexiques bilingues à l'étude de la créativité lexicale en latin médiéval," *Bulletin Du Cange: Archivum Latinitatis Medii Aevi* 63 (2005): 109–17; and his "Translation and Definition in the Medieval Bilingual Dictionary," in Jeanette Beer (ed.), *Translation Theory and Practice in the Middle Ages* (Kalamazoo, 1997), pp. 199–214.

ninth-century Iraqi philologist al-Aşma'ī, whose treatise on desert plant life was, fascinatingly, primarily intended as a companion to explain botanical references in the anthology of pre-Islamic poetry he produced for a later, culturally different, urban readership. While Hopley notes that Idrīsī must have been motivated by an anxiety to preserve his threatened Mediterranean heritage, his treatises also testify to his participation in the dynamic adaptability and renewal of human knowledge.

Chapter 1
Dictionaries, Definitions, and Databases

Brian Merrilees

Translatio est expositio sententie per aliam linguam.
—Johannes Balbus *Catholicon*, 1286

Bilingual dictionaries are and have for centuries been indispensable tools in translation and teaching. In this essay we will look at Latin-French lexicons from the fourteenth and fifteenth centuries and examine how their compilers rendered meaning from one language to the other.[1] Our concentration here is largely restricted to two families of texts, one including the large *Dictionarius* of Firmin Le Ver, completed in 1440, and an incunable *Vocabularius familiaris et compendiosus* published around 1490 by Guillaume Le Talleur, a printer of Rouen, and one of the earliest attempts at a French-Latin dictionary, the *Glossarium gallico-latinum* perhaps from around 1430–1450.[2] The second group is loosely labelled the *Aalma*, a title given by Mario Roques after the first lemma in several of its 14 known versions, the earliest of which is possibly from the mid-fourteenth century.[3]

---

1 This paper is part of a larger and ongoing program of research in early French lexicography, "Le dictionnaire bilingue en France avant 1500." We cannot list here all the medieval Latin-French glossaries and dictionaries that have survived to our time and will limit ourselves to a few with which we are particularly familiar. Margarete Lindemann's superb survey gives both a broad and detailed picture: *Die französischen Wörterbücher von den Anfängen bis 1600: Entstehung und typologische Beschreibung* (Tübingen, 1994).

2 *Dictionarius Firminis Verris: Dictionnaire latin-français de Firmin Le Ver*, ed. William Edwards and Brian Merrilees, Corpus Christianorum: Continuatio mediaevalis, Lexica Latina Medii Aevii: Nouveau Recueil des lexiques latins-français du moyen âge 1 (Turnhout, 1994); *Dictionarius familiaris et compendiosus: le dictionnaire latin-français de Guillaume Le Talleur*, ed. William Edwards and Brian Merrilees, Corpus Christianorum: Continuatio mediaevalis, Lexica Latina Medii Aevii: Nouveau Recueil des lexiques latins-français du moyen âge 3 (Turnhout, 2002); *Glossarium Gallico-Latinum: le Glossaire français-latin du ms. Paris lat. 7684*, ed. Brian Merrilees and Jacques Monfrin, Corpus Christianorum: Continuatio mediaevalis, Lexica Latina Medii Aevii: Nouveau Recueil des lexiques latins-français du moyen âge 2 (Turnhout, 1998), pp. 141–269.

3 Mario Roques, *Recueil général des lexiques français du Moyen Age (XIIe–XVe siècle) I: Lexiques alphabétiques*, Tome I (Paris, 1936). The following versions of the *Aalma* are referred to in this paper:

Paris 13032 = Paris, BnF, MS lat. 13032
Paris 14748 = Paris, BnF, MS lat. 14748
Paris 17881 = Paris, BnF, MS lat. 17881

My colleagues and I are in the process of putting some versions of the *Aalma* online through the Canada-wide TAPoR (Text Analysis Portal for Research) project and we look forward to a multiversion printed edition with Brepols Publishing. The *Aalma* seems to have been associated with basic learning of Latin and one version gives it the title *Mirouer des nouveaulx escoliers*, stating also that its intention was to help translate Latin into French and, more surprisingly, French into Latin.[4] The Le Ver *Dictionarius*, on the other hand, is directed at an educated audience, likely Le Ver's own fellow monks, as well as being the personal creation of a highly sophisticated linguist.

Definitions

The link between these texts and the theme of translation is, of course, through the definitions that are supplied in the second language, per the definition of translation from Johannes Balbus that heads this paper. Balbus was bishop of Genoa in the second half of the thirteenth century and his *Catholicon* (completed 1286) is the basis for many of the dictionaries of medieval Western Europe. It should be noted, however, that definitions in dictionary texts can often be a mixture of Latin and French: medieval compilers called definition in the same language *ethimologia*, definition in another language *translatio*.

As one might expect, many of the French definitions chosen by the compilers are unexceptional, simply equivalents that would seem inevitable choices. In their simplest form, this means a single French gloss for a Latin lemma:

> Ablativus .tiva .tivum—*ablatif*—o
> Abluo .is .lui .luere .lutum—*laver*—a
> Ablucio .cionis—*lavemens*—f [washing]
> Abnegacio .cionis—*denoiemens*—f [denial]
> (*Aalma* Paris 13032)[5]

Soon, however, this must have seemed insufficient and multiple equivalents were given, as well as secondary and tertiary meanings:

Exeter 3517 = Exeter, the Dean and Chapter Library, MS 3517
Lille 147 = Bibliothèque municipale de Lille, MS 147 (formerly 388)
Metz 510 = Metz, Bibliothèque municipale, MS 510
Metz 1182 = Metz, Bibliothèque municipale, MS 1182
St. Omer 644 = Bibliothèque de l'Agglomération de St. Omer, MS 644
Salins 44 = Bibliothèque municipale de Salins, MS 44

4 Brian Merrilees, "Le Mirouer des nouveaulx escoliers: l'*Aalma* du manuscrit Paris, BnF lat. 14748" in Yvan Lepage and Christian Milat (eds), *Por s'onor croistre. Mélanges de langue et de littérature médiévales offerts à Pierre Kunstmann* (Ottawa, 2008), pp. 131–40.

5 See note 3.

> Abominor, abominaris, abominatus sum vel fui, abominari—*avoir en desdaing, en horreur ou en despit, abominer* [disdain, despise, abominate]
>
> Acus, acus, acui—*aguille ou espingle ou ce a quoy on desmelle les cheveux* [needle or pin with which one untangles hair]
>
> Admitto .tis, admisi, admittere, admissum—*recevoir ou pechier ou legierement tourner un cheval, eslaxier* [receive or sin or gently turn a horse, let go] (*Aalma* Paris 13032)

This is all still rather straightforward, though the example of "Acus" here shows how the compiler leads away from an equivalent to something of an explanation. This tendency increased as dictionaries grew in complexity and sophistication. Further examples we can give are as follow:

> Abacus ou Abax est oussi vergue de geometrie ou taule que ont les philosophes ou il font figures en pourre sousmise qui est appellee aultrement emax.cis ... abax oussi ou abacus est piere quadrangulee qui est mise sur coulonnes et oussi cascune table de marbre est ausi ditte. (*Aalma* St. Omer 644)
> [*Abacus* or *Abax* is also a geometrical measuring stick or a table used by philosophers where they draw figures in the dust that has been spread, also known as *emax* ... *abacus* is also a square stone placed on the top of columns; any marble table may also be called such.]
>
> Abdicativus .va .vum—.i. negativus .va .vum—negatif, niiés, refusés—quod componitur Superabdicativus .va .vum surnegatif dont celle negation est dite surnegative qui est ajoustee a negation et ne fait nient plus que celle de devant, si comme on dit communement: ego non habeo nichil le quel cose ne vault nient plus que se on disoit ego nichil habet. (*Aalma* St. Omer 644)
> [*Abdicativus .va .vum—.i. negativus .va .vum*—negative, denied, refused—the compound form is *Superabdicativus .va .vum*, double negative, this is a negative called double negative which is added to a negative but does nothing more than the first one, as if one said in common speech: *ego non habeo nichil*, 'I do not have nothing,' which does not mean more than if one said: *ego nichil habeo*, 'I have nothing.']
>
> Apostrophus .phi—verghelle, rieule a le samblance de le partie dextre de cercle qui est mise en le fin de diction qui demontre la defaillir ung voyel ut: tribunal' pro tribunale, pirrin' pro Pirrine. (*Aalma* St. Omer 644)
> [*Apostrophus .phi*—a comma, stroke like the right part of a circle which is placed at the end of a word to show a vowel is missing, as in: tribunal' for tribunale, Pirrin' for Pirrine (this last is perhaps a proper name.)]

These are nonetheless staying close to the source, in this case the *Catholicon* of Balbus.

Definitions are of particular interest in that one can detect the working of the compilers' minds as translators and creators of neologisms, showing a creative spirit that sometimes contributes permanently to the target language and sometimes remains a fascinating effort that does not survive the work in which it is found.

One such example is the equivalent given for the Latin *accessibilitas* by Le Ver, who was a brilliant fifteenth-century lexicographer from a Cartusian monastery near Abbeville in northwestern France. His choice is to create the word *approchableté* ("approachability"), a term that is never seen again but which we can admire as witness of Le Ver's linguistic inventiveness. Others similar in approach are discussed later in this paper.

Other examples show diversity of forms, steps on the way to a resolution of a final choice. The endings *-able* and *-ible*, both common in French, can be found with the same stem, for example *comprehensible* and *comprehensable*, *corrigible*, and *corrigable*. Feminine endings, too, vary, raising perhaps more questions about medieval female activity than one might imagine. Below is a longish list of apparent neologisms culled from a number of lexicons, but a full treatment may be found in Margarete Lindemann's comprehensive historical study of feminine endings in French:[6]

affermeresse	assistrix [helper, servant]	(Mtp H110, St N78)[7]
agenoilleresse	suffragatrix [supplicant]	(St N78)
aiguisseresse	acutrix [seamstress]	(St N78)
alleresse	itrix [walker]	(*VFC*)
assemblerresse	coactrix [who brings together]	(*Aalma* Paris 13032)
baptiseresse	baptisatrix [baptizer]	(*VFC*, *DLV*)
blasmeresse	vituperatrix [who blames]	(St N78)
bouleresse	bolliatrix, bulliatrix [who boils]	(Mtp H110, St N78)
coeulleresse	lectrix [gatherer]	(*DLV*)
complai(n)gneresse	questrix [complainer]	(Mtp H110, St N78)
consoleresse	consolatrix [consoler]	(*VFC*)
cornemusaresse	mima [player, musician]	(*GGL*)
embaxaderesse	ambaxiatrix [ambassadress]	(*VFC*)
embraseresse	incentrix [who lights]	(Mtp H110)
enchaineresse	catenatrix [who enchains]	(*VFC*)
escriveresse	libraria [writer]	(Mtp H110)
nombreresse	calculatrix [who calculates]	(*VFC*)
nourrisseresse	altrix (nutrix) [who nourishes]	(*VFC*)
tainderesse	tintrix [dyer]	(*Aalma* Paris 17881)

Almost every example could merit further investigation. Whether there were female trumpeters or bagpipe players as *cornemusaresse* suggests—there is also a *cornemuseuse* elsewhere—one cannot say, and the Latin *mima* has a much more general sense of "player, actor." Certainly there were many female writers, as *escriveresse* reminds us, along with the creation *escrivaine* also used to gloss

[6] *Zum Suffixwechsel von "-eresse" zu "-euse" und "-trice" im Französischen* (Tübingen, 1977).

[7] Mtp H110 = Montpellier, Bibliothèque de la Faculté de Médecine, MS H110; St N78 = Stockholm, Royal Library, MS N78.

libraria in Stockholm, Royal Library, MS N78. Many see the modern *écrivaine* as a twentieth-century creation and it was certainly then that it became common, especially in Quebec where other feminine forms such as *auteure, professeure* have become standard. We should point out that *escrivaine* also appeared in medieval texts as Godefroy noted over a century ago.[8] The term has still not been recognized by the *Trésor de la langue française*, which gives: "En règle générale, il n'y a pas de féminin à *écrivain*."

The feminine examples are also witness to the importance of derivation as a generating principle. The model for the process is the twelfth-century Italian Hugutio, whose *Magnae derivationes*[9] were used by later lexicographers such as Balbus. Derivation frequently led to the creation of Latin words that were never used or at least never found in surviving texts. The example *itrix* above is one such creation, found in Le Talleur's *Vocabularius familiaris et compendiosus* as well as in Le Ver's *Dictionarius*, where it is glossed by "viatrix *femme qui chemine*." In the *Vocabularius*, the isolated term *itrix* brought forth a French neologism *aleresse* (not to be confused with *alerresse*, "midwife").

Derivation produced whole families of words in the source language, often then an inspiration to new terms in the target language:

> HOSPITABILIS et hoc .bile—*hostelables* .i. qui libenter hospitatur vel qui dignus est ut recipiatur in hospicium et comparatur et dicitur ab *hospitor .taris et componitur.
> [*hospitable* .i. who freely gives hospitality or who is worthy of being received as a guest.]
> Inhospitabilis et eciam comparatur [inhospitable]
> Hospitabiliter—adverbium—*hospitablement* [hospitably]
> Hospitabilitas .tatis—*hospitabletés* [hospitality, state of being hospitable]

This example is much shorter than most entries but chosen to illustrate the point. The adjective *hostelables* looks very French, yet it is not found in any narrative texts, just in three dictionaries to our knowledge.[10] Yet it is important to notice the difference between the adjective and the accompanying adverb and noun. In our conventional terms as teachers of the history of the French language, the adjective would be described as *populaire* and the two others *savants*. Robert Martin uses the terms *authentique* for a French word deriving from another French word, and *historique* for those deriving clearly from the Latin form.[11]

---

[8] Frédéric Godefroy, *Dictionnaire de l'ancienne langue française et de tous ses dialectes du IXe au XVe siècle* (10 vols, Paris, 1881–1902), vol. 3, p. 442a.

[9] *Derivationes/Uguccione da Pisa: Edizione Critica Princeps*, ed. Enzo Cecchini and Arbizzoni Guido et al. (Tavarnuzze, Florence, 2004).

[10] Besides the *Dictionarius* of Le Ver, the term *hostelable* is found in the *Aalma* versions in Paris 13032 and St. Omer 644.

[11] Robert Martin, "Le préfixe A-/AD- en moyen français," *Romania* 119 (2001): 289–322.

The *Dictionarius* of Le Ver has many articles wherein the derived forms can number ten, a dozen, or even more, though not necessarily evoking new derived forms in French. The headword DUBITO in Le Ver generates by a cursory count 17 derivatives and several compounds—*dubtitans*, *dubitanter*, *dubitantia*, *dubitilabilis*, *dubitilabiliter*, *dubitabilitas*, and so on—with at least one French neologism, *doubtabletés*, among the definitions. This last example shows a French definition that derives from the adjective form, the process that Martin calls *authentique* rather than a definition that is closely based on the Latin form, which in this case might have been **dubitabilité*. The *historique* method was probably the most common in creating words in the target language and we can cite such examples as the following:

dampnabilitas	*dampnabletés* [damnability]
desiderabilitas	*desiderabletés* [desirability]
expedibilitas	*expediabletés* [deliverability]
favorabilitas	*favorabletés* [agreement]
finibilitas	*finabletés* [capability of being finished]
habitabilitas	*habitabletés* [habitability]

Le Ver, however, also exploits the other approach, the *authentique*, in a manner one might describe as "deconstructive," as we saw above in the examples of *approchables*, *approchablement*, *approchabletés*. That is, he goes to the root meaning of a Latin term, translates with a French form that is patent in its sense but is not a gallicized mirror form of the Latin. Unfortunately these terms seldom survive: *approchable* will lose out to *accessible*, which was already in the language, while *accessibilité* will later become the noun, though it will not appear until the seventeenth century. Nonetheless, the process provides insight into the way in which Le Ver was approaching his task, as we can further see from these examples:

acomparabletés	equiperantia [comparability]
apaisabletés	mulcibilitas, pacabilitas [appeasability]
aperchevabletés	advertibilitas [perceivability]
blechabletés	ledibilitas [woundability]
confortabletés	consolabilitas [consolability]
decourabletés	fluxibilitas [flowability]

Sometimes the same text can give "learned" versus "popular" forms, as in an *Aalma* version from Metz 510: "productibilis" has both *productible* and *produisable* as definitions, while the closely related *Dictionarius* of Le Ver and the *Vocabularius* of Le Talleur, some 50 years apart, define "conducibilis" respectively by *conduisible* and *conducible*.

Although it was not our intention to deal here with the mixing of Latin and French in definitions, we must at least do so in part simply to understand the methods used by the compiler of a version of the *Aalma* found in the municipal library of St. Omer in the Pas-de-Calais region of northern France. The St. Omer

Aalma is by far the longest version, almost twice as long as the version Mario Roques published in 1938, the version from Paris 13032, which likely dates from the mid-fourteenth century. St. Omer 644 is, we estimate from the watermark, to be dated around 1430–1440, and appears to have been reconstructed with reference to an early version of the *Aalma* and to a copy of the Latin source, the *Catholicon*, as well as other lexicons, including Le Ver's *Dictionarius*.

St. Omer 644 is indeed part of the *Aalma* group and many entries do not differ or differ only slightly from other versions that we have examined. We initially constructed an Access database of the letter B for our first comparisons, but we have since transcribed complete texts of seven versions and partial transcriptions of four others. All this material has been processed by a DOS program called WordCruncher, which has become the key tool in our analyses. The following examples show simple similarities:

Baculo—*batre de baston* [beat with a stick] (all versions except Metz 1182)
Baiulatrix—*porteresse* [woman who carries] (all versions except Lille 147, which gives *qui porte* for both masculine and feminine)
Biangulus—*ce qui a ii angles* ut hoc: < > [that which has two angles as in: < >] (Paris 13032, 14748, 17881, Salins 44)
– *qui a deux ongles* (Metz 510, 1182)
– *qui a ii cloqettes* [which has two small bells, conical forms] (Lille 147)
– habens duos angulos, id est *cornes* [horns] (Exeter 3517)
– *qui a double angheles, deux angheles* [which has double angles, two angles] (St. Omer 644)
Caliendrum .dri—*mitre ou ce de quoy le tieste est envolepee pour avoir caut* [mitre or that with which the head is covered to keep warm] (St. Omer 644)
– *mittre ou ce de quoy on envelope la teste pour avoir chaut* (Paris 13032, Metz 510, 1182, Lille 147, Salins 44, Exeter 3517)

Other examples in the St. Omer *Aalma* share part of the definition with one or more of the other versions, but the St. Omer compiler has added further definitional material, mostly, it would seem, by going back to the *Catholicon* and translating the Latin into French, as in the following cases (the first example is each time taken from St. Omer 644):

Bibliator—*vendeur ou aourneur de livres, qui les repare affin qu'il les vende plus quier* [seller or decorator of books who repairs them in order to sell them at a dearer price]
Bibliator .toris—.i. venditor vel politor librorum [seller or polisher of books] (Exeter 3517)
Catholicon: ... venditor et ornator librorum quia polit et pumicat ut carius vendat [seller and decorator of books since he polishes and scrubs them so that he might sell them at a dearer price]

Cippus .ppi—*cep, prison a mettre les malfaiteurs ou tronc ou tombe de mort ou cimentiere* [shackle, prison for housing criminals, or trunk, tomb for the dead or cemetery]

– *ceps a mettre en prison les malfaitteurs* (Paris 13032, Metz 510, Lille 147, Salins 44)

– *chep en prison ou chartre* vel cumulus terre aut lapis mortuo supposito (Exeter 3517)

Catholicon: … pro trunco et pro cumulo terre et pro lapide mortuo suppposito et pro cimiterio; et pro instrumento quo reorum pedes restringuntur, quasi capiens pedes [for a trunk and a mound of earth and for a stone laid over the dead and for a cemetery].

Emeritus .ta .tum—*franc, quite et delivré de plus labourer* [free, quit and free from working any more].

– *bien desserviz, frans* [well earned, free] (Paris 13032, etc.)

– iam extra meritum positus .i. miles iam solutus et liberatus a labore sui officii [already rewarded .i. a soldier free and liberated from his assigned task] (Exeter 3517)

Catholicon : … liberatus et solutus est a labore officii sui …

It is not surprising, then, to find that the St. Omer compiler gives a total of 248 specific citations of the name 'Catholicon' and more than 100 references to other sections of the work. There are also some examples where he has expanded a definition or added something of his own that does not necessarily correspond precisely to the *Catholicon* reading:

Cacumen .minis—*hautesce ou le bout hault d'une cose* [height or the high end of something]

– *hautesse* (Paris 13032, etc.)

– *haultece* .i. summitas (Exeter 3517)

Catholicon: … summitas

Elisus .sa .sum—*flatis a tierre, acraventés, blechiés, hurtés* [thrown to the ground, knocked down, wounded, bumped]

– *bleciez, hurtez* (Paris 13032, etc.)

– *hurté, blechié* .i. evidenter lesus (Exeter 3517)

Catholicon: … elisus valde vel extra vel evidenter lesus [hurt somewhat or clearly hurt]

Extrico .cas .cavi .care—*deslier, despecchier, ouvrir, manifester, deffaire treiches de queviaux, destrecchier* [untie, unpick, open, show, undo horses' manes, disentangle]

– *deslier, destrecier* (Paris 13032)

– *desliier, despecier* (Lille 147)

– expedire, exsolvere .i. *deslier, destrechier* (Exeter 3517)

Catholicon: … expedire, exsolvere [disentangle, untie]

We have noted some other connections of St. Omer 644 to the contemporary production of Firmin Le Ver and to another very long compilation found in Montpellier, Faculté de Médecine, H110 and Stockholm, Royal Library, N78. We are currently looking further into these relationships, as well as the relationships between the *Aalma* versions themselves, trying not to make leaps of assumption that will later be found shaky. What we are doing is using definitional translations as a guide to textual transmission, always acknowledging, of course, that there are many links missing in the chain.

All of this is made easier by the technologies at our disposal, from using simple database programs on our own machines to accessing the Internet for larger and more complete reference material. For the study of determining first occurrences of words and the creation of neologisms, online sources are of indispensable value. We also still rely on the major printed dictionaries such as Godefroy, Tobler-Lommatzsch, and the *Französisches Etymologisches Wörterbuch* (*FEW*) though some of their material is now accessible electronically through the *Dictionnaire du moyen français* (*DMF*) in Nancy.[12] For a number of years, the *DMF* was intended to be a printed dictionary, and a preliminary volume of the letter A-AH was circulated in 1998. However, it soon became apparent that the advantage of an electronic dictionary was the possibility of easy updates, corrections, and additions. In 2003 ATILF (Analyse et Traitement Automatique de la Langue Française) produced a first version containing close to 33,000 lemmata and 85,000 fiches. There followed a second version in 2007 with 60,000 lemmata and 118,000 fiches, the latter being in effect mini-articles. A third enlarged version came online in 2009. One useful feature is the possibility of checking citations from modern dictionaries of medieval French (Godefroy, Tobler-Lommatzsch, and the *FEW* among them), though we still wait for full electronic versions of these works. The *DMF* has a number of other features to allow the researcher to view materials from different aspects. One encouraging thing for our project has been the inclusion of hundreds of citations from the *Dictionarius* of Firmin Le Ver, the *Vocabularius* of Guillaume Le Talleur, and the *Glossarium gallico-latinum*.

The Le Ver *Dictionarius* is also searchable online through the *Database of Latin Dictionaries*, a subscribable site set up by Brepols Publishers of Belgium.[13] The database contains two medieval Latin-modern French compilations by Albert Blaise, the *Dictionnaire latin-français des auteurs chrétiens* and the *Dictionnaire latin-français des auteurs du moyen-âge*. There is also the *Lexicon totius latinitatis* begun by Egidio Forcellini in the early eighteenth century and continued in various editions until the twentieth. Another important resource is a searchable PDF copy of Du Cange's *Glossarium mediae et infimae latinitatis*, using the 1883–1887 edition which has quite a number of French terms among its definitions, including *approchable* with a reference to Le Talleur. A PDF copy of the well-known *Latin Dictionary* by Charlton Lewis and Charles Short was added in 2008.[14]

The *Anglo-Norman Dictionary*, first published in paper over a number of years from 1977 to 1992, is currently being reworked at the University of Wales in Aberystwyth as an online source, though two revised printed volumes, A–C and

---

12 See <http://atilf.atilf.fr/dmf.htm> (January 2009).

13 See <http://www.brepolis.net/> (January 2009).

14 First ed. (Oxford, 1879).

D–E, have been printed already.[15] This is a very user-friendly site and although its title might suggest a limited stock, it is a very full lexicon.

On a more modest level, our research program is putting several versions of the *Aalma* online, mostly for purposes of comparison, using the services of the Canadian TAPoR project. The site is not yet public.

It is often argued that the French found in medieval dictionaries is sometimes limited to those very compilations, but even the hapax legomena and neological creations are worth our attention. Lexicographers like Le Ver and the St. Omer compiler were very sophisticated scholars and making their work available has, I believe, been a significant contribution to our discipline.

[15] The first edition of the *Anglo-Norman Dictionary* was published under the general editorship of Louise Stone and William Rothwell, in five fascicles (London, 1977–1992). A second revised edition, *Anglo-Norman Dictionary*, in two volumes (*A–C* and *D–E*), ed. Stewart Gregory, William Rothwell, and David Trotter, was published by the Modern Humanities Research Association in 2005. The online site directed by David Trotter both includes and adds to this base; it is found at <http://www.anglo-norman.net/> (January 2009).

Chapter 2
The Translation of Nature: Al-Sharīf al-Idrīsī on the Plant Life of the Western Mediterranean

Russell Hopley

The interest in plant life evinced by Muslims was from its earliest stages closely tied to the task of translation. Arabic philologists and lexicographers working in cities such as Baṣra, Kūfa, Baghdad, and Damascus devoted a great deal of their energies to recording, deciphering, and interpreting the poetry composed by pre-Islamic Arab poets, the beauty of whose verse was considered second only to the language of the Qur'ān. Yet there remained much about pre-Islamic poetry that early Muslims found vexingly opaque. The myriad references to desert vegetation found throughout the verse of the pagan Arabs were poorly understood in the newly urbanized centers of the faith, and it fell to the likes of the Arab lexicographer from Iraq, Abū Sa'īd 'Abd al-Malik al-Aṣma'ī (d. 828),[1] not only to anthologize the poetry of pre-Islamic Arabia but also to elucidate and gloss the intricate descriptions of desert plant life found therein. The treatise al-Aṣma'ī produced, the *Kitāb al-nabāt wa 'l-shajar*[2] [*The Book of Plants and Trees*], was undoubtedly intended to accompany his poetic anthology, translating the bewildering array of terms and allusions to desert plant life that were increasingly lost on an urban readership, much of which was no longer of Arab stock. Indeed, one suspects that this early effort aimed as much at collecting and explicating the botanical vocabulary of the desert Bedouin as it did at rescuing from oblivion a store of uniquely Arab knowledge that was being lost in an ever more urbanized and multiethnic, that is to say Persian-inflected, civilization.

The centuries following al-Aṣma'ī witnessed a marked growth in the works Muslims devoted to the description of plant life, particularly in those non-Arab lands recently brought into the fold of the Islamic faith, where indigenous knowledge of plants was often highly developed and considered worthy of translation into Arabic, the prestige of which effectively conferred sanction upon a body of knowledge that would have otherwise been neglected or regarded with suspicion. Arabic writings in the field of botany most often maintained the early philological focus,

[1] Biographical details given in *The Encyclopedia of Islam*, ed. H.A.R. Gibb et al. (12 vols, Leiden, 1986–2004) (*EI*²), s.v. al-Aṣma'ī.

[2] Quotations from this work are found in Louis Cheikho and August Haffner, *Dix traités de philologie arabe* (Beirut, 1914), pp. 17–62.

but moved progressively in the direction of medicinal use, agricultural application, and philosophical speculation.[3] This is nowhere more true than in the lands of the Islamic west, namely al-Andalus and North Africa, where the great diversity of terrain and topography has produced a stock of plant life that is especially rich. The indigenous inhabitants of North Africa, the Berbers, have historically shown a keen interest in plant life, yet have more often than not relegated to others the task of recording and translating their venerable botanical knowledge, an inclination that seems emblematic of the larger relationship that existed between al-Andalus and North Africa, the regions of the Islamic western Mediterranean that Muslims called *bilād al-'udwatayn*, "the land of the two coasts."

The intellectual centers of al-Andalus—Cordoba, Seville, and Granada—are best known as the points at which Greek learning passed into Arabic and emerged in Islamic guise bearing the names of Averroes, Avempace, and Avenzoar, Latinized appellations more familiar to a Muslim ear as Ibn Rushd, Ibn Bajja, and Ibn Zuhr. Alongside their interest in Greek learning, Andalusīs felt a certain curiosity regarding their Berber coreligionists to the south. This interest in things Berber was particularly true among Andalusī geographers and botanists, many of whose works show a keen desire to familiarize the Muslims of Iberia with the history, geography, and plant life of the Berber lands of North Africa. As the tide of Christian reconquest of al-Andalus quickened in the eleventh and twelfth centuries and the fortunes of Iberian Muslims progressively worsened, the Arabic literature of al-Andalus continued to direct its gaze south to the Berbers of Africa. This was no doubt tied to the recognition that Berbers, good fighting men, would henceforth be called upon in increasing numbers to slow the momentum of Christian reconquest. Iberian Muslims could thus expect to encounter Berbers in their midst with growing frequency, with all that entailed for the need to make sense of their strange tongue, odd forms of dress, and alien modes of behavior, some of which appeared decidedly un-Islamic to orthodox Andalusīs. Thus the Berbers, a people who had hitherto been relegated to the geographic and cultural periphery of the Islamic west, now found themselves summoned with growing urgency to play a crucial role in the farthest western outpost of Islam, saving it from collapse and, in the fullness of time, restoring it to its past glory.

I would suggest that it is within this complex relationship between al-Andalus and Berber North Africa that the work of al-Sharīf al-Idrīsī can be located. Born in 1100 in the Moroccan city of Sabta, now known as Ceuta, al-Sharīf al-Idrīsī[4] undertook his early education in Cordoba and subsequently spent time in Malaga, an Andalusī city that had at one point been ruled by the Banū Ḥammūd, a family

---

[3] Max Meyerhof, "Esquisse d'histoire de la pharmacologie et botanique chez les Musulmans d'Espagne," *Al-Andalus* 3 (1935): pp. 1–41, provides detailed treatment of the development of botany and pharmacology in al-Andalus. See also *EI*², s.v. Nabāt.

[4] Biographical details given in Henri Bresc and Annliese Nef, *Idrîsî: la première géographie de l'Occident* (Paris, 1999), pp. 13–53; and Muhammad Hadj Sadok, *Al-Idrīsī: le maġrib au 6e siècle de l'hégire (12e siècle après J.-C.)* (Paris, 1983), pp. 11–46.

of Arab noblemen descended from the Prophet to which Idrīsī was related by blood, but which had fallen afoul of the Berber Almoravids after their annexation of al-Andalus in 1092. Idrīsī's grandfather, Idrīs II, had been the final Arab ruler of Malaga,[5] and the family's fortunes suffered considerably in the wake of the Almoravid occupation, an event that proved decisive in determining the course of Idrīsī's life.

Idrīsī's stay in Malaga seems to have been cut short by political turmoil, a turn of events most probably related to his status as a scion of the deposed ruling family, and he next appears in Palermo in 1139, where he was given sanctuary at the Norman court of Roger II.[6] Given his status as a descendent of the Prophet, this flight to Sicily must have been particularly troublesome for Idrīsī; the young prince was undoubtedly aware that in seeking haven in Sicily, he was effectively turning his back on the realm of the faith, the *dār al-Islām*, and moving into the abode of unbelief, the *dār al-kufr*, among peoples who were actively hostile to Islam, many of whom harbored aggressive designs upon Muslim territory. In fact, Idrīsī's flight to Palermo seems especially disconcerting when one considers that the Norman kingdom of Sicily was established on territory formerly under Islamic rule and from which Muslims had been uprooted, many of them either forced to renounce their faith or compelled to return to North Africa.[7] Curiously, however, the Islamic tradition appears not to hold this questionable act against Idrīsī. In fact it is largely silent concerning the Andalusī prince, and this silence is perhaps indicative of the ambivalence with which Muslim biographers regarded Idrīsī. On the few occasions that Arab authors do mention him, they bestow upon him the honorific *al-'Alī bi-llāh*, "he who has been raised high by God."[8] This, however, may be related to Idrīsī's status as a descendent of the Prophet and the widely held belief that impugning a descendent of the Prophet is tantamount to insulting the Prophet himself, *sabb al-nabī*, a capital offense in Islam. Idrīsī registers his own sense of regret about seeking permanent exile in Sicily in the following verse:

> Layta shiʿrī ayna qabarī / ḍāʿ fī 'l-ghurbati umrī
> Lam adʿ lil-'ayni / mā tashtāqu fī barri wa baḥri
> Wa khabartu al-nasa wa 'l-arḍa / ladā khayri wa sharri
> Lam ajid jāran wa lā dāran / kamā fi ṭayyī ṣadrī
> Fa-ka'innī lam asir / illā bi-mayyiti aw bi-qafri
> [If only my true sentiment were where my tomb shall be / My life has been lost in exile.

---

[5] The Idrissid line is venerated in Morocco to this day. A full account of this important family is given in *EI*[2], s.v Idrissids.

[6] Bresc and Nef, pp. 15–20.

[7] A detailed history of Norman rule in Sicily is found in Donald Matthew, *The Norman Kingdom of Sicily* (Cambridge, 1992).

[8] A discussion of Idrīsī's treatment in the Arabic tradition is found in Muṣṭafā al-Shaka', *Al-Maghrib wa –'l-andalus: afāq islāmiyya, wa ḥaḍāra insāniyya, wa mabāḥith adabiyya* (Beirut, 1407/1987), pp. 201–9.

I've recorded for the eye what it desires / of both land and sea.
I've given detail of peoples and lands / both good and evil.
Yet I've found neither companion nor home / except in my innermost breast.
As if going forth I were little more / than a dead man in a barren land.][9]

While resident at the Norman court in Palermo, Idrīsī composed the monumental geographic treatise for which he is best known, the *Nuzhāt al-mushtāq fi ikhtirāq al-afāq*,[10] the title of which translates delightfully as "The Pleasant Diversion for Those Wishing to Cross the Horizons." Idrīsī completed the work in 1154 after 15 years of labor, and dedicated it to his patron, Roger II, under whose name it bears the more prosaic title *kitāb Rujer*, "the book of Roger." Some 70 maps and a large silver planesphere accompanied the treatise, all designed by Idrīsī to serve as a physical guide to the locations described in the text. A second work followed the first, this time dedicated to Roger's son, William I, and bore the title *Uns al-muhaj fī rawḍ al-furaj*[11] [*The Companion of Souls in the Meadow of Delight*], also known as "the little Idrīsī." This latter work is an enumeration of the principal routes and roadways of the known world, including North Africa and, significantly, provides information concerning the distances between the major cities of each region. This invites a somewhat sinister interpretation: the Normans undertook an invasion and occupation of coastal Tunisia in 1148, at which time Idrīsī was composing these two treatises, and one cannot avoid the suspicion that his intimate knowledge of the region was instrumental in supplying the Normans with intelligence needed for their military operations against the Tunisian coastal cities of Mahdia, Susa, and Sfax. It should be pointed out that these three cities were terminal points for the lucrative trans-Saharan trade, and they receive considerable attention in his work.[12] Idrīsī was almost certainly aware of the military use to which his work would be put by the Normans, and it is not entirely outlandish to suggest that he did so hoping to settle a score with the North African Berbers who had brought ruin to his family in al-Andalus.[13]

---

9 Translation mine. The notice concerning Idrīsī is entry 94 in *al-Wāfī bil-wafayāt* by al-Ṣafadī (vol. 1, pp. 163–4).

10 Many editions of this work are extant. I have relied primarily on the edition of Muhammad Hadj Sadok. Cf. note 4 supra.

11 Arabic manuscript published in facsimile edition under the title *The Entertainment of Hearts and Meadows of Contemplation* (Stuttgart, 1984). The original manuscript, MS 1289, is found in the Hüsnü collection of the Süleyminye Library, Istanbul.

12 Tunisia experienced considerable turmoil during the lifetime of Idrīsī, enduring both the Norman occupation of its coastal cities and the significant devastation of its hinterland by the Bedouin tribesmen of the Banū Hilāl and the Banū Sulaym.

13 Idrīsī's attitude toward the Berber dynasties that ruled North Africa and al-Andalus during his lifetime is complex. He supplies the title "amīr" for the Almoravid ruler ʻAlī b. Yusūf b. Tāshfīn, a recognition of the legitimacy of his claim to rule. However, he fails to provide the title "mahdī" to Ibn Tūmart, founder of the Almohad dynasty. The Almohads eventually expelled the Normans from coastal Tunisia and Idrīsī's reticence to supply Ibn Tūmart's title may be a reflection of the enmity that existed between his Norman patrons in Palermo and the Almohads.

Of similarly broad scope, yet not nearly as well known, is the extensive botanical treatise Idrīsī wrote while resident at the Norman court, *al-Jāmi' lī-ṣifāt ashtāt al-nabāt wa ḍrūb anwā' al-mufradāt* [*A Compendium of the Characteristics of Diverse Plants and the Varieties of Simple Medications*]. The work, extant today in manuscript form in two recensions, one found in Istanbul, the second in Tehran, is an ambitious attempt to give a synoptic description of the plant life of the Mediterranean world and the medicinal uses to be derived from these plants.[14] It is, in a way, an expansion of his earlier geographical work which makes frequent brief mention of the plant life found in various regions of the Islamic world without going into great detail. Idrīsī's botanical treatise is remarkable for its breadth of learning, and it represents an important work of translation: each plant is initially identified by its Arabic name, and its designation is frequently provided in classical Greek, Byzantine Greek, Hebrew, and, not infrequently, Sanskrit, Turkish, Kurdish, and Berber. Indeed, we find several passages on the plant life of North Africa that reveal Idrīsī's familiarity with the Berber tribes and customs of central Morocco, a knowledge he most probably gained at first hand as a young man traveling in the region. As for the Greek and Hebrew terms employed in the Arabic text, these are no doubt the result of Idrīsī's close consultation with the Byzantine and Jewish physicians resident at the Norman court in Sicily. He also remarks on his consultation with the work of an individual named Abū Yūsuf al-Ṣiqillī, "the Sicilian," a figure about whom we know very little, yet whose mention reveals that Roger II had other Muslims in his employ.[15]

The three works Idrīsī composed while resident in Palermo should thus be viewed as a significant part of the translation project undertaken in Sicily following the Norman conquest of that island. Much has been made of Baghdad as the primary point through which classical Greek learning passed into the Islamic world and Toledo as the point at which it returned to Christendom in Islamic garb. However, comparatively little attention has been given to Norman Sicily as an important center for the transmission of Islamic and Byzantine science to Western Christendom. Muslim and Byzantine civilizations were, of course, the principle inheritors of the Hellenistic scientific heritage, and the Normans, especially Roger II, were in the unique position to oversee the preservation and transmission of much

---

[14] Both Arabic manuscripts are published in a single facsimile edition under the title *Compendium of the Properties of Diverse Plants and Various Kinds of Simple Drugs* (Mörlenbach, 1995). The German Arabist Helmut Ritter first located the manuscript of Idrīsī's *Jāmi'* in 1928 in the Fatih collection of the Süleyminye Library, Istanbul. Meyerhof subsequently provided a description and brief analysis of the text. The Istanbul manuscript, MS 3610 in the Fatih Collection, is incomplete. The Tehran manuscript, MS 18420 in the Majlis-i Sanā, is complete, but omits many of the translated plant names found in the Istanbul recension.

[15] Matthew, pp. 219–28, provides several important details concerning the role of Muslims and Arabic speakers in the administration of Norman Sicily. His contention that Idrīsī was a second-rate thinker is questionable.

of this learning.[16] Idrīsī's work, his botanical treatise in particular, stands as a compelling example of the Greek heritage in the natural sciences as it passed into the Islamic tradition, whence it was subsequently transmitted to Latin Christendom.

Idrīsī opens the *Jāmi'* with a brief preface in which he cites the sources he drew upon while composing the work. First mention goes to the Greek polymath Dioscorides, whom he considers preeminent in the field. Dioscorides's treatise, the *Materia medica*, was translated from Greek into Syriac, most likely in Baghdad, and then put into Arabic in the ninth century and given the title *Kitāb al-adwīya al-mufrada* [*The Book of Simple Medications*].[17] The Arabic translation of the work made its way to the western lands of Islam where it found an especially fertile reception in cities such as Cordoba and Granada.[18] After the mention of Dioscorides, Idrīsī provides an enumeration of the works of eastern scholars he consulted while preparing his treatise; these include Ḥunayn ibn Isḥāq, Ibn Sarābiyūn, Ibn Juljūl, Ibn al-Jazzār, Ibn Samajūn, and Ibn al-Kattanī. The first of these, Ḥunayn ibn Isḥāq, a Syriac-speaking Christian living in Baghdad, is of particular importance in the field of translation as he is known to have played a central role in translating both Dioscorides and Galen into Syriac and then into Arabic. Idrīsī offers this impressive mix of authors only to disparage those who have come in their wake, namely his contemporaries, whose work he finds lacking in knowledge, based on insufficient research, full of useless repetition, and either overly long or too brief. He asserts, in short, that his contemporaries suffer from a weakness in their religion, *ḍa'f fī dīyānatihim*, a rather remarkable explanation for a perceived failure of science.[19]

Regarding the work of Dioscorides, Idrīsī states that it is *al-kunz alladhī minhu istaslafū* [the treasure from which all those working in the field of botany and pharmacology have drawn].[20] Furthermore, the *Materia medica* is a work he claims to have made his holy book, *ja'ltuhu muṣḥafī*, a term synonymous with the Qur'ān and which he has largely committed to memory, a practice that most Muslims would associate with the Qur'ān. Idrīsī's veneration of Dioscorides's treatise brings him perilously close to blasphemy, but his intent seems merely to emphasize the estimation he feels for the Greek physician and to point out the considerable time he spent with the work on a daily basis, just as a believer would with the Muslim holy text.

---

16 Houben, p. 104, notes that a number of Roger's achievements are preserved in a trilingual inscription, in Latin, Greek, and Arabic, on the wall of the Palatine chapel, a fine indication of the prestige these three languages enjoyed during his period of rule.

17 A full discussion of Dioscorides's role in the development of Arabic medicine is found in *EI*², s.v. Adwīya.

18 César Dubler, "Los Nombres Arabes de Matéria Medica en la Obra del Doctor Laguna," *Al-Andalus* 16 (1951): pp. 142–8, discusses various aspects of the Arabic translation of Dioscorides.

19 These details are given by Idrīsī in the preface to his treatise and are preserved in both manuscripts.

20 Idrīsī., *Jāmi'*, p. 2. Citation preserved in both manuscripts.

Dioscorides serves as the initial reference point for each plant identified in Idrīsī's treatise and he notes whether mention of the plant is to be found in the *Materia medica*, where such mention is located, and what Greek term Dioscorides employs to identify the plant in question. After this, the designation for each plant is given in Persian, Latin, Frankish, Sanskrit, and Berber.[21] It is interesting to note that Idrīsī frequently provides a variety of Arabic designations for a single plant and he observes on occasion that the inhabitants of al-Andalus and Sicily differ from their eastern counterparts in the terminology they choose to employ for a number of plants. This in itself seems indicative of an identity among Muslim scholars of the western Mediterranean that was in the process of becoming more self-confident, assertive, and unwilling to take a backseat to the scholarship of the eastern Islamic lands. It is unfortunate, then, that the manuscript copyist found so many of these terms cumbersome or unintelligible, so that many lacunae exist in the text where one would expect to find the translated plant names. In fact, the copyist of the Tehran manuscript has largely omitted from the text any reference to foreign plant names, presumably either for reasons of space, prohibitive cost, or lack of interest on the part of the individual who commissioned the copy.

On the subject of the botanical life of North Africa, Idrīsī shows a distinct interest for in the plants to be found in the mountainous region surrounding Bijāya, a coastal city of Algeria that was largely inhabited by Berbers at the time he composed his treatise.[22] Idrīsī informs us that the slopes of the mountain that surround the city are replete with plant life, much of which has medicinal use. Among the plants he mentions in this regard are *al-afsantīn* (*artemesia absinthium*, i.e., absinthe), *al-zarāwand* (*aristolochia rotunda*, variously known as smearwort, mercury goosefoot, allgood, and "fat hen"), *al-quṣtūn* (*costus*), *shajar al-ḥuḍaḍ* (*lyceum*, a thorny shrub which grows in mountainous regions), *al-barbārīs* (*berberis*, i.e., pepperidge bush), and *al-qanturiyūn al-kabīr* (*centauria*, i.e., star thistle). Idrīsī also notes that yellow scorpions abound in the area but that they are largely harmless, this latter detail perhaps an indication that Idrīsī visited the area in person prior to his departure from North Africa.

Idrīsī provides extensive entries for several of the plants mentioned above. *Al-afsantīn,* wormwood or absinthe, is the first entry in the treatise, and an entire page is devoted to its description. He notes that Dioscorides makes reference to the plant in the third section of his treatise, where it bears the name *afsanin* in Greek. He tells us further that in Latin the plant is termed *ansansa*, Sanskrit *parina*, Syriac *afsantihana*, Persian *hir*, Frankish *afsantim*, and Berber *tashtalt*.[23] Idrīsī remarks that the plant is small, has one stem from which many branches grow,

21 "Frankish" most likely refers to German.

22 Idrīsī's description of Bijāya is given in Sadok, pp. 107–8.

23 Idrīsī shows considerable interest in the Berber designations for many plants. He may have relied on a local informant for these designations, but it is equally probable that he gained much of his knowledge of Berber terminology while traveling through North Africa as a young man.

and that each of these branches in turn produces numerous leaves that are thin, white, and moss-like in texture. The blossom of the plant is small and white with a yellow stem; its seeds are likewise small and thin, and by turns bitter and sweet in taste. The plant is particularly effective, he observes, for treating ailments of the stomach. It can be used to stimulate the appetite and also acts as a natural laxative, whence it can be used to purge the body of black bile and phlegm. The juice of the plant can be used as a cleaning agent to remove stains from fabric and it can also be used to clean spots from the pages of books. As for the plant's other medicinal applications, Idrīsī points out that it can be used to reduce fatigue and to cleanse an infected or otherwise irritated eye.

The plant known as *zarāwand* is entry 301 of the treatise and Idrīsī notes that Diosciorides makes mention of the plant in the second section of the *Materia*, where he terms it *aristolochia* in Greek. In Latin it bears the name *misqar*, in Syriac *sanilaus*, Frankish *aristolojia*, and Berber *lursia*. The names in Persian and Sanskrit have been left blank, perhaps because they contained sounds for which Arabic had no equivalent letters, and so the copyist preferred simply to omit them. The designations coming from foreign tongues have been given Arabic transliterations that are in many cases wildly inaccurate, especially those coming from non-Semitic languages such as Latin, Greek, and Sanskrit, but this in itself provides an intriguing glimpse at how Arabic speakers heard and chose to transliterate terms coming from languages very different from their own.

Zarāwand was known to be quite important for Arab alchemists of the Middle Ages but Idrīsī unfortunately provides no information on the plant's uses for alchemy. He does mention, however, that the plant is effective for aborting a fetus without doing any harm to the womb, an interesting detail in its own right. Frequent indeed are the notices of plants which may do harm to fetuses in the womb. Such is the case for the plant called *ḥadsā*, a Persian name for which Dioscorides provides the Greek designation *onoma*,[24] but which other Greeks call *asmata*, a detail perhaps supplied by Idrīsī's Byzantine colleagues at Palermo. He remarks that if the leaves of this plant are crushed and ingested with water, it will immediately clear the womb. This, according to Idrīsī, explains how the plant received its designation in colloquial Arabic, *musqiṭ al-ajanna*,[25] a detail that suggests how folk medicine pertaining to women was practiced among Muslims of the western Mediterranean.

Regarding the plant life of Sicily, Idrīsī makes mentions of a plant the Sicilians call "the mountain raisin," *zabīb al-jabal*, but which Andalusīs prefer to call *ḥabb al-rā's*, and the eastern Arabs *zabīb barrī*, "wild raisin." This is in fact none other than staphisagria, more commonly termed lice-bane, a plant known to be especially efficacious at destroying body lice. Idrīsī observes that the plant as found in Sicily resembles the wild fig in size, and if crushed and dried can be used as snuff to clear nasal ailments.

---

[24] Lit. "name." Perhaps an indication of a faulty transmission on the part of Idrīsī.

[25] Lit. "the aborter of fetuses."

Finally, a plant known to abound in the lands of the western Mediterranean, *al-ḥandaqūqī al-barrī*, the wild lotus, which Idrīsī says the Sicilians call *sala*, is said to bear the same name in Berber, a suggestion of the close interaction and linguistic borrowing between these two Mediterranean peoples. The narcotic effects of the plant are duly noted and Idrīsī observes that the plant can be used to reduce pain in the bladder, the womb, and the ribs, as well as pain arising from scorpion bites. It is curious that only the Istanbul manuscript has an entry for this important plant, the Tehran manuscript having omitted it entirely.[26]

There is little doubt that Idrīsī intended his botanical treatise for an Andalusī audience, hoping in part to familiarize Andalusīs with the plant life of North Africa and the botanical knowledge of the Berbers. Given the cosmopolitan character of much of Andalusī society, the population of whose large conurbations was frequently multilingual, the plethora of plant designations from a host of languages found throughout Idrisi's work would have had a special appeal. This seems especially true of those plant names derived from Latinate languages, with which an educated Andalusī readership would have had at least a passing familiarity. When he refers to al-Andalus in the text, he frequently designates it as "our land," *arḍuna*, or "our country," *bilāduna*. In doing so, he is of course signaling his affiliation with his Iberian homeland and perhaps registering some sadness at having left it permanently behind to take up residence in a non-Muslim land, or rather a land that was once Muslim but has now left the fold of the faith.

It would seem, then, that Idrīsī is himself a work of translation, moving across one line of faith into the realm of another, translating the vocabulary of one culture into that of a second, and sometimes of a third and fourth. Moreover, Idrīsī's treatise is strongly influenced by a non-Muslim, Greek source in its method of identifying, describing, and classifying plant life. His work thus represents an important example of the remarkable reliance of Muslim scholarship on Greek sources after the eleventh century, a development for which a fully satisfying explanation has yet to be offered. The treatise is at the same time deeply indebted to the Muslims in the east who expanded the horizons of botany and pharmacology far beyond the point where pagan Greeks had left them, and there is much about the work that tells us how the methods of eastern scholarship crossed the Mediterranean and were received and occasionally reworked by learned Muslims in cities such as Cordoba and Granada.

One might plausibly suggest in conclusion that Idrīsī resembles in no small measure al-Aṣma'ī, the Iraqi philologist cited at the beginning of this paper who wished to save a venerable store of botanical knowledge from oblivion. Residing in Sicily in the twelfth century, Idrīsī almost certainly recognized that Islam's days in Iberia were numbered. His impressive treatise can be seen in this light as an effort to translate and preserve the accumulated botanical and pharmacological knowledge of a Mediterranean civilization that was on the brink of profound change.

---

[26] This may be a reflection of the opprobrium with which some doctors of the law regarded the plant's narcotic effects.

PART 2
Translation and Devotional Selfhood

The essays in this section explore how translation constructs and recuperates medieval literary approaches to spirituality with respect to individuals and to communities, and all three draw in some way, as part of their interpretative methodology, on the material cultural circumstances of the written. Aden Kumler's contribution, "Translating the Reader-Viewer: Visual Appropriation and the Promises of Devotional Literature in Paris, BnF, MS n.a.fr. 4338," interpreting translation as primarily a transposition, a relocation, of meaning, considers how image and text work together to transform the reader into a pious subject.[1] Kumler shows how the miniatures in an early fourteenth-century compilation of religious texts, known from its first item as the *Legiloque*, invoke iconography familiar from other contexts in books of hours and liturgies, as also in secular writing, and also incorporate images of its patron/owner in novel and thought-provoking ways, as part of its project to define and organize both the manuscript's contents and the appropriate response from its female reader. The three illustrations in which the female devotee appears engage in subtle metaphoric play with their subject in ways that incorporate secular courtly reference as well as religious injunction. The layers of interpretation that Kumler expertly unfolds in the meeting between text and picture, and the sophisticated cultural work she shows is expected of the reader, seem to grow from that play of metaphorical and literal reference familiar from, for example, Psalter iconography.[2] The study of translation across word and image promises to be a powerful instrument for the further understanding of the richness of medieval intertextuality.

My essay, on "'Foul Fiends and Dirty Devils': Henry, Duke of Lancaster's *Book of Holy Medicines* and the Translation of Fourteenth-Century Devotional

1 Richard Rouse and Mary Rouse identify the patron of the original compendium as Marie de Bretagne (d. 1339), and give an account of this manuscript (which cannot itself be directly associated with her) in the broader context of the literary patronage she and her family exercised, in "French literature and the counts of Saint-Pol ca. 1178–1377," *Viator* 41.1 (2010): 101–40 at 122–9.

2 On the literal and metaphorical in Psalters, see Lucy Freeman Sandler, "The Images of Words in English Gothic Psalters," in Brendan Cassidy and Rosemary Muir Wright (eds), *Studies in the Illustration of the Psalter* (Stamford, UK, 2000), pp. 67–86. On the multilayeredness of relations between language and imagery in medical manuscripts, where practical instruction, prayer, and devotion may all inform an image of healing, see Peter Murray Jones, "Image, Word, and Medicine in the Middle Ages," in Jean A. Givens, Karen M. Reeds, and Alain Touwaide (eds), *Visualizing Medieval Medicine and Natural History, 1200–1550* (Aldershot, 2006), pp. 1–24.

Literature," investigates the difficulties of translating an insular, penitential, noncanonical text, for which the surviving material contexts supply diverse interpretative perspectives and emphases. An instance of this phenomenon is evident in the Paris manuscript that is the focus of Kumler's essay, suggesting as it does interesting points of comparison and contrast between Henry's text and continental European constructons of devotional selfhood. The translation has to convey the treatise's avowedly spiritually abject tone, and also to signal its place in a religious practice that emerges as both worldly and aristocratic. I reflect on modern perceptions of a multilingual medieval past and on the ways in which a modern translation might encode and convey the cultural complexity of the medieval text. Alan Shapiro, in his account of the difficulties of translating the *Oresteia*, demonstrates how the translator is in negotiation with previous versions of the text and, by extension, with other literature in her/his own language, as well as with the work itself: "No translation can ever escape the history of style."[3] As the translator of a text with little history of internal translation, I both emphasize the provisional nature of my linguistic engagement with that text and make explicit my decisions about the style of the Modern English, to present it as contribution to a larger, continuing conversation with our collective knowledge of, and reconstitution of, the past.

With "Languages Low and High: Translation and the Creation of Community in the Chester Pentecost Play," Robert W. Barrett, Jr. moves discussion to the public stage, to consider what is lost and elided by an overeagerness to read the Chester plays primarily against a backdrop of the cultural changes brought about by the shift to Protestantism and to make the concomitant uncritical assumption that Latin in this context is synonymous with Catholicism, while the English vernacular is automatically part of a Protestant doctrinal agenda. Barrett's analysis repositions Play 21, the Fishmongers' *Pentecost* (which refers to the events of Acts 1:15–26 and 2:1–12) as central to Chester's exploration of redemptive language, and demonstrates how its macaronic switches between Latin and English contribute in highly complex ways to the pageant's verbal construction of community.

Barrett observes how this community nevertheless occludes women, and the lower classes in general, whom the play implicitly disenfranchises. At the same time, one might again take a cue from Ricoeur's emphasis on internal translation, and find particularly apposite the play's concluding conversation between the two *Alienigenae*, astonished witnesses to the Disciples' ministry. The first says he understands these Galileans to be speaking "our language" perfectly, "as ever eate I bread!" (words that recall for the Chester audience both the Eucharist and the events they have recently experienced theatrically, in representations of the Last Supper, and of the recognition of Christ at Emmaus). His companion's throwaway colloquialism is equally suggestive:

[3] Shapiro, "Translation as 'Linguistic Hospitality,'" p. 142.

"Well I wotte, by my lewtee,
that within theise dayes three
one of them could not speake with mee
for to have binne dead."[4]
[By my faith, I know well that,
only three days ago,
not one of them could have spoken with me,
upon his life!]

In speaking more truly than they know, the men, with their idiomatic banter, remind the onlookers of their shared spiritual and doctrinal truths. In the course of the performance, the Chester audience members, if excluded on one level, are also invited, from their perspective of religious conviction, to see as a gift of grace their ability to translate the language of the everyday into spiritual blessing.

[4] *The Chester Mystery Cycle*, ed. R.M. Lumiansky and A.D. Mills, Early English Text Society, s.s. 3 and 9 (2 vols, London, 1974, 1986), vol. 1, pp. 394–5, ll. 370; 371–4. For the Last Supper and the Road to Emmaus, see, respectively, Plays 15 (pp. 268–83) and 19 (pp. 356–68).

Chapter 3
Translating ma dame de Saint-Pol: The Privilege and Predicament of the Devotee in the *Legiloque* Manuscript[1]

Aden Kumler

> Ci commence la dedication de l'ame que nous appelons sanctification. Car lors est la chose a dieu dediee quant elle li est sanctifiee.[2]
> [Here begins the dedication of the soul that we call sanctification. For a thing is dedicated to God when it is sanctified to Him.]

Like all devotional literature, the beginning of a treatise on the sanctification of the soul in Paris, Bibliothèque nationale de France, MS naf 4338 claims to effect a change of state in the person it instructs. The *before*-and-*after* calculus of devotional literature implies a triangulation between a historical reader, a text, and an ideal reader. No construct of modern critical interpretation, the ideal reader often explicitly anticipated by devotional literature is the historical reader *after* his or her encounter with the text. In the European Middle Ages, a context in which devotional literature was understood as effective, useful literature, its ideal reader was its every historical reader transformed.

Medieval devotional literature's claim to transform historical reader-viewers into ideal reader-viewers may best be understood as a form of translation. Both the Latin *translatio* and the Old French *translation* referred primarily to physical transferral, and only secondarily to linguistic translation; the primary sense of both words was that of movement from one place to another.

---

[1] I am grateful to Karen L. Fresco, Charles D. Wright, and Anne D. Hedeman for inviting me to participate in the "Translating the Middle Ages" conference. My thinking about medieval practices of translation benefited from the contributions, questions, and comments of the conference participants. I am also grateful to Geneviève Hasenohr and Mary and Richard Rouse for generously sharing their insights concerning Paris, BnF, MS naf 4338. Jeffrey Hamburger's suggestions and critiques helped to shape this argument at a formative stage and I remain indebted to him for his contributions to my thinking.

[2] Paris, BnF, MS naf 4338, f. 193r. In transcriptions from the manuscript, I have silently expanded abbreviations, omitted words that are vacated, and supplied punctuation when required for sense. Latin scripture is cited from the Vulgate; English translations are cited from *The Holy Bible: Douay Rheims Version*, trans. Bishop Richard Challoner (Rockford, IL, 2000; reprint, rev. ed.). Unless otherwise noted all translations are my own.

In the context of Latinate Christianity, *translatio* also referred to the ritual movement of the relics of a saint from one location to another.[3] As Amy Hollywood has argued, this application of the term *translatio* implies the conflation of bodies with language;[4] following Hollywood's insight, I would suggest that in *translatio* we may discern not only the conflation of bodies with language but also the movement of meaning from place to place. It is this sense of translation that informs the medieval concepts of *translatio imperii* and *translatio studii.*[5] In the European medieval context, *translatio* connoted a transfer: a transfer of meaning, of holiness, of power, of knowledge.

Accordingly, medieval devotional literature in the vernacular accomplishes a double translation: it transfers the teaching of faith and the provision of salvation from a Latinate linguistic register into a vernacular language and, if it is to live up to its name, it transfers its reader from a lesser spiritual state to a greater one. In the later Middle Ages, as vernacular devotional literature came to be illuminated in luxury manuscripts designed for elite audiences, a further, visual form of translation began to play an important part in the transformative calculus of devotion.[6]

In this essay I explore how a fourteenth-century illuminated manuscript designed for moral and spiritual instruction attempted to translate its anticipated female reader-viewer. My analysis focuses on three representations of an aristocratic woman painted within the manuscript's ambitious visual program (Figures 1, 4, and 5). In collaboration with the Middle French texts they accompany, these representations collectively incorporate the figure of the female devotee within the visual framework of the manuscript. Rather than seeing these depictions as conventional painted reflections of a female patron or book-owner, I will instead suggest they—like many translations—were appropriative figures,

---

[3] On hagiographic and ritual *translationes*, see Patrick J. Geary, *Living with the Dead in the Middle Ages* (Ithaca, 1994), pp. 213–14, and passim; Martin Heinzelmann, *Translationsberichte und andere Quellen des Reliquienkultes*, Typologie des sources du Moyen Age occidental 33 (Turnhout, Belgium, 1979).

[4] Amy Hollywood, "'Beautiful as a Wasp': Angela of Foligno and Georges Bataille," *Harvard Theological Review* 92.2 (1999): 219–36 at 233–6.

[5] These two cultural conceptions of *translatio* are intimately linked in the medieval period. For a point of entry into a vast bibliography, see Ulrike Krämer, *Translatio imperii et studii: zum Geschichts- und Kulturverständnis in der französischen Literatur des Mittelalters und der frühen Neuzeit*, Abhandlungen zur Sprache und Literatur 98 (Bonn, 1996); Serge Lusignan, *Parler vulgairement: Les intellectuels et la langue française au XIIIe et XIVe siècles*, ed. Pierre Boglioni, 2nd ed., Études médiévales (Montréal, 1987); Colette Beaune, *The Birth of an Ideology: Myths and Symbols of Nation in Late-Medieval France*, trans. Susan Ross Huston (Berkeley, 1991), pp. 266–82; A.G. Jongkees, "Translatio Studii: les avatars d'un thème médiéval," in D.P. Blok (ed.), *Miscellanea Mediaevalia in Memoriam Jan Frederik Niermeyer* (Groningen, 1967), pp. 41–51.

[6] For further discussion see Aden Kumler, *Translating Truth: Ambitious Images and Religious Knowledge in Late Medieval France and England* (New Haven and London, 2011).

both aggressive and authorizing, that attempted to implicate an anticipated reader-viewer in the privileges and predicament of the role of devotee.

Paris, BnF, MS naf 4338: The First of the *Legiloque* Manuscripts

Paris, BnF, MS naf 4338 (hereafter the *Legiloque* manuscript, after the title of its first treatise) belongs to a popular, but largely forgotten genre of late medieval manuscript: vernacular illuminated compendia, designed to instruct their reader-viewers in the curriculum of the faith, moral rectitude, and sacramental participation.[7] Comprised of 209 folios,[8] the volume provided its original reader-viewer with no fewer than 19 improving texts, in prose and verse, as well as 27 images.[9]

7 First discussed by Léopold Delisle in 1869, the compendium has only recently attracted the attention it deserves: Jeffrey Hamburger, "Body vs. Book: The Trope of Visibility in Images of Christian-Jewish Polemic," in David Ganz, Thomas Lentes, and Georg Henkel (eds), *Ästhetik des Unsichtbaren: Bildtheorie und Bildgebrauch in der Vormoderne*, KultBild 1 ([Berlin], 2004), pp. 113–45 at pp. 115–16; Léopold Delisle, "Notice sur un recueil de traités de dévotion ayant appartenu à Charles V," *Bibliothèque de l'École des Chartes* 6ème sér. 5 (1869): 532–42; Sylvia Huot, "The Writer's Mirror: Watriquet de Couvin and the Development of the Author-Centred Book," in Bill Bell, Jonquil Bevan, and Philip Bennet (eds), *Across Boundaries: The Book in Culture & Commerce* (Winchester, Hampshire, UK, and New Castle, DE, 2000), pp. 29–46 at pp. 30–32; Sylvia Huot, "Polytextual Reading: The Meditative Reading of Real and Metaphorical Books," in Mark Chinca and Christopher Young (eds), *Orality and Literacy in the Middle Ages: Essays on a Conjunction and its Consequences in Honour of D.H. Green*, Utrecht Studies in Medieval Literacy 12 (Turnhout, 2005), pp. 203–22 at pp. 206–9; Mary Rouse and Richard Rouse, "French Literature and the Counts of Saint-Pol ca. 1178–1377," *Viator* 41.1 (2010): 101–40 at 122–9, 135–9; Anne-Marie Legaré, "L'Image du livre comme adjuvant mémoriel dans le *Conte des trois chevaliers et des trois livres*," in Frank Willaert, Herman Braet, Thom Mertens, and Theo Venckeleer (eds), *Medieval Memory: Image and Text*, Textes et études du moyen âge 27 (Turnhout, 2004), pp. 129–43; François Avril and Jean Lafaurie (eds), *La Librairie de Charles V* (Paris, 1968), pp. 73–4 (no. 139). The BnF has made a full digital facsimile of the manuscript available through its Gallica portal: <http://gallica.bnf.fr/ark:/12148/btv1b84557917> (August 2012).

8 The manuscript's folios (210 x 150 mm) are organized into 26 regular quaternions with the addition of a preliminary singleton flyleaf (formerly an initial pastedown). Catchwords at the end of each quire confirm that the sequence of the quires has not been disturbed. The manuscript is foliated by a contemporary hand in inked roman numerals and is partially foliated (ff. 79–207) in a modern hand in pencil; both systems of foliation become inaccurate in sections of the manuscript. Folio references in my discussion will not depend on either of the foliations found in the manuscript. My folio 1 is currently foliated as "A" in the manuscript; my folio 2 is currently foliated as "B" in the manuscript; my folio 3 is currently foliated as "I" in the manuscript, etc.

9 The textual contents of the manuscript are inventoried in Rouse and Rouse, "Counts of Saint-Pol," pp. 135–9.

Several internal references showcase the compendium's aristocratic pedigree. The author of the *Legiloque* manuscript's *petit trectie de nostre dame* is explicitly identified as a count of the House of Saint-Pol. We find a second reference to this comital family in a lengthy account of the foundation of the Carthusian order that occurs in both the *nouuelletez dou monde* (ff. 110r-111v) and the *trectie dou saint esperit* (ff. 175v-177r). In both recitations of the foundation legend the author authorizes his account by claiming that it is "selonc ce que ie oi conter deuant madame la contesse de saint pol a j. des greigneurs hommes et des plus anciens de celle ordre de chartresuse" ["according to what I heard related before Madame the Countess of Saint-Pol by one of the greater men and one of the oldest men of this order of the Chartreuse"].[10]

Recently, Mary and Richard Rouse have made a convincing argument that the countess of Saint-Pol mentioned in the manuscript should be identified as Marie de Bretagne, the wife of Gui II de Châtillon, Count of Saint-Pol and *Grand Boutellier* of the King of France, who, following her husband's death in 1317, was dowager countess of Saint-Pol until her own demise in 1339.[11] A colophon to the compendium suggests that the Countess of Saint-Pol was not a passive recipient of the volume's instructions, but rather the curator of its program for spiritual perfection.[12] In this valediction, we encounter an unusual *patronal* statement of purpose:

> Ci acheuerons nostre traitie. Et redant [*sic*] graces a dieu et a sa benoite mere. Et suppliant a ceus qui laront et liront que il se tiennent apaiez de nostre petite information. Que charite et deuotion nous a ainssi fait ordener pour lessier apres nous aucune chose en quoi se puissent espirituement occupier noz bons amis et nos bonnes amies. Et nos seigneurs et nos dames. Aus quiex et aus queles nous nous recommandons tres humblement. Et a uie et a mort especiaument.
> [Here we shall end our treatise. And giving thanks to God and to his blessed Mother, and entreating those who shall hear and read it that they shall consider themselves satisfied with our little instruction, which charity and devotion thus made us prepare in order to leave behind us some thing with which our good friends (male and female) and our Lords and our Ladies might occupy themselves spiritually. To whom (male and female) we recommend ourselves very humbly, both in life and especially in death.]

The survival of two other fourteenth-century copies of the compendium suggests that Marie de Bretagne's desire to provide moral-spiritual direction for her children and her *bons et bonnes amies* was fulfilled. Dated within a decade of BnF, MS naf 4338, BnF, MS fr. 1136 and Chantilly, Bibliothèque du Château, MS 137, contain precisely the same collection of texts, in the same order, with nearly identical visual programs. In each exemplar a single female figure appears in three miniatures.

10 Paris, BnF, MS naf 4338, ff. 111v and 177r.

11 Rouse and Rouse, "Counts of Saint-Pol," 117–18, 119, 123–9.

12 Ibid., p. 127.

The consistency of the visual program preserved in all three fourteenth-century exemplars of Marie de Bretagne's purpose-built compilation is, no doubt, an index of the deliberated, bespoke character of its assemblage of texts and images. It is also, almost certainly, the result of an artistic monopoly: each copy of the *Legiloque* compendium was painted by a single illuminator, named Mahiet.[13] Working at the epicenter of elite manuscript painting in Paris, Mahiet's chief period of production seems to span the years from c. 1323 and to c. 1350.[14] On stylistic grounds, BnF, MS naf 4338 has been dated to the mid-period of Mahiet's career, c. 1330–1340.[15] An emergent consensus sees BnF, MS naf 4338 as the earliest of the three fourteenth-century copies of the compendium. Subsequently, BnF, MS fr. 1136 and Chantilly, Bibliothèque du Château, MS 137 were produced in short succession, likely within a decade.[16]

As Mary and Richard Rouse emphasize, to identify Marie de Bretagne as the original commissioner and supervisor of the *Legiloque* compilation is "not the same as saying that any of the three extant manuscripts belonged to her."[17] This note of caution is particularly relevant to the interpretation of the female figure who appears three times in BnF, MS naf 4338, and applies also to her "sisters" in the two nearly contemporary exemplars of the compendium.[18] Traditionally, art historians have interpreted similar contemporary figures painted or drawn on the medieval

---

13 Formerly dubbed "The Master of the Lives of Saint Louis" and "The Master of the Long Fingers," François Avril and Marie-Thérèse Gousset have made a compelling case for identifying this illuminator as Mahiet, alias Mathieu le Vavasseur: Richard Rouse, "Mahiet, the Illuminator of Cambridge University Library, MS Dd.5.5," in Stella Panayotova (ed.), *The Cambridge Illuminations: The Conference Papers* (London, 2007), pp. 173–86; *Les Fastes du gothique: Le siècle de Charles V: Galeries nationales du Grand Palais, 9 octobre 1981–1er février 1982* ([Paris], 1981), pp. 299–300, no. 247; Marie-Thérèse Gousset, "Libraires d'origine normande à Paris au XIVe siècle," in Pierre Bouet and Monique Dosdat (eds), *Manuscrits et enluminures dans le monde normand (Xe–XVe siècles): Colloque de Cerisy-la-Salle (octobre 1995): actes* (Caen, 1999), pp. 169–80. I am grateful to Beth Morrison for drawing my attention to Richard Rouse's essay.

14 Richard H. Rouse and Mary A. Rouse, *Manuscripts and Their Makers: Commercial Book Producers in Medieval Paris, 1200–1500: Illiterati et uxorati* (2 vols, Turnhout, 2000), vol. 2, pp. 94–5, 96. For a tentative chronology of Mahiet's work, see Jane Geein Chung-Apley, "The Illustrated 'Vie et Miracles de Saint Louis' of Guillaume de Saint-Pathus (Paris, B.N., Ms. fr. 5716)," PhD dissertation, University of Michigan, 1998, pp. 144–71.

15 Avril and Lafaurie (eds), *La Librairie de Charles V*, pp. 73–4, no. 139.

16 Rouse and Rouse, "Counts of Saint-Pol," 126–7.

17 Ibid., p. 127.

18 Interpretation of the female figure in Paris, BnF, MS naf 4338 becomes even more complicated when she is visually compared to her "sisters" in Paris, BnF, MS fr. 1136 and Chantilly, Bibliothèque du Château, MS 137. In this essay, I hope to suggest, if only by implication, that the ambiguous identity of the devotee figure may be integral to her role in the visual program as an exemplar of a matrilineal ideal of female spiritual excellence.

manuscript page as surrogates for the patron or recipient of an illuminated book.[19] Often seen as idealized "reflections" of specific medieval reader-viewers, such figures feature prominently in liturgical and paraliturgical books (such as psalters, psalter-hours, and books of hours). In other types of manuscript, these kinds of figures are usually found in introductory frontispiece or "dedication" miniatures celebrating the patronage (either through commission or receipt) of a manuscript.[20] Less frequently attested in the Middle Ages, the presence of contemporary figures in the visual programs of didactic manuscripts has similarly been described as belonging to a visual tradition of idealizing surrogates or proxies.[21]

The single female figure—notably unencumbered by heraldic markers of identity—depicted three times in the *Legiloque* compendium's visual program poses a real challenge to our taxonomies of owner surrogates or patronal proxies. Despite the manuscript's insistent referencing of its aristocratic provenance, no internal textual or visual evidence settles the question of the female figure's identity. By contrast, as I will suggest in the remainder of this essay, the aristocratic female figure who inhabits three of the manuscript's miniatures might best be understood as a kind of function, a *figura translata* that proleptically and aggressively asserts the efficacy of the devotional economy constructed and perpetuated by the compendium as a whole.

---

[19] For further discussion see Stephen Perkinson, *The Likeness of the King: A Prehistory of Portraiture in Late Medieval France* (Chicago, 2009); Kathryn A. Smith, "Book, Body, and the Construction of the Self in the Taymouth Hours," in Katherine Allen Smith and Scott Wells (eds), *Negotiating Community and Difference in Medieval Europe: Gender, Power, Patronage, and the Authority of Religion in Latin Christendom*, Studies in the History of Christian Traditions 142 (Leiden and Boston, 2009), pp. 173–97; Hugo van der Velden, *The Donor's Image: Gerard Loyet and the Votive Portraits of Charles the Bold*, Burgundica 2 (Turnhout, 2000); Madeleine Caviness, "Anchoress, Abbess, and Queen: Donors and Patrons or Intercessors and Matrons?" in June Hall McCash (ed.), *The Cultural Patronage of Medieval Women* (Athens, 1996), pp. 105–54.

[20] Further examples and analysis in Elizabeth Salter and Derek Pearsall, "Pictorial illustration of late medieval poetic texts: the role of the frontispiece or prefatory picture," in Flemming Gotthelf Andersen (ed.), *Medieval Iconography and Narrative: A Symposium* (Odense, 1980), pp. 100–123; Dhira B. Mahoney, "Courtly Presentation and Authorial Self-fashioning: Frontispiece Miniatures in Late Medieval French and English Manuscripts," *Mediaevalia* 21 (1996): 97–160; Anne D. Hedeman, "Constructing Memories: Scenes of Conversation and Presentation in Pierre Salmon's *Dialogues*," *Journal of the Walters Art Gallery* 54 (1996): 119–34; Anne D. Hedeman, "Pierre Salmon's Advice for a King," *Gesta* 32.2 (1993): 113–23.

[21] See the important analyses in Lucy Freeman Sandler, "The Image of the Book-Owner in the Fourteenth Century: Three Cases of Self-definition," in Nicholas Rogers (ed.), *England in the Fourteenth Century: Proceedings of the 1991 Harlaxton Symposium*, Harlaxton Medieval Studies 3 (Stamford, UK, 1993), pp. 58–80; Sylvia Huot, "A Book Made for a Queen: The Shaping of a Late Medieval Anthology Manuscript (B.N. fr. 24429)," in Siegfried Wenzel (ed.), *The Whole Book: Cultural Perspectives on the Medieval Miscellany*, Recentiores (Ann Arbor, 1996), pp. 123–73.

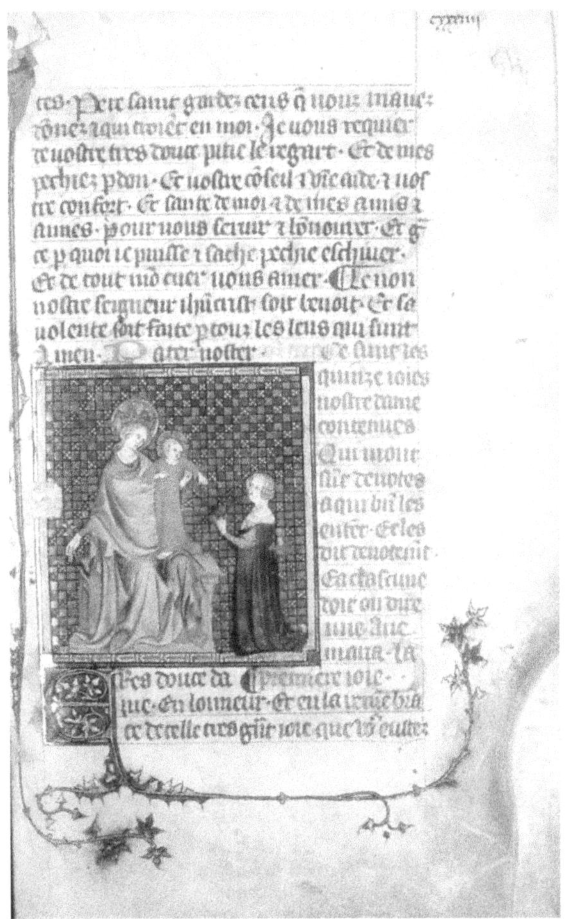

Fig. 3.1 Paris, BnF, MS naf 4338, f. 134r (photo BnF).

Translation in the Space of Devotion

The figure of the female devotee first appears in an image placed at the end of *.Vij. peticions tres deuotes et tres profitables pour requerre l'aide et le conseil et la grace nostre seigneur* [*Seven very devout and useful petitions to request the aide, counsel and grace of Our Lord*] and before *Les quinze ioies nostre dame* [*The fifteen joys of Our Lady*] (Figure 3.1). The miniature in which the devotee debuts is the last of a suite of three images in the *Legiloque* manuscript that derive from an iconographic repertoire associated with liturgical and paraliturgical books.

Fig. 3.2 Paris, BnF, MS naf 4338, f. 131v (photo BnF).

The first miniature in the series introduces the *.Vij. peticions* tract (Figure 3.2). This half-page illumination takes the form of a *maiestas domini*, an iconographic formula closely associated with the Canon of the Mass in late medieval illuminated missals. In the second miniature in the series, placed between the end of the third petition and start of the fourth, Christ appears crucified between the Virgin and John within an ambiguous space defined only by a patterned ground (Figure 3.3).

The inclusion of a representation of the Crucifixion at this particular point in the text is motivated by a shift that occurs between the third and fourth petitions. The third petition concludes in a three-part evocation of Christ's life from the Incarnation through his ministry. In the fourth petition a series of memorial evocations of events in the Passion narrative begins, culminating in Christ's Ascension.

Fig. 3.3 Paris, BnF, MS naf 4338, f. 132v (photo BnF).

The Crucifixion image is thus placed as if it were a frontispiece to a new text: the text of Christ's Passion and his subsequent Resurrection. Despite its indeterminate treatment of pictorial space, the miniature provides a visual memorial of the historical Crucifixion, an event belonging to the scriptural past, witnessed by the historical figures of Mary and John the Evangelist. Simultaneously, viewed in tandem with the *maiestas* image that precedes it, the second miniature of the *Peticions* evokes the visual repertoire of missals, in which a Crucifixion miniature might introduce the Canon of the Mass (in place of a *maiestas*), and of books of hours, in which Crucifixion images usually prefaced the Hours of the Cross and a *maiestas* often initiated the Penitential Psalms.

The third miniature in the series, featuring the aristocratic devotee, marks the transition from the *Peticions* to the *Les quinze ioies nostre dame* (Figure 3.1). Like the *Peticions*, the *Joies* are structured through a series of prayers in the first-person that collectively commemorate events from Christ's life; in the *Joies*, these commemorations are mediated through the Virgin's experience of the vita Christi. The image accompanying the *Joies*, however, does not represent a moment from this Christological narrative. The miniature instead depicts the female devotee's adoration of the Virgin and Christ Child. In the *Legiloque* manuscript, this scene is visually unmoored from the scriptural past. It is instead a vignette that clothes devotional prescription in the compelling guise of visual description, interpellating the devotee in a present-tense relationship with the deity. At the same time, like the *maiestas domini* and Crucifixion that precede it, the iconographic formula of kneeling devotee and seated Virgin and Child evokes the visual repertoire of contemporary liturgical use books and prayer books. In this way, the miniature associates the *Joies*, an expository vernacular tract of more recent vintage, with the authoritative visual signifiers of church ritual and accepted forms of paraliturgical prayer.

Derived from an established canon of "devotional images," the series of three images that constitute this prayer-book-in-miniature section of the compendium are the exception rather than the rule in the *Legiloque* manuscript. Referencing books used in, or in parallel with the liturgy, these illuminations form a cohesive and anomalous interlude within the manuscript. Significantly, in the later Middle Ages, prayer books often served as primers for young aristocrats, initiating them in the "polytextual" protocols of reading, viewing, and interpretation that Sylvia Huot has described as crucial to aristocratic formation in the period.[22] An imaginative hermeneusis that encompassed real and imagined books, the material page and the page as trope, polytexual reading involved elite readers and viewers in an "active and inventive" encounter with the illuminated and inscribed page.[23] Within the larger conceptual and visual framework of the *Legiloque* manuscript, the manuscript's prayer book subsection overtly evokes the polytexual promise of psalters and books of hours, those primers of literacy, devotion, and the art of interpretation in late medieval aristocratic households.

The *Joies* miniature performs a double role in the manuscript. First, it terminates a sequence of three images that emulate the content and illustration of a prayer book, thus defining a kind of (prayer) book within a book (of didactic instruction). Second, the miniature accomplishes the manuscript's first translation of its anticipated female reader-viewer. The iconographic formula into which the figure of the devotee is transposed and the literal frame painted about the image are not separative devices; they collapse the space of devotion inhabited by the laywoman, as she holds the *Legiloque* manuscript, with the pictorial space of an

---

22 Huot, "Polytextual Reading."

23 Ibid., p. 222.

image in that book that prescribes a form of devotion to her. Representing the book-owner's devotion as consummated, and her prayer as effective, the image asserts a proleptic claim for its own translative efficacy.

Although the first appearance of the *Legiloque* compendium's female figure can be accommodated within established art historical conceptions of donor or patron figures, the *Joies* miniature's visual appropriation of the devotee is but the first maneuver in a sustained campaign to translate her into the very fabric of the compendium, and so into the terms of its prescriptive vision of moral, spiritual, and aristocratic formation. In subsequent appearances, this female figure increasingly frustrates art historical desires to read a singular, stable historical identity from painted representation.

Translation in the *Livre de vie*

The *Legiloque* compendium's second presentation of the female figure situates her in privileged proximity to Christ crucified (Figure 3.4, p. 46). This, however, is no generic image of devotee and suffering incarnate deity. Regular bands of pale green wash painted over linear under-drawing delimit the angular space of reserved parchment behind the figure of Christ on the cross as a book. The seven almond-shaped pendants hanging from the codex's lower edges indicate that this volume should be identified as the apocalyptic codex of John's Revelation. The introductory rubric that precedes the miniature confirms this reading of the image:

> Ci commence un petit trectie qui a bon droit est apele. liure de uie et aguillon d'amour et de deuotion. dont l'escripture et les lettres sunt de la croiz ihesucrist trestes et de sa sainte passion.[24]
> [Here begins a little treatise that is quite properly called the Book of Life and the Prick (or Goad) of Love and of Devotion; the writing and the letters of which are drawn from the cross of Jesus Christ and from his holy Passion.]

The "book of life," described in Apocalypse 20:15 ("And who so ever was not found written in the book of life, was cast into the pool of fire"), is *not*, however, the book with seven seals described in Apocalypse 5:1 ("And I saw in the right hand of him that sat on the throne, a book written within and without, sealed with seven seals.") The combined effect of rubric and image suggests that we are confronted not with any book, nor even with one book, but rather with the deliberate conflation of three elements: the book of life, the book with seven seals, and Christ's Cross, described in the introductory rubric as a textual source for the treatise that follows.

This multiplication of referents, hovering within and about the miniature, is only further complicated by the treatise that follows: for in this *Liure de uie*

[24] Paris, BnF, MS naf 4338, f. 143r.

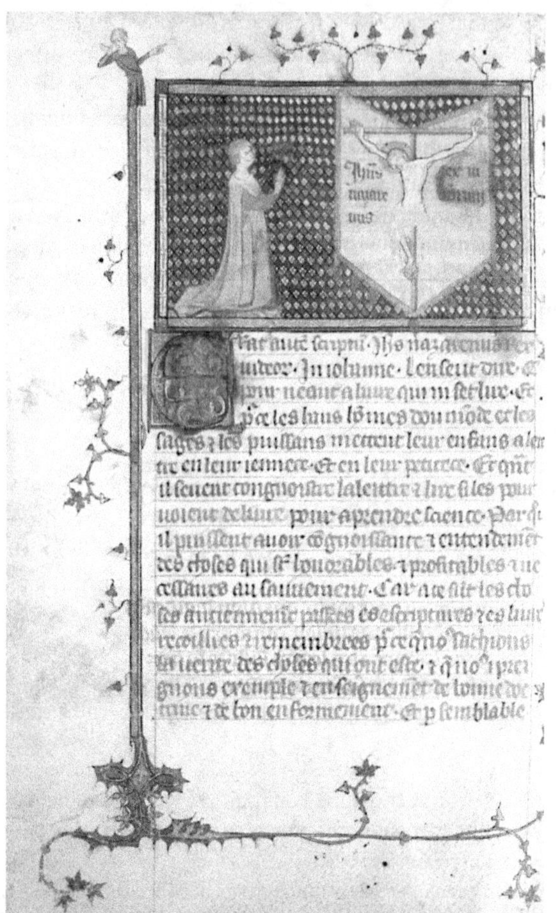

Fig. 3.4 Paris, BnF, MS naf 4338, f. 143v (photo BnF).

[*Book of Life*] we receive explicit instruction in learning to view and read the book that is Christ. The treatise, in fact, teaches us that Christ is both one and many books and, over the course of 28 folios (ff. 143v-170r), it describes a proliferation of Christ-Books.[25]

[25] The tract's title—*le Liure de uie et aguillon d'amour et de devotion*—evokes the *Stimulus amoris* tract, written by the thirteenth-century Franciscan James of Milan: Jacobus Mediolanensis, *Stimulus amoris fr. Jacobi Mediolanensis*, Bibliotheca franciscana ascetica medii aevi; 4 (Quaracchi, 1905). I have not been able to identify any significant correspondence between the *Stimulus* and the Middle French treatise found in the *Legiloque* manuscript.

The bookish multiplication begins with a comparison of the *titulus*, written by Pilate, and placed above Christ's head on the cross, to a table of contents:

> Et tout aussi comme uous ueez que l'en seut escrire au commencement dou liure et touchier briement la matiere que il contient. Tout aussi pilate … ou temps et ou iour de la sainte passion au benoit ihesucrist qui est le liure dont nous parlons escript en une table que il mist sus son chief une suscription ou il toucha briement la matiere que il contient.[26]
> [And, as you see, just as one is wont to write at the beginning of a book and to briefly touch upon the material that it contains, so too Pilate … in the time and on the day of the holy Passion of Jesus Christ, who is the book of which we speak, wrote a superscription on a tablet that he put above his (Christ's) head, in which he briefly touched upon the material that it contained (i.e., Christ).]

The contents of the book of Christ are identified as the knowledge (*science*) and the teaching (*doctrine*) of three things: all perfect salvation, every gracious ornament (*parement*), and all holy governance (*gouuernement*).[27] As the treatise pursues each of these topics, however, the Christ-Books continue to multiply. Identifying Christ with the book described in Apocalypse 5:1 as "written within and without," the treatise glosses this external and internal writing in the following fashion:

> Et en signe de ce uit Saint Jehen en l'apocalipse un liure escript dedanz et dehors seignie de .vij. seaus. En cest liure est le benoit filz dieu ihesucrist escript dedanz quant a sa benoite deite. ou les anges et les ames beneurees lisent tres clerement toutes les choses qui onques furent sunt et seront. Ensement il est escript par dehors quant a sa uraie humanite. ou nous pouon lire et ueoir sa tres grant perfection de sa tres sainte conuersation et de sa tres glorieuse predication.[28]
> [And as a sign of this Saint John, in the Apocalypse, saw a book written within and without, signed with seven seals. In this book the blessed Son of God, Jesus Christ, is written within with respect to his blessed deity, in which the blessed angels and souls read very clearly all the things that ever were, are, and shall be. Likewise, he is written without with respect to his true humanity, in which we can read and see his very great perfection, both of his very holy way of life and of his very glorious preaching.]

Focused on an exegesis of the internal and external writing of this Christ-Book, the treatise continues the deliberate conflation of apocalyptic books that permeates its introductory miniature.

---

26 Paris, BnF, MS naf 4338, f. 145r. It should be noted that the aside *comme uous ueez* in this passage refers the reader to a citation of John 19:19 in the tract's first line: *erat autem scriptum Ihesus Nazarenus rex Iudaeorum* (Paris, BnF, MS naf 4338, f. 143v). As the manuscript itself begins with a table of contents (ff. 1r-2r), an extratextual reference to the compendium's prefatory apparatus may also be construed from this remark.

27 Paris, BnF, MS naf 4338, f. 145v.

28 Paris, BnF, MS naf 4338, f. 151r.

Following a discussion of the Book of the Cross (ff. 155v-157r), we learn that Christ-as-Book may be understood to beget three additional treatises or booklets (*liurets*). The text describes the derivation of these tracts from the ur-Book in terms that echo the structure and character of the *Legiloque* manuscript itself:

> Et de cest benoit liure de uie sunt estrez .iij. petiz liures. Qui nous sunt donnez pour nous enformer en uie espirituele par quoi nous puisson uenir a uie pardurable. Et de ces .iij. liures Le premier est appele le liure de la conscience … le secont liure est de la deuine congnoissance … Et le tiers est le liure de la souueraine et de la pardurable sapience …[29]
> [And from this blessed Book of Life are extracted (*estrez*) three little books which are given to us in order to instruct (*enformer*) us in spiritual life, by which we may come to eternal life. And of these three books, the first is called the Book of the Conscience … the second book is of Divine Knowledge … And the third is the Book of the Exalted (*souueraine*) and Eternal Wisdom …]

In a further passage, the final booklet—the Book of the Exalted and Eternal Wisdom—is also identified with the book written within and without.

> Et de cest liure de la souueraine sapience parle ezechie le prophete en vne uision que nostre sires li monstra. Ie vi dist il que nostre sires me monstra vne main que il m'enuoia ou estoit .i. liure enuelope escript dehors et dedanz Et celui liure fu deuant moi estendu. Ou il auoit escript et contenu pleurs et lamentations Ioies et consolations et meschiez et tribulations (Ezek. 2:9). Et entendez que ceste main qui fu au prophete monstree et a nous en cest monde enuoie fu le benoit filz dieu ihesucrist … Et en ceste main c'est ou benoit ihesucrist fu enuelope le liure de la souueraine sapience. Escript par dehors quant a sa uraie humanite. Et par dedanz quant a sa glorieuse deite qui fu deuant nous estendu. quant il fu pour nous en la croiez o clous rudes et groz atachie et cousu …[30]
> [And concerning this Book of the Exalted Wisdom Ezekiel the prophet speaks in a vision that Our Lord showed to him. "I saw," he says, "that Our Lord showed me a hand that he sent to me in which was wrapped (*enuelope*) a book written without and within. And this book was stretched out (*estendu*) before me, in which he had written and contained tears and lamentations, joys and consolations and misfortunes and tribulations" (Ezek. 2:9). And understand that this hand that was shown to the prophet and sent to us in this world was the blessed son of God, Jesus Christ … And in this hand, that is, in the blessed Jesus Christ, was wrapped the Book of the Exalted Wisdom, written on the outside with respect to his true humanity, and written on the inside with respect to his glorious deity, who was stretched out (*estendu*) before us when, for us, he was fixed and sewn (*cousu*) to the cross with crude nails …]

In the last folios of the treatise we have come full circle, returning to the complex layering of referents first encountered in the miniature that prefaces the tract.

[29] Paris, BnF, MS naf 4338, f. 160r.

[30] Paris, BnF, MS naf 4338, f. 169r-169v.

In a final elaboration of the many and the singular Christ-Book(s), the treatise evokes the Crucifixion codex represented within the space of its introductory miniature.

It is, in part, a feat of the treatise's French text that Ezekiel's vision of the book can be so specifically linked to a notion of Christ as both metaphorically and *materially* the Book. In this vernacular treatise the Vulgate's *inuolutus liber* becomes *un liure enuelope*; a translation that brings with it the implications of being clothed or wrapped, rather than closed or concealed.[31] The material quality of Christ-as-Book is further emphasized through the French text's choice of words at the end of the passage cited above. Describing Christ on the Cross as both "stretched out" (*estendu*) and "sewn" or "laced" (*cousu*), the *Liure de uie* recasts the Passion in the guise of book production. Christ's flesh is stretched, just as animal skins are stretched in the preparation of parchment; Christ is both "fixed" and "sewn" to the Cross, a choice of words that explicitly couches the Crucifixion as a literal and material codification or binding of Christ-as-Book.

As textually elaborated by the *Liure de uie*, Christ is both one and many books. Christ's Passion looses humanity from Satan's bonds and binds him like a book. His abundance as an authoritative codex yields three little tracts made of his humanity and divinity: Christ is the ideal *compendium* of salvific instruction. The title given to the treatise, *The Book of Life and the Prick* [or *Goad*] *of Love and Devotion*, encourages us to encounter the treatise *itself* as yet another book-avatar of Christ.

The tract's prefatory miniature responds to this invitation. In the image we may discern a visual *précis* of all the elements that the text will subsequently disclose. Christ's crucified body is aligned so that his torso and the vertical bar of the Cross coincide visually with the inner sewn fold of bound bifolium. The expanded text of Pilate's *titulus* is executed in letters of burnished gold that shine from fictive verso and recto. And kneeling before the bound and titled codex of Christ crucified is the second representation of the *Legiloque* manuscript's female figure.

The treatment of the fictive book within the miniature's frame insinuates that the female devotee's engagement with Christ crucified on the book must also be understood as a visualization of her engagement with the very *Liure de uie* treatise introduced by the image. The open book behind Christ, displayed to the female figure—and to the viewer of the manuscript page—is the only unpainted zone within the miniature. When the manuscript is viewed *in situ*, the words inscribed on the verso of the folio are visible, hovering on the other side of the semi-transparent parchment surface that defines the opening of the book depicted on the recto. Subtly, the miniature conflates the figured book, the *Liure de uie* treatise, and the apocalyptic book of life. Christ-as-Book is really Christ-as-Books: ineffable logos-creator, source of metaphysical treatises, object of vernacular interpretation, and painted devotional image.

---

31 The *liuret dou Rossignolet* likewise describes Christ as *tout enuelope de la nostre pourete*: Paris, BnF, MS naf 4338, f. 180r.

Through a sometimes dizzying explosion of textual and visual predication, the *Legiloque* manuscript refuses to choose between the metaphorical and the material. In visibly collapsing such distinctions it again elides the difference between its actual viewer and the ideal viewer represented in its miniatures. The *Legiloque* manuscript's first depiction of the female devotee translated her to a fictive space of already-rewarded devotion; its second representation of the female figure redoubles this effort with an important change: in the *Liure de uie* miniature the space of devotion that the devotee inhabits is explicitly rendered as the didactic and vernacular space of the treatise itself, radically embodied as the Book of Life that is Christ crucified.

Translation in the Space of Metaphor

The third and final appearance of the female devotee occurs in a miniature that also contains the manuscript's final crucifixion scene (Figure 3.5). The chief elements of this composition—kneeling female devotee, Christ on the Cross, seated male writer, and tree with small bird—all collaborate to identify the space of the miniature as the space of the text that it introduces: the *petit liuret a l'essample dou rossignolet* [little book (made) after the *exemplum* of the nightingale].

The *Rossignolet* treatise is a verse meditation on Christ's life and Passion.[32] Exalting the singing nightingale as a compassionate witness to Christ's redemptive sacrifice, the *liuret dou Rossignolet* offers the reader a series of meditative subjects, each designated for one of the canonical hours. The poem's central motif—the nightingale—is successively a figure for the holy man-poet, for Christ, for the human soul, and for the female recipient of the poem (the holy man's *bonne amie*).

The shifting identities assigned the nightingale within the text are the very figural elements that populate the prefatory miniature's landscape, with a subtle difference. In the miniature, the holy man identified as the poem's author is conspicuously absent: no "poor man of religion" inhabits the fictive landscape. In his place, a courtly youth sits hunched over a piece of parchment. In this way, the miniature subtly translates the landscape of the text from a world of devout correspondence to a more ambiguous space encompassing both the poem's fiction and the elite social ambient of the *Legiloque*'s anticipated viewer. The miniature's visual translation is accomplished through a further form of dramatic substitution: here, for the first time, the female devotee is represented not simply as "herself" but also as the poem's addressee, the holy man's *bonne amie*. As a consequence, perhaps, her spiritual correspondent is transformed into a youthful figure more suited to court life than to the rigors of the monastic cloister or scriptorium.

---

[32] The *Legiloque*'s nightingale poem is explored further in Masami Okubo, "Le rossignol et le mystère de Jésus-Christ. A propos d'un poème inédit: Le livret du rossignolet," *Reinardus: Yearbook of the International Reynard Society / Annuaire de la Société internationale renardienne* 4 (1991): 137–46; Masami Okubo, "Le rossignol sur la croix: une figure du rossignol-Christ dans la poésie médiévale," *Reinardus: Yearbook of the International Reynard Society/Annuaire de la Société internationale renardienne* 6 (1993): 81–93.

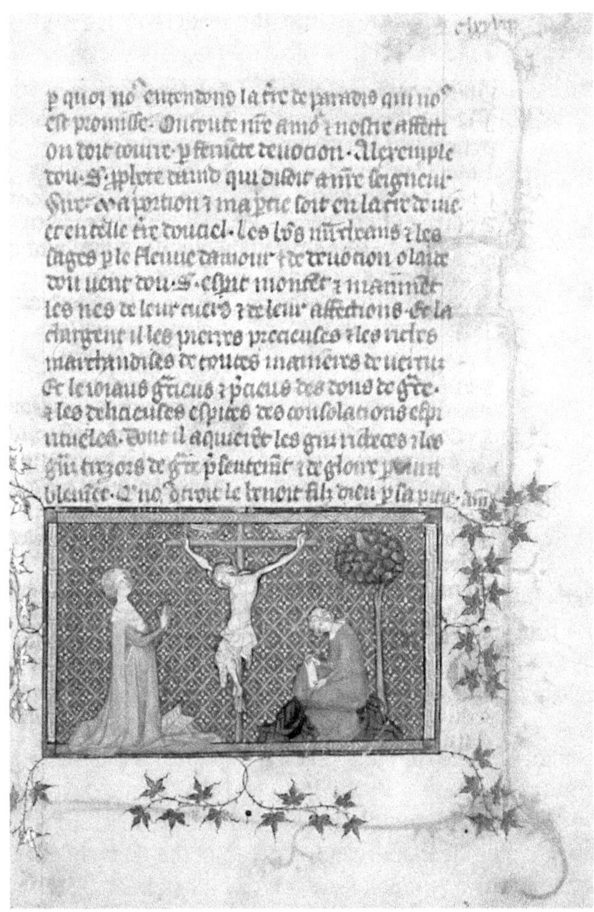

Fig. 3.5 Paris, BnF, MS naf 4338, f. 178r (photo BnF).

The presence of the titular nightingale in the image further suggests that the *liuret dou Rossignolet*'s miniature is something between an illustration of text and a visualized fiction of the *Legiloque* book-owner's patronage of, or participation in, the production of the text. The painted bird identifies the space of the miniature with the content of the poem that follows, while simultaneously standing as a legible element within a legibly articulated landscape. The question here is not one of attempted naturalism, but rather of a fusion of interpretive horizons.[33]

---

33 My conception of the fusion of horizons accomplished in the *liuret dou Rossignolet* miniature is indebted to Hans-Georg Gadamer's analysis of the fusion of historical horizons involved in the work of interpretation: Gadamer, *Truth and Method*, 2nd rev. ed., trans. Joel Weinsheimer and Donald G. Marshall (New York, 2000), esp. pp. 300–307 and 369–79.

In the *liuret dou Rossignolet* miniature the reader-viewer is presented with a devotional landscape generated in response to a textual metaphor. The prefatory image is visually constructed from the very textual elements that mark the poem as a literary work: authorial persona, addressee, and central metaphor (the nightingale as both the devout soul *and* Christ). The inclusion and integration of the female devotee, the nightingale, *and* Christ into the same unified landscape as the author-youth reveals the metaphorical structuring of both poem and image.

It would, however, be a mistake to understand image and text as only visualizing an invisible metaphor. The fusion of horizons realized in both the poem and its image is grounded in the phenomena of the visible world: the nightingale is chosen as the central device of the poem because of its "observed" behavior and cry. The poem explains that the dying nightingale sings more loudly at every canonical hour until, exhausted by its loving song, the bird collapses. Transliterated into the vernacular, the nightingale's song—*occi occi*—provides the poem's central vehicle: in Old French *occi* is the imperative "kill!" In the *liuret dou Rossignolet* this imperative refrain is identified as Christ's song when he accepts the Passion, as the soul's cry as it desires a death to the world, and as the song of the elect commemorating Christ's redemptive sacrifice.[34] Through the repetition of the *occi* refrain, the poem asserts that its central metaphor—nightingale as Christ, nightingale as soul—is grounded in the natural phenomenon of the nightingale's call.

Employing a parallel approach, the miniature describes a fictive landscape that is both of the text and of the observed world. The combination of elements that defines the prefatory image (in particular the juxtaposition of the crucified Christ with the youthful author, the tree, the bird, and the female devotee) suggests an order of reality beyond the mundane. Simultaneously, the formal integration of these elements into a unified landscape asserts that the metaphoric, the mundane, and the theophanic are not mutually exclusive phenomena. Indeed, the image claims that these phenomena find a common ground in the devotional practice prescribed to the *Legiloque*'s reader-viewer.

The Privilege and Predicament of the Devotee

Although each appearance of the aristocratic laywoman in the *Legiloque* compendium exploits the iconographic conventions we have come to associate with "donor" and "owner" figures, this repeated female figure cannot be assimilated to our conventional conceptions of the surrogate or the proxy. Visually presented as the same figure, she is, nonetheless, always implicated in a local hermeneutic situation. From one folio to another, we find both identity and difference: a gesture toward an anticipated flesh and blood female reader-viewer for whom the manuscript would be transformative, and an aggressive insistence that she

---

[34] Paris, Bnf, MS naf 4338: f. 180r (Christ's song); ff. 181r, 183r (soul's song); f. 184r (elect's song).

was already, definitively translated into the idealized female devotee painted on the page. Visibly, even seductively, the manuscript at once enacts and lays bare the claim of all medieval Christian devotional literature and of many devotional images to translate from an imperfect *before* to a more perfect *after*.

In terms that would have been readily apparent to a contemporary viewer, the manuscript's textual contents, its luxurious program of illuminations and the artist chosen to realize those paintings, as well as its repeated references to the comital House of Saint-Pol, collectively proclaim the compendium's elite Parisian provenance, its aristocratic pedigree, and its royal affiliations. The valediction that closes the manuscript further identifies the volume as an artifact of a matrilineal economy of moral-spiritual authority and dynastic distinction. And so, by design, perhaps even by gift, the *Legiloque* manuscript involved its anticipated reader-viewer in a gendered tradition of moral-spiritual translation, a tradition both authorizing and, inevitably, conscriptive.

Gazing at the compendium's pages, the aristocratic book-owner was invited to find herself in a vision of female spiritual excellence predicated upon an aggressive appropriation of subjectivity and perpetuated as an economy of aggrandizing promises and exacting, perfectionist demands. As the manuscript translated the reader-viewer into the form of the devotee, it asked her to participate in the fiction of her own idealization. This was—at least within the painted pages of the *Legiloque* compendium—an offer that no *Dame de Saint-Pol* could refuse: before she opened her book of spiritual improvement, she was, already, inscribed within it.

Chapter 4
Foul Fiends and Dirty Devils: Henry, Duke of Lancaster's *Book of Holy Medicines* and the Translation of Fourteenth-Century Devotional Literature

Catherine Batt

> Quant a vostre cors estes vous ore plus vil ke nul fymer. Vous estes engendré de si graunt ordure ke c'est hunte a nomer e abominacion a penser. Vous serrez livré a crapauz por vous devorer e manger.
> [As for your body, you are now viler than any dung-heap. You are conceived in such great filth that it is shame to mention it and disgusting to think about. You will be given up to toads, to consume and devour you.]
>
> —*Mirour de Seinte Eglyse*[1]

In his *Livre de seyntz medicines* [*Book of Holy Medicines*], written in 1354, a penitential treatise remarkable for the detail with which it works through the ancient metaphor of the sinner as wounded body in need of the spiritual medicine Christ's own wounds provide, Henry, Duke of Lancaster (c. 1310–1361), has taken to heart his devotional culture's stark association of *ordure*, "filth," with the human condition. In the course of his exposition, he returns repeatedly to self-castigating expressions of self-disgust, both at the foulness of his sins—often imagined as suppurating wounds—and at his similarity to the arch-enemy of his Lord God, the devil, with whom he paradoxically finds himself too often in alliance. As he confesses to God: "jeo cheitif dolent comme malveys et faux traitre qe jeo sui … j'ai plus servi, honouree et creu le ord deable d'enfern qe vous" ["I, miserable wretch, like the wicked and disloyal traitor that I am … have served, honoured and believed in the foul fiend of hell rather than you"] (2).[2] The reiteration of the words *ord* and *ordure* to characterize Henry's sin and vile nature sets them in vivid contrast to his continually invoked "douz Sire Jesus Crist" ["sweet Lord Jesus Christ"] (19) whose redemptive love Henry acknowledges, seeks, and declares himself unworthy of. When, over halfway through his treatise, he recounts how

1 *Mirour de Seinte Eglyse*, ed. A.D. Wilshere, Anglo-Norman Text Society 40 (London, 1982), p. 9. All translations in this essay are my own unless otherwise indicated.

2 This and all subsequent quotations from the *Livre* are taken from *Le Livre de Seyntz Medicines*, ed. É.J. Arnould, Anglo-Norman Text Society 2 (Oxford, 1940) and are cited parenthetically by page number.

Adam and Eve's sin of disobedience to God necessitates Christ's sacrifice for the redemption of human kind—"de celle mordure vient la mort dure a le douz Jesu" ["from that bite bitter death came to sweet Jesus"] (146)—his punning articulation of personal moral and spiritual culpability in relation to the Son's redeeming sacrifice (*mordure* can be read as *m'ordure* "my filth") adds a further layer of meaning to the wordplay linking Adam's action to Christ's death.[3]

I begin by contextualizing and commenting on one phrase, *ord deable*, "foul fiend," because the problem of how best to translate it serves to focus local and general questions regarding present-day access to and engagement with both this text and medieval culture at large. Charged with translating the *Livre* for the French of England Translation Series, I am required by the editorial protocols to "aim at the highest possible faithfulness to meaning and to stylistic effect"; and yet, to identify local "stylistic effect" in a text composed in a still little-studied medieval vernacular and to mediate it through translation involves several interpretative processes, which in turn produce their own "effects." As Robert Stein notes (in the context of a discussion of insular medieval multilingualism) a translated text "enters into networks of intertextual affiliation that create very different meanings out of even its smallest elements."[4] The phrase *ord deable* does not, from the readily available evidence, have the same currency in Anglo-Norman texts as its (to me) equivalent term in Middle English, "foul fiend," which crops up in both secular and devotional literature, whether (for example) in the opening exhortative prayer of the Middle English *Sir Gowther* ("God … Shilde us from the fowle fende"),[5] or in the homiletic *Tretis of Discrescyon of Spirites*' warning against "þat cursid spirite, þe foule feend of helle."[6] A full study of the *Livre*'s lexis has yet to be undertaken, but it is even possible that, with *ord deable*, Henry is translating the Middle English phrase "foule fende," rather than employing a familiar Anglo-Norman term. The very process of translating Henry's monolingual text into Modern English, then, can uncover aspects of its original polyglot cultural context.[7] The modern educated nonspecialist reader, meanwhile, might well be put in mind of the "foul fiend" with mention of whom Edgar punctuates his ravings as Mad Tom in *King Lear*: "Away, the foul fiend follows me."[8] In Shakespeare's

3 Thanks to Francis Ingledew for drawing attention, via e-mail communication, to this pun.

4 Robert Stein, "Multilingualism," in Paul Strohm (ed.), *Oxford Twenty-First Century Approaches to Literature: Middle English* (Oxford, 2007), p. 33.

5 Sir Gowther, in *The Middle English Breton Lays*, ed. Anne Laskaya and Eve Salisbury (Kalamazoo, 1995), ll. 1–4.

6 *A Tretis of Discrescyon of Spirites*, in *The Cloud of Unknowing and Related Treatises*, ed. Phyllis Hodgson (Salzburg, 1982), pp. 147–53 at p. 147.

7 Another possible example is Henry's use of the saying "plenté n'est pas deynté" ["plenty is no dainty"] (133): *The Anglo-Norman Dictionary* <www.anglo-norman.net>, s.v. deinté, glosses the phrase as proverbial, but supplies only this instance; see also *The Middle English Dictionary* <http://quod.lib.umich.edu/m/med>, s.v. deinte.

8 William Shakespeare, *King Lear*, ed. Jay L. Halio (Cambridge, 1992), 3.4.44.

shadow, the term "foul fiend" in my translation inevitably gives Henry's prose a literary cast, but "vile fiend" sounds somewhat melodramatic, and to translate an *ord deable* into an equally alliterative "dirty devil" would arguably introduce too distracting an element of low comedy (even though it might, on occasion, be in keeping with Henry's wry self-deprecating mode), as well as lose the connection with the Middle English collocation.

Translation decisions, then, set up, but are also assimilated into, interpretative processes and networks at once cultural, literary, linguistic, and historical. An individual translation of a medieval canonical text, one that has a history in postmedieval culture, of its nature adds to a continuing body of work by means of which one can chart cultural responses to, engagements with, and constructions of, a particular medieval text and its context over time. Roy Liuzza, while expressing the wish that his translation of *Beowulf* might communicate "some sense"[9] of the poem that has brought him such pleasure, contextualizes his own achievement with an appendix[10] containing examples of a passage from the poem translated 20 different ways, from readers and poets as distant in time as 1805 and 1991. The various translations simultaneously offer a history of English literary language and the fashions and tensions of modern literary critical response to a poem that belongs to a "half-alien culture"—to adopt for the earlier medieval period Stephen Medcalf's characterization of the later Middle Ages.[11] A noncanonical text such as Henry's *Livre* has little such history of engagement, but because, as a consequence, it arguably belongs to an even more "alien" Middle Ages, the translator is more pressingly aware of the need, not only to make explicit, but to reconstruct (even rewriting postmedieval assumptions) its contexts and procedures in the very act of translating it.

My brief account of the imagery of *ordure*, for example, claims a place for such a register in mainstream later-medieval devotional language, and for the *Livre*'s embeddedness in such language, that might surprise the writer of the brief introduction to the two pages of *Livre* extracts (corresponding to 161 and 194 of Arnould's edition) anthologized in *English Historical Documents*,[12] apparently as curious examples of a quasi-baroque sensationalism. In these excerpted passages, Henry, following established medical authority and, for all his extravagance of expression, conforming to precedents in devotional literature that discuss the spiritual relationship of the soul to God in terms of medicine or food, compares Christ to a cockerel, disembowelled as a remedy for those suffering from delirium, and further, to the beneficial effects of chicken soup. The editor appears to leave

[9] *Beowulf: A New Verse Translation*, trans. R.M. Liuzza (Peterborough, Ontario, 2000), p. 10.

[10] Ibid., pp. 212–31.

[11] Stephen Medcalf, "On Reading Books from a Half-Alien Culture," in Stephen Medcalf (ed.), *The Later Middle Ages* (London, 1981), pp. 1–55.

[12] *English Historical Documents*, gen. ed. David C. Douglas, vol. 4: *1327–1485*, ed. A.R. Myers (London, 1969).

one to decide whether such imagery is idiosyncratic, or typical of the period: "However distasteful and far-fetched some of the imagery may be to people at the present time, it is at any rate of great interest in the light it throws on the type of devotion which appealed to a man who was immensely admired in his own day as a pattern of chivalry."[13] More recently, William Rothwell, while celebrating Henry's happy facility with wordplay in French, similarly anticipates an aesthetic gulf between modern and medieval reception of (in his example) Henry's punning on the production of medicinal rosewater as a way of meditating on Christ's Passion (150–51): "this kind of verbal play may not be to the taste of modern readers."[14] Both writers identify "taste" as the principal marker of cultural difference across time, and both in this way implicitly raise but avoid the question of what kind of distance obtains between medieval texts and modern perceptions and interpretations; and neither addresses how translation might interrogate or mediate this distance. While Rothwell does not translate his examples, the *EHD* translations seem to aim at fidelity to the original by employing its French words where possible, as when the line "jeo siu si fiebles et si degastee par ma maladie qe jeo ne puisse longement endurer si je ne soie temprement socoruz et enforcee par ceste medicine" (194) is rendered as: "I am so feeble and wasted by my malady that I can no longer endure if I am not succoured at once and strengthened by this medicine."[15] It seems important to make one's translation strategies visible, especially where an apparent attempt at faithful reproduction makes for an unidiomatic prose that reinforces for the reader the sense of the "half-alien."

Michelle Warren notes the importance of registering how Middle English texts belong to a translation culture, within which it is productive to think of translations "less as linguistic events and more as manifestations of culture."[16] This helpful formulation applies as well to twenty-first-century translations of medieval texts as to the texts themselves. While my own researches make clear to me the need to uncover and communicate the *Livre*'s insular cultural and devotional contexts if one is to translate the text into Modern English as accurately as possible, and so to supply both "equivalences (literal translation) and explanatory context (metaphorical translation),"[17] I should want to emphasize the way in which a multilingual cultural context gives its productions a particular density of meaning, just as those cultural contexts for the *Livre* themselves suggest for it a range of interpretative emphases. The "original" text is already plural, rather than singular. For Umberto Eco, writing about translating a novella, the footnote is "always a

---

[13] Ibid., p. 812.

[14] William Rothwell, "Henry of Lancaster and Geoffrey Chaucer: Anglo-French and Middle English in Fourteenth-Century England," *Modern Language Review* 99 (2004): 313–27 at 325.

[15] Trans. Myers, *English Historical Documents*, vol. 4, p. 813.

[16] Michelle Warren, "Translation," in Strohm (ed.), *Twenty-First Century Approaches*, p. 51.

[17] Ibid., pp. 65–6.

sign of weakness on the part of a translator";[18] the intimation is that the translated text should be able alone fully to perform the work of cultural transmission. In a pedagogical translation, the note is surely less a "sign of weakness" than a necessary part of the supporting contextualization: the translator into Modern English under these conditions has, moreover, to think how she might employ her "metaphorical" translations, the critical apparatus she is supplying, to inform her "literal" translation, and how the two might operate in dialogue one with the other so as to offer the reader an understanding of the very processes of writing and its mediation.

What kinds of cultural space, then, does the *Livre* occupy? Its author's own character is ostensibly contradictory: "sage, glorious et prus, et ensa iuuent reueillous en honour et armys, et deuaunt soun descesse, durement bon Cristien" ["wise, full of glory and valiant and in his youth eager for honour and feats of arms, and before his death, a fiercely devout Christian"], as Thomas Gray reports in the *Scalacronica*.[19] Soldier, diplomat, cousin to Edward III, one of the most powerful men of his time, Henry is an aristocrat whose work, with what Lynn Staley calls "its message of devotional abjection," appears both to defend and to express regret for, his chivalric aristocratic lifestyle.[20] Andrew Taylor detects a propensity for "chastising himself for his sins but never fully abandoning them ... his penitence ... tinged ... with nostalgia and even ... pride."[21] The two full surviving manuscripts give material witness to different ways of placing the text culturally in the fourteenth century.[22] The manuscript that serves as the base for Arnould's 1940 edition, and my translation, Stonyhurst College, Lancashire, MS 24, the surviving exemplar closest to the original date of composition, features, in the decorative frame of its opening page (f. 1r), a number of coats of arms, some of them now obscured; in the large initial B in the body of the text are the arms of the Duchy of Lancaster, while Arnould has identified, among the arms in the frame, those of Henry's recently acquired earldom of Lincoln, and those of Jean de Grailly, and of Henry's cousin, the Earl of Warwick. All three are founder

[18] Umberto Eco, *Experiences in Translation*, trans. Alistair McEwen (Toronto, 2001), p. 50.

[19] *Scalacronica 1272–1363*, ed. and trans. Andy King (Woodbridge, 2005), p. 196. My translation.

[20] Lynn Staley, *Languages of Power in the Age of Richard II* (University Park, 2005), p. 207.

[21] Andrew Taylor, "Reading the Body in *Le Livre de Seyntz Medecines*," *Essays in Medieval Studies* 11 (1994): 103–18 at 115.

[22] Fragments of the second part of the treatise were later (carelessly and unsystematically) misbound with medical material in Latin and English, in what is now National Library of Wales, Peniarth MS 388.2, and a mid nineteenth-century catalogue identifies it as a medical text. See Jeanne Krochalis and Ruth J. Dean, "Henry of Lancaster's *Livre de Seyntz Medicines*: New Fragments of an Anglo-Norman Work," *The National Library of Wales Journal* 18 (1973–1974): 87–94.

members of the Order of the Garter.[23] The effect is similar to that of the tomb brass for Lord Hastings (d. 1347) that survives at Elsing Parish Church, Norfolk.[24] Beneath images of the Coronation of the Virgin and of Saint George, the central figure of Hastings is flanked by mourners—including Edward III and Henry, Duke of Lancaster—who are Garter knights, companions-in-arms, and kin: "Sir Hugh's tomb thus expresses a form of corporate identity, embedded in shared military honour and badges of allegiance."[25] In the Stonyhurst presentation, the devotional text is made the occasion for the proclamation and memorialization of aristocratic and military ties, status and comradeship, and those very honors for which Henry confesses himself formerly more eager than for the love of God (72). The later fourteenth-century Corpus Christi College, Cambridge, MS 218, meanwhile, has no such ornate frontispiece; but, squeezed into the remaining space at the end of the manuscript, is a Latin translation, by Geoffroy de Beaulieu, Saint Louis' confessor, of his king's epistolary *Instructions* to his son, a text that also features in its original French in the early fourteenth-century devotional compilation, Paris, BnF, MS naf 4338,[26] which Aden Kumler discusses elsewhere in this volume. Where one manuscript acknowledges Henry's worldly standing, the other emphasizes the *Livre*'s links—already evident internally in its debts to such texts as the *Somme le roi* of Laurent d'Orléans, written in 1279 for King Louis's son, Philip III—with particular continental aristocratic devotional material, and further invites comparison and contrast with continental procedures and practices.

The cultural material contexts for the *Livre*, then, together reflect its dual status as a confidently aristocratic book that nonetheless proclaims spiritual abjection. The work of a high-status male, it seems surprisingly sympathetic to the female condition, observes M. Teresa Tavormina[27] in the preface to her fine translation of the *Livre*'s meditation (207–28) on "The Holy Bandages of Mary's Joys," a translation itself part of an anthology of devotional piety intended in part to revise modern assumptions about the reach and nature of spiritual writings in medieval England. At the same time, it is worth noting the extent to which aristocratic men and women appear to share the same registers of devotion, and partake in a common religious culture. For the rest of this essay I want to consider the strategies by which a translation might mediate the contradictions and difficulties of Henry's text, by way of examples of the use of French, wordplay and punning, grammatical gender, and the question of authority and biblical citation.

---

23 *Livre*, pp. lxvii–lxviii.

24 Illustrated in Paul Binski, *Medieval Death: Ritual and Representation* (London, 1996), p. 106.

25 Ibid., p. 104.

26 Described in Henri Omont, *Bibliothèque Nationale: Catalogue général des manuscrits français*, vol. 2 (Paris, 1900), pp. 167–9.

27 M. Teresa Tavormina, "Henry of Lancaster: *The Book of Holy Medicines*," in Anne Clark Bartlett and Thomas H. Bestul (eds), *Cultures of Piety: Medieval English Devotional Literature in Translation* (Ithaca, 1999), pp. 19–40 at p. 25.

Henry's brief animadversions on the writing of his text may seem self-alienating. Toward the end of his work, his announces his general unfitness for the task:

> Par trois choses me puisse jeo resonablement escuser de defautes de cest livre: l'une est que jeo n'ai pas le sen de moy entremettre de haut chose; l'autre si est, si le franceis ne soit pas bon, jeo doie ester escusee, pur ceo qe jeo sui engleis et n'ai pas moelt hauntee le franceis; la tierce chose est qe jeo ne sui pas bon escryvene, car unqes ne l'apris forsqe tard, de moy meismes. Siqe par ces trois chosez il me semble qe jeo puisse escuser les defautes de ceste livre et moy. (239)
> [I may justifiably excuse myself for the shortcomings of this book, on three counts. The first is that I lack the ability to engage with such profound matters; the second is that if my French is not good, I should be excused, because I am English and have not had very much to do with French; the third reason is that I am not a good writer, for I only learned how to do it late in life, and am self-taught. And so, for these three reasons, it seems to me, I may excuse the shortcomings of this book and of myself.]

Henry's "defense" rewards closer examination. He would have encountered the French of England, and continental French, on a daily basis, in courtly, household, literary, political, diplomatic, legal, economic and medical, as well as devotional, contexts, and his own book demonstrates an easy acquaintance with all of those registers, so it seems surprising for him to declare himself working beyond the limits of his professional expertise. Henry's treatise shows knowledge of a wealth of post-1215 Lateran Council works designed to instruct the laity in spiritual matters, including prayers, books on vices and virtues, Franciscan homiletic material, the Bible and biblical commentary, and with the teachings of such as Augustine, Gregory, Bernard, and Anselm, and his locutions suggest the medium of pious instruction was primarily (if not uniquely) Anglo-Norman. By claiming ignorance of French, Henry is perhaps disavowing specifically his ability fully to realize the forms of spiritual practice available to him in that medium; it forms part of his self-construction as abject. Richard Ingham's researches into the *Livre*'s syntax conclude that it is written by a bilingually competent individual.[28] At one point, Henry, employing a familiar metaphor of the soul as a besieged castle, is able to observe how it is pertinent to his argument that the *dounggeon* (81), the "keep" of the castle, also means, *en engleis* "in English" (81), the prison at its base, for he imagines the "enemy" sins already gathered at the base of his tower, compromising the spiritual integrity the keep is meant to signify. Thus, Henry furnishes an example of how "monolingual texts become sites of multilingual transactions."[29] *Engleis* may well operate here as shorthand for "insular vernaculars," as Anglo-Norman (unlike continental French) witnesses to both meanings of "keep" and of (Modern English) "dungeon," and seems to have

[28] Richard Ingham, "Bilingualism and Syntactic Change in Medieval England," *Reading Working Papers in Linguistics* 8 (2005): 1–25 at 23.

[29] Warren, "Translation," p. 58.

influenced English in this respect.[30] The translator, in this instance, has to explain Henry's observation extratextually, but there are ways in which Henry's extended wordplay might also be reproduced integrally within the text.

I have written elsewhere about how the process of translating Henry's puns engages with the *Livre*'s tacit argument that wordplay acknowledges the divine in human systems of signification, and also makes the translator's work most visible at the very point at which it is attempting to be most faithful to the text.[31] A conspicuous example is Henry's comparison of his unconfessed soul, festering with evil, to a fox's den:

> Beau Sire Dieux, donetz moy grace qe jeo puisse prendre ensample par le renard coment jeo doie destruire les ords pecchés qe sont en la court de mon corps; et court se bien poet nomer le corps, car court serra son cours, et nul ne siet come court il court. (106)
> [Lord God, give me grace that I might heed the example of the fox as to how I should destroy the filthy sins that are in the earth of my body; and the body may well call itself earth, for earth will be but of earth, and no-one knows the time of earth on earth.]

The original plays on *court* "fox's hole"; *court* "brief"; *cours* "lifespan"; and *court* as third-person singular of the verb "to run." My translation cannot reproduce the headlong rush to death, nor the frustration of human endeavor registered by having *court* communicate both the verb of motion and the static location of sin—and *court* might, in that respect, also pun on Henry's own aristocratic household court—but it does exploit the technical term for a fox's den, an "earth," and chooses to emphasize a multilingual cultural context for Henry's work by taking inspiration from the riddling lyric extant in the early fourteenth-century London, British Library, MS Harley 2253, which meditates ruefully on birth, procreation, and death, the cycle of human existence (but which also riddlingly evokes Original Sin and Salvation history):

> Erþ toc of erþe erþe with woh
> Erþe other erþe to the erþe droh
> Erþe leyde erþe in erþene þroh
> Þo heuede erþe of erþe erþe ynoh. (f. 59v)
> [Earth took earth of earth with sorrow
> Earth drew other earth down to earth
> Earth laid earth in an earthen grave
> Then earth had earth enough of earth.]

---

[30] Rothwell, "Henry of Lancaster and Geoffrey Chaucer," p. 326.

[31] Catherine Batt, "'De celle mordure vient la mort dure': Perspectives on Puns and their Translation in Henry, Duke of Lancaster's *Le Livre de Seyntz Medicines*," in Jacqueline Jenkins and Olivier Bertrand (eds) [8th International Conference on the Theory and Practice of Translation in the Middle Ages], *The Medieval Translator / Traduire au Moyen Âge* 10 (Turnhout, 2007), pp. 405–17 at p. 417.

The translation emphasizes a particular devotional and literary milieu for Henry's writing, one that not only exploits language for devotional ends but also prompts awareness of the multilingual context in which that language operates.

Wordplay invites the reader to participate with the text in games that are both devotional and literary, but the puzzle of how to translate another aspect of Henry's French raises the question of how the reader might respond to the spiritual persona the *Livre* presents. Grammatical gender in Anglo-Norman "tends to be fluid,"[32] and may seem in some respects unimportant, but in translation what may appear originally neutral can become starkly marked. So, for example, when Henry confesses that he has damned "la cheitive alme" ["my wretched soul"] (12), delivered into his care, my translation has no feminine pronoun:

> cel poure alme ai jeo malement et fausement mourdry en moun conduyt et en ma garde … et en point de la getter mult parfond en enfern … (12)
> [I have wickedly and falsely murdered this poor soul while it was under my protection and in my charge … and I am on the point of casting it into the very depths of hell …]

And yet, one might object that it is depersonalizing to refer to the soul as "it." There is a similar problem with translating *homme*, which is used as the indefinite pronoun, but also often appears primarily to signify "man." Whether to translate as "man," "one," or "you" depends on a fine set of judgments, and can make for shifts and difficulties of tone, now perhaps too formal, now too casual, where the original (just as it offers the option of perceiving the soul as feminine) leaves readers to supply their own nuances of interpretation.

Henry, as cited above, denies deep knowledge of spiritual matters; the extant manuscripts' marginalia are bare of learned notes and cross-references, and yet (to take one example) Henry's incorporation of Psalm commentary into his spiritual autobiography demonstrates his familiarity with a particular form of fourteenth-century pious self-representation that depends on both biblical and patristic knowledge. When Henry describes how he cannot rise from his bed of sin without the grace of Christ the Physician (129), and how sometimes amputation, followed by cauterization, is the only course of treatment advisable (164), it is a translation of a now-lost Anglo-Norman commentary on *The Seven Psalms*, made in the following century by Eleanor Hull, that is closest in language and spirit to the *Livre*: just as Henry "shows" his sin-poisoned wounds to Christ, and begs they might be cured, so Hull's commentary on Psalm 6 explains the Psalmist's language: "And I haue dyscouryd the venym of the wonde and ther-for, Lord, I requere you that ye hele me for ye be wysyst leche, fre and true in thy promessys."[33] How best to reproduce Henry's biblical allusions? Jenny Rytting's study of

32 Ian Short, *Manual of Anglo-Norman* (London, 2007), p. 123.

33 *The Seven Psalms: A Commentary on the Penitential Psalms translated from French into English by Dame Eleanor Hull*, ed. Alexandra Barratt, Early English Text Society, o.s. 307 (Oxford, 1995), p. 12.

how Modern English translators of *Pearl* employ the King James Version of the Bible for the Middle English poem's biblical paraphrasing notes the difficulty of balancing "literal meaning, biblical resonance, and poetic form,"[34] and implicitly raises interesting questions about whose culture is being represented through this strategy. The French of England series editors have wisely mandated use of the New Revised Standard Version (New Oxford Annotated Bible); the resonance of the King James Bible would not convey, to the modern reader, an appropriate sense of the state of vernacular translations of the Bible at the time Henry is writing, nor of the way Henry authorizes his text by means of a complex intercalation of biblical reference and established scriptural commentary. The reader needs to have a sense of the range of Henry's biblical knowledge, and the circumstances in which he would be familiar with it, without being overwhelmed by too much information.

This brief account of translating the *Livre* shows how that process cannot be isolated from a reconstruction of the conditions of the original text's production and reception, and how, inevitably, the translation also constitutes in itself a critical reading and appraisal. Lawrence Venuti has charted the traditional "invisibility" of the translator in English-language translation, and the tendency to "domesticate" a "foreign" text, rather than to respect cultural difference. He proposes that one read a translation as "both communication and interpretive inscription."[35] The luxury of an academic translation project lies in its freedom to make the text accessible by means of metaphoric as well as literal translation, and so to make the conditions of its own production visible, and to historicize itself in turn, as Venuti recommends.[36] The conference "Translating the Middle Ages" suggests a continuous present of engagement with the medieval period. To what extent the French of England translation I have undertaken will be judged as satisfactorily conveying a sense of the cultural complexity and richness of the *Livre* remains to be seen, but I would hope that the work (in parts self-conscious, awkward, and all-too-aware of its provisionality) might at least contribute to and reflect on modern perceptions of a multilingual medieval past, and that disagreements with my choices and procedures might spark productive dialogues over the text, and the nature of our critical response to it, which is the best way to continue our encounters with the Middle Ages.

---

[34] Jenny Rebecca Rytting, "*Pearl* and the Translation of Scriptural Paraphrase," in Rosalynn Voaden, René Tixier, Teresa Sanchez Roura, and Jenny Rebecca Rytting (eds), *The Medieval Translator: The Theory and Practice of Translation in the Middle Ages*, The Medieval Translator / Traduire au Moyen Age 8 (Turnhout, 2003), pp. 281–93 at p. 291.

[35] Lawrence Venuti, *The Translator's Invisibility: A History of Translation* (London, 2008), p. 276.

[36] Ibid., p. 276.

Chapter 5
Languages Low and High: Translation and the Creation of Community in the Chester *Pentecost* Play

Robert W. Barrett, Jr.

The festive implications of England's northern cycle plays have been well studied in recent decades, particularly with regard to the plays' connections to the Feast of Corpus Christi (the Thursday after Trinity Sunday). The primary point of departure for this line of inquiry was the embodied model of civic community outlined by Mervyn James in 1983:

> I propose to argue that the theme of Corpus Christi is society seen in terms of body; and that the concept of body provided urban societies with a mythology and ritual in terms of which the opposites of social wholeness and social differentiation could be both affirmed, and also brought into a creative tension, one with the other. The final intention of the cult was, then, to express the social bond and to contribute to social integration.[1]

Indeed, although subsequent critics (like Sarah Beckwith and Claire Sponsler) have had reason to critique and refine James's analysis, they still maintain his focus on the metaphorical possibilities of the Body of Christ.[2] Recent study of the York cycle, a Corpus Christi event throughout its fifteenth- and sixteenth-century performance history, continues to dwell extensively (and productively) on this somatic emphasis.[3]

Chester cycle scholarship has also benefited from the current state of affairs. After all, the biblical plays from this northwestern city do repeatedly focus on

---

1 Mervyn James, "Ritual, Drama, and Social Body in the Late Medieval English Town," *Past and Present* 98 (1983): 3–29 at 4.

2 See Sarah Beckwith's *Signifying God: Social Relation and Symbolic Act in the York Corpus Christi Plays* (Chicago, 2001) and Claire Sponsler's *Drama and Resistance: Bodies, Goods, and Theatricality in Late Medieval England* (Minneapolis, 1997) for their most developed discussions of embodiment.

3 Examples include the exploration of embodied spectatorship in Jill Stevenson's 2006 "Sensual Bodies and Devotional Encounters: The Influence of Performance on Lay Visual Piety in Late Medieval York," PhD dissertation, City University of New York, and the pervasive awareness of male bodies in Christina M. Fitzgerald's 2007 *The Drama of Masculinity and Medieval English Guild Culture* (New York).

the wounded body of Christ and the Christian community that body subtends. But the Chester cycle is not a Corpus Christi play at all. It almost certainly began as such no later than the first quarter of the fifteenth century: we have a record of a 1422 dispute between several guilds over the parameters of their shared responsibility for producing part of the Passion sequence "in luso Corporis christi."[4] The Early or Pre-Reformation Banns describe the path the city's Corpus Christi procession took en route to the performance of its play: "They come from saynt maries on the hill / the church of saynt Iohns vntill."[5] But these same Banns are also the last document to treat Chester's Corpus Christi play as a going concern. They appear to have been first written down between 1505 and 1521, revised at least once between 1521 and 1532, and then recopied in 1539–1540 as part of London, British Library, MS Harley 2150—their only extant witness.[6] By the time of Harley 2150's inscription, the Whitsun plays had become an established civic custom, first mentioned as such in a 1520–1521 agreement between the Founders-Pewterers and the Smiths to share the costs of "whitson playe & Corpus christi light."[7] It is this sequence of 24 Whitsuntide pageants—performed in three segments on the Monday, Tuesday, and Wednesday of the Octave of Pentecost—that survives to the present day in multiple manuscripts. The Corpus Christi play was almost certainly defunct by 1548, the year in which the Protestant government of Edward VI suppressed the feast that gave the play its name.

None of these facts are new or recent discoveries; early English drama scholars have known them for decades.[8] Instead, what proves most surprising here is not the Whitsuntide context of the Chester plays, but their persistent treatment by critics as a collection of Corpus Christi pageants. Possible explanations for this oversight are legion: the long-standing influence of V.A. Kolve's 1966 *The Play Called Corpus Christi*, the critical dominance of the York plays, and so on.[9] However, the essay that follows is less interested in determining *why* scholars have hitherto downplayed performance at Pentecost than in exploring *what* the

---

4 *Cheshire including Chester*, ed. Elizabeth Baldwin, Lawrence M. Clopper, and David Mills, Records of Early English Drama (2 vols, Toronto, 2007), vol. 1, p. 47.

5 Ibid., vol. 1, p. 86. For a detailed discussion of the route's history and political significance, see David Mills, *Recycling the Cycle: The City of Chester and Its Whitsun Plays* (Toronto, 1998), pp. 106–12.

6 *Cheshire including Chester*, ed. Baldwin, Clopper, and Mills, vol. 2, p. 890.

7 Ibid., vol. 1, p. 69.

8 Clopper's "History and Development of the Chester Cycle," *Modern Philology* 75 (1978): 219–46 is still authoritative on these points 36 years later and counting.

9 A subject search of the online *MLA International Bibliography* reveals the following hierarchy of critical interest in individual cycles: "York cycle" is first with 230 hits; "Towneley cycle," second with 215 hits; "Chester cycle," third with 164 hits; and "N-Town cycle" last with 120 hits. These numbers are of course not conclusive evidence for scholarly preference, but they do suggest that research on the York plays—benefited by the cycle's abundance of archival records—sets the agenda for work on the other three cycles.

implications of such performance might be. Chief among the latter—and in sync with this volume's thematic emphasis—is the Chester cycle's frequent recourse to macaronic language.[10] Characters speak in English, French, and Latin throughout the cycle; stage directions switch back and forth between English and Latin.[11] The plays' multilingual character makes them particularly suitable for Whitsuntide performance: Robert Stanton tells us that the Pentecost narrative (Acts 2) was routinely read by patristic and early medieval writers like Gregory the Great, Isidore, and Bede as "the miraculous reattainment of linguistic unanimity."[12] However, as Stanton goes on to note, such "unanimity" is purely figurative in nature:

> Pentecost reversed the negative miracle of Babel, but not by eliminating the differences between human languages. Instead, it united all languages in the saving effect of preaching and conversion. Linguistic fragmentation was not swept away, but rather served as the basis of a new miracle whereby difference was both possible and divinely sanctioned.[13]

This is a key qualification where Whitsun-focused analysis of the Chester plays is concerned. Christian theology enables a multilingual redemption: the Church contains many languages, but only one spirit. The cycle's frequent code-switching unites the different languages (and language communities) of Tudor Chester under a single evangelical identity.[14] In doing so, each of the languages employed in the plays acquires a salvific character.[15]

Strangely enough, this linguistic point—common enough in analyses of Pentecostal themes in other medieval and early modern texts—is rarely made

---

[10] Throughout this essay, I rely on Siegfried Wenzel's broad definition of "macaronic" as "any kind of verse that mixes English and Latin (or French) in different structural forms and for a variety of rhetorical purposes" (*Macaronic Sermons: Bilingualism and Preaching in Late-Medieval England* [Ann Arbor, 1994], p. 5).

[11] French is primarily reserved for such upper-class characters as Herod and the Magi: see Deanne Williams's discussion of Play 8, the Vintners' *Three Kings*, in her *The French Fetish from Chaucer to Shakespeare* (Cambridge, 2004), pp. 79–81.

[12] Robert Stanton, "Linguistic Fragmentation and Redemption before King Alfred," *Yearbook of English Studies* 36 (2006): 12–26 at 12.

[13] Ibid., p. 14.

[14] The one Cestrian language conspicuously absent from the cycle is Welsh. Play 7, the Painters' *Shepherds*, does acknowledge the city's Welsh community by bringing three Welsh shepherds and their boy to town, but these Welshmen all speak English. For more on the exclusion of Welsh from the plays, see my "Leeks for Livery: Consuming Welsh Difference in the Chester *Shepherds' Play*," in Catherine A.M. Clarke (ed.), *Mapping the Medieval City: Space, Place, and Identity in Chester, c. 1200–1600* (Cardiff, 2011), pp. 184–200.

[15] That redemptive potential is not present in every utterance of a given language: the French of Herod and his knights will not lead them to accept the authority of the Christ Child. But the French of the Magi ensures that the language is not wholly fallen.

by the best critics of the Chester pageants.[16] They occasionally acknowledge Pentecost's potential influence on the content of the cycle, but their analyses thereof are minimal. Lawrence Clopper postulates that "The shift to Whitsuntide and the subsequent alteration in the procession route may have arisen from the city's desire to separate its play from the ecclesiastical auspices of the Corpus Christi celebrations in order to emphasize civic sponsorship."[17] Kevin Harty sees Whitsuntide performance as broadly symbolic: the plays take on the task of "announcing the good news to those assembled in the city—and by extension to the members of the Chester audience who live in the age of the Holy Spirit."[18] Writing about Play 21, the Fishmongers' Pentecost, Rosemary Woolf has little more to say than that the pageant's use of the Pentecostal hymns "Veni creator spiritus" and "Accipite spiritum sanctum" seems "appropriate to the occasion."[19] Clifford Davidson lets the shift to Whitsuntide speak for itself, stating that there should be "no puzzlement" about the appropriateness of such a move.[20] Finally, although David Mills identifies the cycle as "an act of evangelism," he nonetheless goes on to note that, "While it is not inappropriate to undertake such an act at the feast of the Holy Spirit, it is not necessary tied to that time."[21]

To the best of my knowledge, only two Chester cycle scholars have produced chapter-length accounts (or longer) of both the rationale behind the Whitsuntide

---

16 For example, John V. Fleming's "The Pentecosts of Four Poets," in Robert F. Yeager and Charlotte C. Morse (eds), *Speaking Images: Essays in Honor of V.A. Kolve* (Asheville, 2001), treats the theme in Wolfram's *Parzival*, Dante's *Commedia*, Chaucer's *Summoner's Tale*, and Camões's *Lusiad*, while William Elford Rogers's *Interpretation in Piers Plowman* (Washington, DC, 2002) explores its function in Passus 19 of the B-Text of Langland's poem (pp. 62–9).

17 Lawrence M. Clopper, "History and Development," p. 245. In a subsequent article, Clopper entertains the possibility that "there was some desire to move the plays away from the celebration of the eucharistic sacrament and toward the salvific words of Christ, away from the body of Christ (Corpus Christi) and toward the words of Christ—the making of the Creed, the evangelical teaching in tongues, both of which are associated with Whitsuntide, a feast that celebrates a scriptural event rather than a feast 'newly' established by men" ("Lay and Clerical Impact on Civic Religious Drama and Ceremony," in Marianne G. Briscoe and John C. Coldewey [eds], *Contexts for Early English Drama* [Bloomington, 1989], pp. 102–36 at p. 111). See below for Theodore Lerud's expansion of Clopper's hypothesis here.

18 Kevin J. Harty, "The Unity and Structure of *The Chester Mystery Cycle*," in Kevin J. Harty (ed.), *The Chester Mystery Cycle: A Casebook* (New York, 1993), pp. 69–88 at p. 72.

19 Rosemary Woolf, *The English Mystery Plays* (Berkeley, 1972), p. 284. She also notes that the playwright's decision to include a dialogue in heaven between Father and Son appears to be taken from John 14:16, "part of a lectio … a response in the liturgy for the vigil of Pentecost" (ibid., p. 285). However, none of her observations about Chester's use of the Pentecost liturgy extend beyond the boundaries of Play 21.

20 Clifford Davidson, *Festivals and Plays in Late Medieval Britain* (Aldershot, 2007), p. 107.

21 Mills, *Recycling the Cycle*, p. 114.

shift and the thematic implications thereof.[22] Peter Travis argued back in 1982 that the apostles' Play 21 recitation of their eponymous Creed functions as the climax of the cycle: "The Chester audience ... as it beheld the unfolding episodes of its cycle, was beholding (among other things) a dramatic 'sacralization' of the twelve articles of the Apostles' Creed."[23] This moment of anagnorisis comes in Play 21 because only then do "Christ's disciples in Chester manage to order their faith sufficiently," only then do they achieve their "final perfection, divinely wrought."[24] Travis identifies the end product of such creedal structure as a "communal society of Christian believers," a "mystical fellowship" that spans worlds and times.[25] As I argue below, community is indeed a theme of Play 21 and of the cycle as a whole. But the vision of holistic communitas that Travis lays out is a curiously bloodless one: its conflicts only take place at high levels of theological and moral abstraction. The social and spiritual fissures that trouble the sixteenth-century Cestrians watching the cycle—the conflicts that Travis designates as part and parcel of *societas*, the "everyday order of society"—never seem to trouble the characters on stage.[26]

More recently, Theodore Lerud has characterized the cycle's shift to Whitsuntide as an instance of "regrounding the civic base under the *Protestant* auspices of Whitsuntide rather than the *Catholic* auspices of the Corpus Christi holiday."[27] For Lerud, Pentecost is "the central holiday of the Protestant calendar," a designation

---

22 While I concentrate in the next few paragraphs on Peter Travis and Theodore Lerud, I do want to acknowledge two other attempts to make significant statements about the function of the Pentecostal theme in the Chester cycle. The first, Lynn Staley's 1994 *Margery Kempe's Dissenting Fictions* (University Park, 1994), argues that, "where dramatizations of Christ's entry into Jerusalem present community as a manifestation of faith and consequently as far less hierarchically ordered than the city that produces and watches the pageant, treatments of Pentecost emphasize the composition of the community of the Church in terms of apostolic succession" (p. 187). The second, Margaret Pappano and Nicole Rice's "'Beginning and Beginning-Again': Processions, Plays, and Civic Politics in York and Chester," *Studies in the Age of Chaucer* 30 (2008): 269–301, considers how evocations of the Pentecost liturgy within the Tanners' *Fall of Lucifer* "work subtly ... to justify and naturalize the shift from Corpus Christi to Pentecost" (p. 296). However, both of these discussions are as brief as they are valuable (Staley's observations cover just two pages, while Pappano and Rice spend approximately four pages on the topic).

23 Peter W. Travis, *Dramatic Design in the Chester Cycle* (Chicago, 1982), p. 202.

24 Ibid., pp. 199 and 205.

25 Ibid., p. 215.

26 Ibid., p. 117. In subsequent work on the cycle (e.g., "The Social Body of the Dramatic Christ in Medieval England," in Albert H. Tricomi [ed.], *Early Drama to 1600*, Acta 13 [Binghamton, 1985], pp. 17–36), Travis has shifted gears, repeatedly calling attention to the plays' larger social contexts and ideologies—albeit without revising his earlier characterization of Play 19's function.

27 Theodore K. Lerud, *Memory, Images, and the English Corpus Christi Drama* (New York, 2008), p. 108.

he ultimately appears to derive from Archbishop Cranmer's decision to introduce the 1549 *Book of Common Prayer* to English congregations on Whitsunday.[28] The Chester cycle time-shift serves then as a civic "response to and potential accommodation of rising Reformation trends."[29] In this newly Protestant context, the individual pageants of the cycle take on reformed meanings: the martyrdoms of Elijah and Enoch in Play 23, the Dyers' *Antichrist*, allude to the narratives of Protestant martyrdom in Foxe; the aforementioned translation and recitation of the Apostles' Creed in Play 21 serves "as an emblem of the Protestant agenda of presenting sacred texts to all believers in the vernacular"; and Christ's anticipation of the Holy Ghost's visit in Play 15, the Bakers' *Last Supper*, is an "apparent echo of the 1552 Prayer Book."[30]

These allusions, emblems, and echoes are of course all possible components of the cycle's sixteenth-century production and reception, especially during the years following the onset of the English Reformation.[31] But Lerud's argument is not that the Whitsun plays gradually accrued Protestant meanings over the decades of their existence—a perfectly acceptable position (and one I adopt below). Instead, he insists upon a Whitsun cycle that was Protestant *ab ovo*, redating or explaining away several of the key documents in the cycle archive. For instance, he suggests that the use of the singular "whitsun playe" in the 1520–1521 agreement between the Founder-Pewterers and the Smiths points to "a time before a significant performance shift had occurred" as well as "a far different creature than the later three-day cycle of Whitsuntide plays ... Perhaps ... a single Whitsun pageant in the earlier Corpus Christi cycle."[32] A singleton Whitsun play is a different generic beast than a multiform Whitsun cycle, and it is this potential distinction that gives Lerud the daylight he needs to separate a clearly pre-Reformation (i.e., Catholic) reference to Whitsun performance from the post-Reformation (i.e., Protestant)

28 Ibid. The point about Cranmer's *Book of Common Prayer* first emerges on p. 116 and is then repeated on p. 121; Lerud provides no other evidence that Pentecost outranks all other holidays in the Protestant calendar. As a contrast, David Cressy, one of the major figures in early modern calendrical studies, only sees fit to mention Whitsuntide in the appendices of his "The Protestant Calendar and the Vocabulary of Celebration in Early Modern England," *Journal of British Studies* 29 (1990): 31–52 at 51–2. His subsequent piece on "God's Time, Rome's Time, and the English Protestant Regime," *Viator* 34 (2003): 392–406, notes that some of the most temporally radical British Protestants—the Scots who produced the 1561 *Book of Discipline*—saw fit to eliminate Pentecost from "one of the most austere calendrical regimes in all of Christendom," reserving holiness for the Sabbath alone (p. 397). While Pentecost may therefore have a particular resonance for Protestants, it does not follow that the holiday is a defining characteristic of the reformed faith.

29 Lerud, *Memory, Images, and the English Corpus Christi Drama*, p. 113.

30 Ibid., pp. 128 and 126.

31 For a paradigmatic statement of ideological shifts in the pageants' meanings over time, see Richard K. Emmerson, "Contextualizing Performance: The Reception of the Chester *Antichrist*," *Journal of Medieval and Early Modern Studies* 29 (1999): 89–119.

32 Lerud, *Memory, Images, and the English Corpus Christi Drama*, pp. 113–14.

play cycle he postulates. Indeed, the earliest reference to the cycle as plural Whitsun "plaies" does postdate 1520–1521, first appearing in a proclamation made by William Newhall, clerk of the Pentice. But David Mills has argued against the assumption that a difference in grammatical number equals a difference in dramatic genre, calling the distinction between "playe" and "plaies" little more than a "vacillation" whose "usage seems to depend on whether the concept is of the total cyclic structure or the individual plays that constitute it."[33]

Lerud attempts to strengthen the evidence for a Protestant cycle by redating the Newhall Proclamation itself. Mills and R.M. Lumiansky initially dated the Proclamation to 1531–1532 on account of the document's closing statement that it was "per me Willelmum Newhall factum tempore Willelmo Sneyde draper secundo tempore sui marioralitatis."[34] (Sneyd's first term as mayor was 1516–1517; his second, 1531–1532.) Lerud ignores the evidence of Newhall's signature, preferring the 1539–1540 (and thus post-Reformation) date of the Proclamation's third manuscript witness, British Library MS Harley 2150. Given what he acknowledges is the Proclamation's "ongoing concern with revision," it seems a stretch for Lerud to claim that a document internally dated to 1531–1532 is actually a post-Reformation "attempt to reinvent the cycle, always already existing as a Protestant enterprise."[35] We are better off recognizing both cycle and Proclamation as texts in motion, undergoing constant modification as cultural circumstances dictate. We cannot follow Lerud's lead and situate the Whitsun plays in discrete religious boxes, Catholic at one moment, Protestant in the next. Instead, we must recognize that, as Theresa Coletti puts it, "the cycle's religious ideology is as mobile as its sixteenth-century pageant wagons."[36]

The remainder of this essay is therefore devoted to the process of taking the "Whitsun" in the Whitsun plays seriously. The cycle needs to be treated as something other than a Corpus Christi play *manqué*. For example, reorienting our approach to the plays in a Pentecostal direction allows us to augment Lawrence Clopper's thesis about the rationale informing the producers' selection of Old Testament episodes for inclusion in the cycle. Clopper has argued that "Much of the uniqueness of the Chester cycle can be directly attributed to the compiler's

---

[33] *Recycling the Cycle*, p. 116. Lerud may be basing his argument here first on Clopper's suggestion in "The History and Development of the Chester Cycle" that the play referenced in the 1520–1521 agreement is probably "the guilds' Corpus Christi play ... shifted to Whitsuntide" (p. 221) and then on the elaboration of that point in R.M. Lumiansky and David Mills (eds), *The Chester Mystery Cycle: Essays and Documents* (Chapel Hill, 1983), pp. 176–81. However, as the above quotation from Mills suggests, he modified his position on this point in the 15 years separating *Essays and Documents* (1983) from *Recycling the Cycle* (1998). Moreover, even if the 1520–1521 version of the play is a single-day event, there is still the pre-Reformation evidence of the Newhall Proclamation to consider (see below).

[34] *Cheshire including Chester*, ed. Baldwin, Clopper, and Mills, vol. 1, p. 72.

[35] *Memory, Images, and the English Corpus Christi Drama*, pp. 117 and 118.

[36] Theresa Coletti, "The Chester Cycle in Sixteenth-Century Religious Culture," *Journal of Medieval and Early Modern Studies* 37 (2007): 531–47 at 535.

decision to use the Old Law-New Law theme as his structuring principle ... the sacrifice-covenant complex accounts for all the Old Testament incidents dramatized by Chester."[37] He thus sees the presentation of the Ten Commandments to Moses in Play 5 (the Cappers' *Moses and the Law*; *Balaam and Balaack*) as "the last formulation of the relationship between God and man before the Advent," the coming of Christ that will usher in the New Law.[38] However, Pentecost goes unmentioned in Clopper's discussion of the New Testament episodes making use of the coventual theme. Adopting a Whitsuntide perspective reveals the feast's relevance to Clopper's theme: Penn Szittya's account of Pentecostal typology notes that, "As the Mosaic Law was given to the twelve tribes on the fiftieth day after the Passover, so the Holy Spirit, the sanctifying grace of the New Law, was sent to the twelve apostles on the Pentecostal day."[39] Ian Lancashire agrees, identifying Moses, "always in his role as receiver of the Law on Sinai from God," as one of "the main types for Pentecost."[40] While I share Clopper's recent opinion that the cycle plays "are not particularly given to typology beyond the simplest sort," figural associations—such as those connecting Sinai with the Cenacle—nonetheless help shape the cycle audience's horizon of reception and thus continue to merit a degree of critical attention.[41]

In the end, though, Whitsun-oriented discussion of the cycle must begin with a reading of Play 21, the Fishmongers' *Pentecost*.[42] The play dramatizes events from Acts 1:15–26 (the election of Matthias to Judas's position) and Acts 2:1–12 (the fiery descent of the Holy Ghost). In the larger narrative of the cycle, it follows Play 20, the Tailors' Ascension, and precedes Play 22, the Clothworkers' Prophets of Antichrist.

---

[37] Lawrence M. Clopper, "The Principle of Selection of the Chester Old Testament Plays," *Chaucer Review* 13 (1979): 272–83 at 280–81.

[38] Ibid., p. 276.

[39] Penn R. Szittya, "The Friar as False Apostle: Antifraternal Exegesis and the *Summoner's Tale*," *Studies in Philology* 71 (1974): 19–46 at 25.

[40] Ian Lancashire, "Moses, Elijah and the Back Parts of God: Satiric Scatology in Chaucer's *Summoner's Tale*," *Mosaic* 14 (1981): 17–30 at 19.

[41] Lawrence M. Clopper, *Drama, Play, and Game: English Festive Culture in the Medieval and Early Modern Period* (Chicago, 2001), p. 210.

[42] In his chapter on Pentecost entertainments, Clifford Davidson calls "the two-part Chester Passion ... *the central point* in salvation history as it was then understood," suggesting that Play 21 and Pentecost are best received as subordinate elements in the cycle narrative: "without Christ's sacrifice of himself, there would have been no possibility of a Christian Church and, of course, no Pentecost" (*Festivals and Plays in Late Medieval Britain*, p. 134). I take his point, but I also feel that it leads back to the status quo of a Corpus Christi-centered biblical drama. What if we fully acknowledge that "salvation history as it was then understood" is actually a moving target during the religious controversies of the sixteenth century? (Here I follow Theresa Coletti's lead in "The Chester Cycle in Sixteenth-Century Religious Culture.") Can we then so easily settle on Corpus Christi and the Passion narrative as the key to the cycle plays? Why not entertain alternate centers and see where doing so leads us?

The pageant therefore serves as the last play of the Christian "past."[43] Plays 22 to 24 (Prophets of Antichrist, Antichrist, and The Last Judgment) are all necessarily set in the audience's future. They represent what is to come, not what is or what has been. Play 21, on the other hand, is the moment of transition from "then" to "now": it depicts the formation of the Church, the community surviving to the present, sixteenth-century day and the one to which all members of the play's audience are presumed to belong (even if the precise nature of that community is in dispute).

How is that community formed? Not through bodies—the play has little explicit interest in direct embodiment. Peter opens the play by reminding us that Jesus has ascended to Heaven, that his body is "from us gonne / to blysse that lasteth aye" (3–4).[44] Countering this absence is his subsequent report of Judas's gruesome end:

> Amonge us nombred that wretch was,
> the fayth to preach in eych place;
> and nowe his hyre fullye hee hasse,
> for hanged himselfe hasse he.
> His bodye bursten for his trespasse,
> soule dampned as a man withowt grace. (25–30)

But even this direct somatic reference involves bodily dissolution, a presence that bursts to leave only absence behind.[45] The central section of the play, a dialogue in Heaven between the Son and the Father that derives from John 14:16 (itself part of the Pentecost liturgy), references the Incarnation and Passion, but in curiously bloodless terms: "Nowe man fullye have I bought / and out of bale to blysse

---

[43] Looking at the cycle's Late Banns (composed and revised during the period of 1548–1575), David Mills observes that a line has been ruled beneath the stanza devoted to Play 21 (*Recycling the Cycle*, p. 142). He argues elsewhere that, in conjunction with the opening lines of the Late Banns' Pentecost stanza ("This of the olde and newe testamente to ende all the storye / which oure author meaneth at this tyme to have in playe"), this rule indicates a stopping point for the final, abbreviated production of the cycle in 1575 ("Some Theological Issues in Chester's Plays," in David N. Klausner and Karen Sawyer Marsalek [eds], "*Bring furth the pagants*": *Essays in Early English Drama Presented to Alexandra F. Johnston* [Toronto, 2007], pp. 212–29 at p. 217). If Mills is correct that Plays 22–4 were cut in 1575, then the Fishmongers' *Pentecost* was truly the last Whitsun play performed as such prior to the cycle's twentieth-century revival. (The 1577–1578 performance of Play 7, the Painters' *Shepherds*, is chronologically the last play performed in the sixteenth century, but it belongs not to the cycle, but to the series of festivities that welcome the Earl of Derby and his son Lord Strange to the city.)

[44] This and all subsequent citations of Play 21 are taken from the text of the pageant edited by R.M. Lumiansky and David Mills in *The Chester Mystery Cycle*, Early English Text Society, s.s 3 and 9 (2 vols, London, 1974 and 1986), by line numbers.

[45] Matthias's election technically fills the gap left in the apostolic community by Judas's betrayal, but the language surrounding his selection is free of somatic references.

brought" (191–2).[46] Even the apostles' fears of physical persecution are effectively groundless: the Father says that he will send the Holy Ghost "in lycknes of fyre freelye, / that they may styffned be therbye" (235–6), but the Judean *inridentes* of Acts 2:13 are nowhere to be found in the Chester pageant (whereas they do make a threatening appearance in York toward the end of the Potters' *Pentecost* play).[47] Taking their place are a pair of what the manuscript speech headings identify as friendly *alienigenae*, foreigners who can be said to double for the equally non-Galilean members of the audience. The second of these generic outsiders ends the play with an exhortation to his companion: "Fellowe, goe we therfore and espye / howe goes this wondrous case" (389–90). Note that even here the verb (*espye*) is one of watching, not of physically interacting. The *alienigenae* are spectators similar to those standing in the streets and rows of Chester; both groups witness the formation of the Church, but they cannot take part in it bodily. That event has already concluded.

Play 21 resolves these difficulties of identity by substituting words for bodies. In the Chester cycle, Christian community is cemented by language, and the glue of that joining is the disciples' article-by-article creation of the Apostles' Creed (à la Rufinus) in the third and final section of the play (303–58). Particularly relevant to the concerns of this anthology is the manner in which that act of communal composition takes place: beginning with Peter, each apostle says an article of the Creed in Latin and then loosely translates it with an English quatrain. Implicitly invoked by Philip's statement that "I that never could speake thinge / save Ebrewe as I learned yonge, / nowe I can speake at my liking / all languages, both lowe and hye" (279–82), Latin (*hye*) and English (*lowe*) stand in for the linguistic miracle brought about by the Holy Ghost. The pageant manuscript's layout mirrors this alternation of tongues. First we encounter a Latin stage direction reading "Tunc Petrus incipiat: 'Credo in Deum, Patrem omnipotentem, creatorem caeli et terrae'" (310+), and then we receive the English translation of Peter's words: "I beleeve in God omnipotent / that made heaven and yearth and fyrmament / with steadfast hart and true intent, / and hee is my comford" (311–14). Andreas continues by pairing up the paratext "et in Jesum Christum, Filium eius, unicum dominum nostrum" (314+) with the dialogue "And I beleeve, where I be lent, / in Jesu, his Sonne, from heaven sent, verey Cryste, that us hath kent / and ys our elders lord" (315–18), and the remaining ten apostles follow suit. The sixteenth-century English audience is explicitly a part of this action: Peter mentions that, once the Creed is complete, "the lewd hereafter . . . we maye lere, / to further them yn the faye" (309–10).

---

[46] Woolf notes that John 14:16 (*Et ego rogabo Patrem, et alium Paraclitum dabit vobis*) is "part of a *lectio* and provided a response in the liturgy for the vigil of Pentecost" (*The English Mystery Plays*, p. 285).

[47] Lynn Staley points out that the York play, along with a less violent N-Town version of *Pentecost*, "present the world as polarized by that moment of rapture, employing a stereotypical community of Jewish elders and citizens as the scoffers and enemies of this newly composed community" (*Margery Kempe's Dissenting Fictions*, p. 188).

This moment is pure metadrama, no less self-reflexive than Play 23, the Dyers' Antichrist (a pageant depicting Antichrist as a producer of perverted spectacles).[48] In its reenactment of the Church community's foundation, Play 21 works to connect past and present, to generate a polity that transcends historical and linguistic boundaries. From our vantage point in the twenty-first century, we can see the social faults the Fishmongers are papering over: the apostles are learned, not lewd; their frequent self-designation as "brethren free" (57) who receive meede (266) from their "mayster free" (269) identifies them as franchised citizens instead of disenfranchised foreigns; and the Chester playwright's decision to eschew tradition and remove the Virgin Mary from the Cenacle (a revision the N-Town and York playwrights do not undertake) reminds us that the Whitsun plays' heavily masculine emphasis also includes women among the disenfranchised.[49] And of course there is no guarantee that all citizens will receive the play as its makers intend. What matters here, though, is the pageant's decision to foreground the spoken word as the basis of community. After all, it is the apostles' spoken glossolalia that attracts the amenable *alienigenae* ("we herden them, witterlye, / prayse God faste," 387–8), not the visible fire of the Holy Ghost.[50]

A similar emphasis is at work in Play 21's use of liturgical music. Unlike the comedic (yet fallen) music of the Welsh shepherds in Play 7, the Painters' *Shepherds*, the songs sung in Play 21 are perfectly harmonized. For example, the first of the songs—the great Pentecostal hymn "Veni creator spiritus," sung by the apostles in lines 121–48—exists as a structural counterpart to the play's subsequent

48 Writing about Apocalypse 13:13 (*et fecit signa magna ut etiam ignem faceret de caelo descendere in terram in conspectu hominum*), Glending Olson notes that Antichrist's "miracle" here is "a fake Pentecost achieved through magic," one that is "among those staged in the Chester Antichrist pageant" ("The End of *The Summoner's Tale* and the Uses of Pentecost," *Studies in the Age of Chaucer* 21 [1999]: 209–45 at 218 and 219). The Fishmongers' *Pentecost* therefore looks forward in sacred time as well as backward.

49 As Christina M. Fitzgerald points out, "the York and Chester cycles were more than incidentally male-oriented; rather, they form a 'drama of masculinity,' a distinct subgenre of dramatic activity specifically and self-consciously concerned with the fantasies and anxieties of being male in the urban, mercantile worlds of their performance" (*The Drama of Masculinity*, p. 1). That said, it is also worth noting that her lengthy analysis of the disciples' homosocial fellowship (ibid., pp. 122–44) ends without saying anything about Play 21 and its depiction of an entirely male Church community.

50 It is telling that Play 21's only reference to bread, the physical symbol of Christian community in the Bakers' *Last Supper* (Play 15) and the Saddlers' *Emmaus* (Play 19), occurs at pageant's end in a proverbial oath: Primus Alienigena marvels that "theise men of Gallilee … Our language the can as well as wee, / as ever eate I bread!" (368, 369–70). His bread is mere material accident, lacking in an animating divine substance—a point brought home by Secundus Alienigena's word choice for the *b*-rhyme that echoes "bread" and closes the stanza: "for to have binne dead" (374). In Play 21, life is not the body broken for you, but flame, spirit, and speech.

creation and recitation of the Creed.[51] The Latin stage direction preceding line 121 tells us that "Tunc omnes apostoli genuflectentes cantent 'Veni, creator Spiritus.'" It is unclear whether the actors portraying the apostles sang the entirety of the hymn in Latin or just the opening verse (all of which is included in the London, British Library, MS Harley 2124 or "H" version of the play). But it is definitely the case that, Latin version completed, the apostles then produce an English translation on stage. Jacobus Major begins with the first verse of the hymn in lines 121–4 ("Come, Holye Ghoost; come, creatour! / Visytt or thoughtes in this store— / thou art mans conquerour— / and grant us, lord, thy grace!"); Johannes takes up the second, and so on until the newly elected Matthias concludes the translation of the Latin in lines 145–8. Marked off by the macaronic translations of Latin hymn and Latin Creed, the episodes comprising the play's triple structure deliberately stress community: the first episode (1–120) depicts Matthias's entry into the apostolic communion of saints; the second (121–302) portrays God's acknowledgment of humanity as his "brethren in companye" (232); and the third (303–90) returns full circle to the first when the recitation and translation of the Creed is overheard by the two *alienigenae*—both of whom seem poised to seek membership in the newly founded Church.

The second piece of music performed in Play 21 comes at the moment of greatest spectacle: as the Holy Ghost descends *in spetie ignis* (238+) from the elevated, heavenly portion of the pageant wagon to the lower, earthly level, two angels sing the antiphon "Accipite spiritum sanctum," another piece from the liturgy of Pentecost.[52] Play 21 would have been performed on the third day of the cycle, the Wednesday after Pentecost and thus the first of the three Ember Days of the feast—a time routinely set aside for fasting and for the ordination of priests. "Accipite spiritum sanctum" is associated with ordination, making it a perfect accompaniment for the Holy Ghost's creation of the apostles as evangelists. Liturgical citations such as these might seem to mark out the play as Catholic, but a look at the writings of sixteenth-century radical Protestant and Chester divine Christopher Goodman suggests otherwise. Goodman includes Play 21 in his 1572 "Notes of the absurdities &c in the Chester plays," one of our few contemporary witnesses to a production of the cycle.[53] He identifies the play's particular "absurdities" as follows:

> Peter onely is said to create Matthias an Apostle
> The Angell bringeth the Holy ghost to the Apostles
> The Creed made in 12 Articles by 12 Apostles every one their portion.

---

51 Pamela King writes that Pentecost was "marked by a special liturgy in the Use of York," one that featured the singing of "Veni creator spiritus" at Terce (*The York Mystery Cycle and the Worship of the City* [Cambridge, 2006], p. 166).

52 Woolf calls it "appropriate to the occasion" (*The English Mystery Plays*, p. 284).

53 The full text of the "absurdities" can be found in *Cheshire including Chester*, ed. Baldwin, Clopper, and Mills, vol. 1, pp. 147–8. All references to Goodman's text will refer to this edition.

> Matthews words these. And I believe throgh godes grace soche beleffe as holy church has that godes bodie granted us was & to use in forme of bred Simons words. And I beleve with devotion, of syn to have remission, throgh penance & contrition, & heven whan I am dead.

These objections are not surprising: Goodman sees a justification of papal authority in Peter's creation of Matthew, rejects Rufinus's extrascriptural origin of the Creed, critiques Matthew's association of transubstantiation with the *sanctorum communionem*, and dismisses Simon's evocation of the sacrament of confession. (The scribes of all the extant manuscripts appear to agree with Goodman in this last instance, replacing Simon's "penance & contrition" with "Christes blood and Passion" in line 349.) What is surprising is Goodman's apparent willingness to overlook the play's liturgical music. Signals we might reasonably take to be Catholic in origin (what Theresa Coletti calls "Catholic red flags") fail to have that particular meaning, even for the most puritan of readers.[54]

An explanation for Goodman's tolerance of the play's music might stick to factual grounds: both "Veni creator spiritus" and "Accipite spiritum sanctum" survived the 1549 Act of Uniformity and made their way into the Anglican *Book of Common Prayer*. But it might be more productive to rethink this Reformation *translatio*, to once again acknowledge (with Coletti) that "stable categories of religious identity have been replaced by a complex cultural field of such identity production."[55] Put another way, just as the Whitsun plays' sixteenth-century (and thus "Renaissance") translation of York and Coventry's fifteenth-century (and thus "medieval") cycle form troubles long-standing notions of literary-historical periodization, so too does its Tudor transformation of earlier forms of lay spirituality and liturgical practice undermine established scholarly understandings of the Reformation. Lerud's confessional certainties give way to Coletti's "toggling back and forth between traditionalist and reformist possibilities for interpretation."[56]

Indeed, such destabilizations are present in Play 21's relatively effortless movement from Latin to English and back again—another aspect of the pageant ignored by Goodman (who clearly worries more about the theological contents of the script than the religious affiliations of the languages conveying that concept). This linguistic "toggling back and forth" calls into question Timothy Rosendale's 2001 assertion that the 1549 *Book of Common Prayer*, with its "mandatory and nationally-uniform English liturgy," merits attention for its "consequential" role in what he calls "the reciprocal constitution of nation and subject."[57] Noting (like Lerud) that the English-language *Book of Common Prayer* became liturgical law on Whitsunday 1549, Rosendale stresses the importance of reading Pentecost's "divinely inspired linguistic profusion" as a Protestant, centralized "work of recuperation, the beginning

54 "The Chester Cycle in Sixteenth-Century Religious Culture," p. 535.

55 Ibid., p. 536.

56 Ibid., p. 535.

57 Timothy Rosendale, "'Fiery toungues': Language, Liturgy, and the Paradox of the English Reformation," *Renaissance Quarterly* 54 (2001): 1142–64 at 1143.

of international evangelism, through which the whole world would eventually be brought back into God's kingdom."[58] The Reformation and the acts of vernacular translation accompanying it are explicitly seen here as instances of global *translatio*, types of Pentecost that overrule the implicitly localized Babel of Catholicism. For Rosendale, the Reformation witnesses "the tyrannous opacity of Latin" give way to "the ideal congruency of realm and language … essential to a sense of national identity."[59] The English nation has at long last an English liturgy.

Or does it? As Reformation historians remind us, the Latin liturgy did not disappear overnight. Christopher Haigh notes that, "throughout the 1560s and 1570s, the Church courts dealt with ministers who tried to 'counterfeit the mass,' by muttering Latin prayers, facing east during the service, or raising the bread and wine in an 'elevation.'"[60] Nor was resistance to vernacularization limited to traditionalist clergy who ostensibly benefited from Latin's "tyrannous opacity." Peter Marshall notes that, during the popular June 1549 West Country rising against the publication of the *Book of Common Prayer*, a group of Devon rebels "forced their rector … to put on his full set of vestments … and to say Mass in Latin."[61] The Marian restoration of the Latin liturgy in the mid-1550s clearly complicates any teleological connection between liturgy and nation. So too does the evidence of Latin's persistence in the early years of Elizabeth's reign: Eamon Duffy notes that, "If we take the destruction by the end of the second year of the reign [1559–1560] of such major cult items as the altars, the Rood and other images, and the Mass-books, as an indicator of prompt compliance, just forty-five of the 180 parishes qualify as having complied promptly with the main requirements of the Elizabethan settlement."[62] In such historical contexts, Rosendale's equation of English national identity with English liturgical practice ends up owing more to Reformation ideology than Reformation actuality.

We might also resituate both the *Book of Common Prayer* and the Chester Whitsun Plays within the *longue durée* history of attempts, both official and unofficial, to make the Latin liturgy comprehensible—a pre-Renaissance history that Rosendale mostly ignores. This alternate history stretches back to the 1281 publication of Archbishop of Canterbury John Pecham's *Syllabus* (with its insistence on four mandatory English language sermons a year) and includes Archbishop of York John Thoresby's 1357 republishing of the *Syllabus* in Latin (as the *Injunctiones*) and English (as the text we now call *The Lay Folks' Catechism*). Lollards belong to this history, but so

---

[58] Ibid., p. 1147.

[59] Ibid., p. 1148.

[60] Christopher Haigh, "The Church of England, Catholics, and the People," in Peter Marshall (ed.), *The Impact of the English Reformation 1500–1640* (London, 1997), pp. 235–56 at p. 237.

[61] Peter Marshall, *The Catholic Priesthood and the English Reformation* (Oxford, 1994), p. 79.

[62] Eamon Duffy, *The Stripping of the Altars: Traditional Religion in England 1400–1580* (New Haven, 1992), p. 573.

too do orthodox writers and readers: as Nicholas Watson notes, "the discussion over the nature of vernacular theology and its uneducated readers (*illiterati*) conducted in many of these highly self-conscious theologies written between 1350 and 1390" is "equivalent in significance to Chaucer's parallel ruminations … on the nature of secular literature and on the problems of creating a courtly style in the English vernacular."[63] While antagonism (either lay-clerical or orthodox-heretical) is certainly part of Watson's historical account, so too are outreach and accommodation. Katherine Zieman's work on "extragrammatical literacies" and lay access to Latinity testifies to the presence of the latter in late medieval English culture.[64]

Play 21 (and, by extension, the rest of the Whitsun plays) extends the argument for negotiated continuity into the third quarter of the sixteenth century: the macaronic language of the play serves as one more piece of evidence undermining Rosendale's Whig history. Of course, some concessions must be made: we cannot say for sure that the manuscripts we have today correspond to the cycle as it was performed in the mid-sixteenth century. (Mills's discovery of Goodman's papers—with their account of a cycle different from any of those attested in the preexisting archive—demonstrated the necessity of this caution.) Precisely coordinating the text of the Chester cycle and the history of the English Reformation is an impossible task; at best, we can suggest possibilities of interpretation and horizons of reception. But the multiple languages of Play 21 do provide an alternative to the sort of stark linguistic and religious binarisms offered up by Rosendale and Lerud. Sixteenth-century Cestrians didn't need the official imprimatur of Archbishop Cranmer and the Westminster-centered state to translate scriptural and liturgical Latin into English; their own civic authorities had sufficient might to make such sociolinguistic calls (and clearly felt comfortable exercising that authority). In fact, the correspondences between Goodman's contemporary account of the 1572 performance and the extant manuscripts suggest strongly that the text as we have it represents a long-standing (and post-Reformation) comfort with Latin.[65] The fluid ease with which a local, lay production like Play 21 shifts between the two languages challenges the nation-centered master narrative of Catholic to Protestant and Latin to English that scholars like Rosendale continue to transmit. What we learn from this initial consideration of the Chester cycle as a Whitsuntide performance is that there were many English vernaculars available for the purposes of translation, that the center holds only fitfully.

---

[63] Nicholas Watson, "Censorship and Cultural Change in Late Medieval England: Vernacular Theology, the Oxford Translation Debate, and Arundel's Constitutions of 1409," *Speculum* 70 (1995): 822–64 at 839.

[64] For more, see her *Singing the New Song: Literacy and Liturgy in Late Medieval England* (Philadelphia, 2008), pp. 114–49.

[65] Goodman's only complaint about Latin comes in his list of absurdities for Play 24, the Websters' *Last Judgment*. Writing about this play (which was the twenty-third pageant in 1572), he notes with disdain "The divell speaking Latin, & setteth forth invocation of Saints" (p. 148). We could read this absurdity as anti-Catholic in nature, but then we have to ask why the anti-papist Goodman would be upset with the devil's use of Latin and not that of the apostles.

PART 3
Translation in Italy

In "Dante's *Comedy*: The Poetics of Translation," Christopher Kleinhenz offers a fine example of how attention to aspects of Dante's art, as of its reception, through the lens of translation (understood on a variety of levels, including that of broader civilization and culture), can synthesize appreciation both of the poet's artistry and his place in a tradition in freshly interesting ways. Kleinhenz rehearses Dante's concern with translation as movement, literal and aesthetic (with a reminder of Dante's own anxieties that a text loses its "sweetness" in translation), to read the *Divine Comedy* as itself a cultural translation of a specific conceptualization of the universe. Dante, notes Kleinhenz, makes possible the Italian literary tradition by means of his borrowings from and reworkings of scripture and classical literature alike. Kleinhenz traces—for example, in his account of the Pilgrim's encounter with his friend Casella, which depends in large part on Virgil for its power—an interconnectedness between Dante's work and other texts and cultures that releases both text and critical perspective from a simple binary of "translation" and "original" to a subtler appreciation of the nature of literary authority, creativity, and continuity, even as the amusing anecdote about Dante's own resistance to unregulated popular dissemination of his work raises important questions about high and low culture and the ownership of intellectual property. Furthermore, the consideration of Dante's deployment of the visual in the *Comedy*, and of the iconographic interpretations the poem engenders, bears continuing witness to the importance of contextualizing the written word within broader artistic cultural practices and responses.

Alison Cornish's "Traces of the Translators in Late Medieval Italian Vernacularizations" complements Kleinhenz's work in further examining translation's "mobility," and in complicating neat distinctions between such terms as scribe, editor, translator, and author, even as medieval writers themselves invoke them by way of explanation. Cornish's careful attention to the details of commentators', translators', copyists', and glossators' methodologies throws light on medieval practice as also on contemporary accounts of that practice. Cornish identifies in the work of Lapo di Neri Corsini, a nonprofessional copyist of *The Fatti dei Romani* (an early fourteenth-century translation of the French *Li Fet des Romains*, itself translated from Latin), a tendency to "Italianize" his text, which is also typical of his fellow copyists, a diligence in his work, and an anxiety for accuracy. Cornish contextualizes Lapo by tracing the ways in which other copyists translated the Fatti, seeing him as primarily a private reader, working independently, but also as a product of his times in his interest in conveying (on his own terms) a fidelity to the source.

Chapter 6
Dante's *Comedy*: The Poetics of Translation

Christopher Kleinhenz

Etymologically, translation—*translatio* from *transferre*—denotes a movement, a transfer from one place to another. More than a half-century ago Ernst Robert Curtius[1] employed it to describe the transmission of learning from Athens to Rome to Paris (*translatio studii*) as well as, in the area of politics, to the migration of Empire (*translatio imperii*) from East to West and, across the centuries, from the Roman Empire to its perhaps less than Holy descendant.[2] These two concepts—*translatio studii* and *translatio imperii*—were very near and dear to the hearts of medieval authors precisely because they emphasized the importance of tradition in the movement of civilization and culture.

Metaphorically, *translatio* refers to the rendering of a text from one language to another, but this was not the only term used to indicate the multifaceted idea of "translation." Indeed, several words in Latin—*transferre*, *vertere*, *convertere*, *interpretari*, *mutare*, and *exprimere*—designate specific varieties of this practice, both oral and written.[3] In their discussions of Dante as translator, scholars have contributed to our understanding of the various sorts of translation-like operations in which the Florentine poet engaged.[4] Dante employs the verb *tras-* or *translatare*

---

[1] Curtius's work, *Europäische Literatur und lateinisches Mittelalter* (Bern, 1948), was first published in the United States for the Bollingen Foundation by Pantheon Books in Willard R. Trask's English translation, *European Literature and the Latin Middle Ages* (New York, 1953). It was reissued by the Princeton University Press with a new afterword by Peter Godman in 1990. I cite from this edition.

[2] See Curtius, *European Literature*, pp. 28–30.

[3] See, among others, Sandro Sticca's fine overview of these terms, "*Traduttore/ Traditore*: *Convertere*, *Vertere*, *Transferre*, *Interpretari* and Leonardo Bruni's *De Interpretatione Recta*," *Mediaevalia* 26.2 (2005): 7–36.

[4] See, among others, the studies by Felicina Groppi, *Dante traduttore* (Rome, 1962); Gianfranco Folena, "*Volgarizzare* e *tradurre*," in his *La traduzione: saggi e studi* (Trieste, 1973), pp. 59–120; and Massimiliano Chiamenti, *Dante Alighieri traduttore* (Florence, 1995). Dante's most sustained effort as translator is his greatly condensed version of the *Roman de la Rose* in the 232 sonnets of *Il Fiore*, if he is indeed its author; the thorny question of attribution lies beyond the scope of this essay. For a translation of this work, see *The Fiore and the Detto d'Amore: A Late 13th-Century Italian Translation of the Roman de la Rose, Attributable to Dante Alighieri*, trans. Christopher Kleinhenz and Santa Casciani (Notre Dame, 2000).

only two times in the *Comedy*,[5] both in *Paradiso* and in its strict etymological sense of movement from one place to another: the movement of the Ark of the Covenant from town to town ["che l'arca traslatò di villa in villa," *Par.* 20:39][6] and the passage of the Pilgrim and Beatrice from one celestial heaven to another: "I saw myself, alone with my lady, translated to a more exalted blessedness" ["vidimi translato / sol con mia donna in più alta salute," *Par.* 14:83–4].[7] In the *Convivio*, however, Dante uses derivatives from *translatare* in the modern sense of "translation"—*translatori* (II xiv 7) and *translazione* (II xiv 6)[8]—in reference to translations of Aristotle and to an apparently contradictory statement concerning the composition of the galaxy in the Stagirite's works, an obvious error that Dante attributes to the "translators" and not to the author ["lo errore de li translatori"].[9] Earlier in the *Convivio* (I vii 14–15) he uses another verb—*transmutare*[10]—in various forms when speaking about the impossibility of rendering poetry into another language without losing the sweetness and harmony of the original: "E però sappia ciascuno che nulla cosa per legame musaico armonizzata si può de la sua loquela in altra transmutare sanza rompere tutta sua dolcezza e armonia" ["Therefore everyone should know that nothing harmonized according to the rules of poetry can be translated from its native tongue into another without destroying

5 See the entry "Traslatare" by Andrea Mariani in the *Enciclopedia dantesca*, 2nd ed. (6 vols, Rome, 1984) [= *ED*], vol. 5, p. 699.

6 Citations from the *Comedy* follow the edition of Giorgio Petrocchi, *La Commedia secondo l'antica vulgata*, Società Dantesca Italiana, Edizione Nazionale (4 vols, Milan, 1966–1967).

7 [7] Translations from the *Comedy* follow, with minor variations, that of Charles S. Singleton, *The Divine Comedy: Inferno, Purgatorio, Paradiso: Italian Text and Translation, Commentary* (6 vols, Princeton, 1970, 1973, 1975).

8 See the respective entries in the *ED* by Andrea Mariani, vol. 5, pp. 689 and 690.

9 The entire passage reads as follows: "E credo che fosse lo errore de li translatori; ché ne la Nuova pare dicere che ciò sia uno ragunamento di vapori sotto le stelle di quella parte, che sempre traggono quelli; e questo non pare avere ragione vera. Ne la Vecchia dice che la Galassia non è altro che moltitudine di stelle fisse in quella parte, tanto picciole che distinguere di qua giù non le potemo, ma di loro apparisce quello albore, lo quale noi chiamiamo Galassia; e puote essere, ché lo cielo in quella parte è più spesso, e però ritiene e ripresenta quello lume. E questa oppinione pare avere, con Aristotile, Avicenna e Tolomeo" (*Convivio* II xiv 7) (*Convivio*, ed. Maria Simonelli [Bologna, 1966]) [I believe that this is due to an error on the part of the translators; for in the New Translation he seems to say that it is a collection of vapors beneath the stars in that region, which attracts them continuously; this does not seem to have any foundation in truth. In the Old Translation he says that the Galaxy is nothing but a multitude of fixed stars in that region, so small that we are unable to distinguish them from here below, though from them originates the appearance of that brightness which we call the Galaxy; this may be so, for the heaven in that region is denser, and therefore retains and throws back this light. Avicenna and Ptolemy seem to share this opinion with Aristotle] (Dante Alighieri, *Dante's "Il Convivio" ("The Banquet")*, trans. Richard H. Lansing [New York, 1990]).

10 See the entry on "Trasmutare (Transmutare, Tramutare)" by Alessandro Niccoli in the *ED*, vol. 5, pp. 699–700.

all its sweetness and harmony," *Con.* I vii 14]. Dante continues by noting that this is the reason why Homer's poetry (unlike Greek works in prose) was not translated into Latin and why the Psalms "sono sanza dolcezza di musica e d'armonia" ["lack the sweetness of music and harmony"], precisely because they were translated—"furono transmutati"—from Hebrew into Greek and then from Greek into Latin, and "ne la prima transmutazione tutta quella dolcezza venne meno" ["in the first translation all their sweetness was lost," *Con.* I vii 15].[11] This is, of course, a common complaint about translations: that they have lost the "music" of the original.[12]

Dante is well aware of the meaning and value of translation for his own literary enterprise, and, in many ways, he is the consummate *translator* of the Middle Ages. He clearly understood the sense of movement and tradition associated with the term, the notion of the necessary, indeed the unavoidable changes that occur, *mutatis mutandis*, in the transferral of something from one place to another, in its *translatio*. Dante was aware of his role as poet, inventor, and architect of his great poetic edifice. We might say that he "translated" the entire cosmos as conceived and understood in the Middle Ages into his poem, inventing the rhyme scheme *terza rima* for this ultimately divine purpose and making his vision of the afterlife come alive. As a "traduttore" Dante is rarely a "traditore," although his verses do, as it were, "betray" everywhere the mark of the master craftsman—he is the

[11] *Convivio* I vii 15: "E questa è la cagione per che Omero non si mutò di greco in latino come l'altre scritture che avemo da loro. E questa è la cagione per che li versi del Salterio sono sanza dolcezza di musica e d'armonia; ché essi furono transmutati d'ebreo in greco e di greco in latino, e ne la prima transmutazione tutta quella dolcezza venne meno" ["This is the reason why Homer has not been translated from Greek into Latin as have been other writings we have of theirs. And this is the reason why the verses of the Psalter lack the sweetness of music and harmony; for they were translated from Hebrew into Greek and from Greek into Latin, and in the first translation all their sweetness was lost"]. Noting that Dante was not the first to hold this view, Chiamenti (*Dante Alighieri traduttore*, p. 202) cites the passage in which Jerome says virtually the same thing (*Interpretatio Chronicorum Eusebii*, Praef. 1–2) and suggests that Dante, who knew neither Hebrew nor Greek, may have received these notions from him.

[12] This shortcoming may also be present in the not very mellifluous prose of the *Convivio*, where Dante proves to be an able, but extremely literal translator of passages from Holy Scripture (Chiamenti, *Dante Alighieri traduttore*, p. 25). Perhaps the serious philosophical nature of the *Convivio* necessitated an accurate, verbatim version of the sacred text. Moreover, given the very personal nature of the treatise, Dante took pains to justify his decision to write it in Italian and not in Latin, and herein may lie the reason for his comments on the impossibility of translating poetry. However, if Dante translates the Bible very literally in the *Convivio*, in the *Comedy* he often presents the biblical text in its original garb, thus maintaining both its integrity and its authority. One term—*volgarizzatore*—never occurs in Dante's works, and this absence may reflect his negative appraisal of the "vulgarizer" as one of lesser ability who plies a lower trade, rendering works in a more mundane, unimaginative, and utilitarian way for a decidedly less well-educated readership (see Folena, "*Volgarizzare*," pp. 82–4). A "volgarizzatore" is not a poet or rhetorician or authority figure, as Dante considered himself.

"miglior fabbro"[13] and is no doubt the sort of poet Ezra Pound had in mind when he titled his collection of essays *Make It New*[14] as a way of both commanding and challenging poets to rise to the task of making new the old and traditional. Dante did "make it new" and, in so doing, made it possible for centuries of readers and commentators to see, experience, and marvel at his achievement.[15] Not only did Dante give new life to earlier works, but he also essentially began, in stunning fashion, the Italian literary tradition.

In his "translation" of the Book of the Universe, whose author is God, Dante achieves his greatest and most sublime goal. Yet he remains humble in his self-description as the diligent amanuensis who transcribes the universal order onto the parchment leaves: "quella materia ond'io son fatto scriba" ["that matter of which I am made the scribe," *Par.* 10:27]. Dante translates portions of earlier works—sacred and profane, literary, philosophical, theological, scientific—from Latin and the vernacular, incorporating them seamlessly into his poem. Dante translates components of the world of nature (rivers, mountains, meadows, constellations) and elements of human experience (emotions, gestures, triumphs, failures) into richly textured passages in his poem. Dante translates works of art and musical expressions into his poetic fabric making it appeal to our senses, both visual and aural. Finally, Dante recognizes the seemingly insurmountable problem inherent in translating the nature and essence of the divine—the ineffable—into comprehensible human language, and yet he succeeds in doing so, even as he protests his inadequacy.

Just as Dante uses his "translations" from so many different sources in the composition of the *Comedy*, so too has his magnum opus been translated in a variety of interesting, provocative, and important ways. Besides the ever more numerous versions of the *Comedy* in many languages worldwide,[16] there

---

[13] In the *Purgatory* Dante has his poetic mentor, Guido Guinizzelli, refer to the troubadour Arnaut Daniel as the "miglior fabbro del parlar materno" ["better craftsman of the mother tongue," *Purg.* 26:117], and T.S. Eliot employed this phrase in the epigraph to *The Wasteland* to pay homage to Ezra Pound.

[14] Ezra Pound, *Make It New* (London, 1934).

[15] The University of Illinois conference featured an evening conversation with the distinguished poets and translators of Dante, Robert Pinsky and W.S. Merwin, who have certainly made Dante's poem come to life, "made it new" for new generations of readers.

[16] In recent years many English translations, either of the entire *Comedy* or of one or more of the three canticles, have been published, including, among others, those by the following translators (in chronological order): Charles Singleton (1970, 1973, 1975), Mark Musa (1971, 1981, 1984), C.H. Sisson (1980), Allen Mandelbaum (1980, 1982, 1984), Tom Phillips (1985), Nicholas Kilmer (1985), James Torrens (1993), Robert Pinsky (1994), Peter Dale (1996), Robert Durling (1996, 2003), Elio Zappulla (1998), W.S. Merwin (2000), James Finn Cotter (2000), Jean and Robert Hollander (2000, 2003, 2006), Michael Palma (2002), Ciaran Carson (2002), Anthony Esolen (2002, 2003, 2004), and Robin Kirkpatrick (2006). For an historical overview of translations of the poem, see Gilbert F. Cunningham, *The Divine Comedy in English: A Critical Bibliography*, 2 vols, 1: *1782–1900*; 2: *1901–1966* (New York, 1965–1967).

are also other translations of his work effected by a host of individuals: 1) by *jongleurs* and others who sang or performed it, faithfully or not, in the town square and elsewhere; 2) by countless scribes who copied from their exemplars, sometimes inventing new readings; 3) by commentators whose glosses may or may not accurately interpret the poem;[17] 4) by musicians whose vocal settings and orchestral compositions provide an aural dimension to the poem;[18] and 5) by artists, manuscript illuminators, and book illustrators whose images assist our visual understanding of the work.[19]

In the following pages I will focus on two distinct aspects of Dante—as "translator" and as "translated," Dante *traduttore* and Dante *tradotto*—and will present some specific examples in each category. As noted above, translation literally means the movement of something from one place to another, and, literarily, it refers to the transfer of a text from one linguistic and cultural context to another. Translation, then, is not simply a question of language, but also of ethos and all that term implies. Thus, Dante puts his "poetics of translation"[20] into practice not only by rendering, for example, the Latin phrases of the Bible into Italian but also by moving them, transferring them in their original garb directly into his poem, where they take on new life in their new context and carry with them the written and visual commentary traditions associated with them. The same phenomenon occurs more generally with all the texts in the classical and medieval literary traditions incorporated in the *Comedy*.

---

[17] For a sampling of the extensive commentary tradition on the *Comedy*, see the Dartmouth Dante Project (<http://dante.dartmouth.edu> [August 2012]) which presents electronic copies of more than 70 commentaries from the fourteenth century to the present.

[18] See, among others, the detailed study by Maria Ann Roglieri, *Dante and Music: Musical Adaptations of the "Commedia" from the Sixteenth Century to the Present* (Aldershot, 2001).

[19] Among the many examples in this category, perhaps the best known are Botticelli's drawings, William Blake's drawings and water colors, Gustave Doré's engravings, and Tom Phillips's set of 139 illustrations that accompany his translation of the first canticle, *Dante's Inferno* (London, 1985).

[20] My earlier research focused on what I term Dante's "poetics of citation," which is a subset of the "poetics of translation." The word "poetics" implies a conscious and programmatic incorporation of certain rules or precepts concerning literary or poetic composition, of which there are many examples in the Middle Ages: in rhetoric [*artes rhetoricae*], in poetry [*artes poeticae*, or *artes versificatoriae*], in letter writing [*artes dictaminis*] and in preaching [*artes praedicandi*]. My earlier work on Dante and the Bible is indebted to the following studies, among others: Giovanni Barblan (ed.), *Dante e la bibbia* (Florence, 1988); Celestino Cavedoni, *Raffronti tra gli autori biblici e sacri e la Divina commedia* (Città di Castello, 1896); Peter S. Hawkins, *Dante's Testaments: Essays in Scriptural Imagination* (Stanford, 1999); David Higgins, *Dante and the Bible: An Introduction* (Bristol, 1992); Robert Hollander, *Allegory in Dante's "Commedia"* (Princeton, 1969); Giulio Marzot, *Il linguaggio biblico nella Divina Commedia* (Pisa, 1956); Edward Moore, *Studies in Dante, First Series: Scripture and Classical Authors in Dante* (Oxford, 1896); Paola Rigo, *Memoria classica e memoria biblica in Dante* (Florence, 1994).

For example, the second canto of *Purgatory* describes the arrival of the ship of souls with the angel at its helm—a "translation" as it were of these souls from the world of the living to their new, albeit temporary home on the island of Purgatory. As they approach, the souls sing, in unison, the 113th Psalm:

> "*In exitu Isräel de Aegypto*"
> cantavan tutti insieme ad una voce
> con quanto di quel salmo è poscia scripto. (*Purg*. 2:46–8)
> ["*When Israel came out of Egypt*" all of them were singing together with one voice, with the rest of that psalm as it is written.]

Dante specifies that they sang the *entire* psalm, and thus we know—for we are told—to think in terms of the entire psalm to understand fully its importance to the events at hand.[21] In its original context this psalm signaled the deliverance from tyranny, the exodus of the children of Israel from bondage in Egypt. Indeed, Dante used this psalm in his "Letter to Can Grande" to exemplify how biblical texts can be interpreted allegorically according to the four levels of meaning: literal/historical, allegorical, moral, and anagogical. Given that exodus is the controlling metaphor for the *Comedy*,[22] it is no accident that we find this theme at this particular point in the journey, for in his journey up the Mountain of Purgatory Dante the Pilgrim will move from the bondage of sin to freedom, to that state of original justice in the Earthly Paradise at its summit.[23] Thus, the authority of the Latin biblical text and its web of associations and resonances are translated into Dante's poem.

In that same canto we witness the Pilgrim's failed attempt to embrace one of the newly arrived souls, his friend Casella:

> Ohi ombre vane, fuor che ne l'aspetto!
> tre volte dietro a lei le mani avvinsi,
> e tante mi tornai con esse al petto. (*Purg*. 2:79–81)
> [O empty shades except in aspect! Three times I clasped my hands behind him and as often brought them back to my breast.]

This scene represents not only a translation of verses from Virgil's *Aeneid* but also their substance, and indeed two moments in the *Aeneid* present identical language: Aeneas attempts, without success, to embrace the shade of his wife Creusa in Book 2 (792–4) and the same thing occurs in Book 6 with the shade of his father Anchises (700–702):[24]

---

[21] See Singleton's commentary to v. 46 of canto 2 of Dante's *Purgatorio* (p. 31).

[22] On this point, see, for example, Charles S. Singleton, "In Exitu Israel de Aegypto," *Seventy-Eighth Annual Report of the Dante Society* (1960): 1–24.

[23] On this point, see, for example, Charles S. Singleton, *Journey to Beatrice*, Dante Studies 2 (Cambridge, MA, 1958).

[24] The text, with slight modifications in the translations, comes from Virgil, *Aeneid*, trans. H. Rushton Fairclough (Cambridge, MA, 1967).

> ter conatus ibi collo dare bracchia circum;
> ter frustra comprensa manus effugit imago,
> par levibus ventis volucrique simillima somno.
> [Thrice there I strove to throw my arms about her/his neck; thrice the form, vainly clasped, fled from my hands, even as light winds, and most like a winged dream.]

More than the mere words, Dante translates here the highly charged emotional content of these two bittersweet encounters: Aeneas the devoted husband who yearns to embrace his wife; pious Aeneas who longs to embrace his father. To capture the tenderness of his meeting with Casella Dante not only imbues his narrative with the resonance of these two Virgilian passages but also transforms them: sadness and melancholy yield to joy and hope, for he recognizes Casella as one of the elect, and thus there is no cause for grief.

In *Inferno* 10 among the burning sarcophagi of the heretics, Dante meets a fellow Florentine, Farinata degli Uberti. An arch-nemesis of Dante, who was a White Guelph, this great Ghibelline warlord identifies the place of the Pilgrim's origin—Florence—by his speech:

> La tua loquela ti fa manifesto
> di quella nobil patrïa natio,
> a la qual forse fui troppo molesto. (*Inf.* 10:25–7)
> [Your speech clearly shows you a native of that noble fatherland to which I perhaps did too much harm.]

We recognize in Farinata's words a precise translation from the Gospel of Matthew—"loquela tua manifestum te facit" (Mt. 26:73)—where the servant maid and her companions are able to identify Peter as a Galilean *by his speech*, by his accent, which is different from the Judean. By employing this particular translation from the Bible, Dante sets in motion a series of intertextual connections between this episode in the *Inferno* and the specific biblical text as viewed in its larger referential context of the Passion, Crucifixion, and Resurrection.[25] Significantly, in the Bible the local accent serves to *differentiate* Peter's speech from that of the others, while in the *Comedy* Dante's Tuscan speech ironically aligns him with Farinata. Ironically, for their political affiliations—the one Guelph and the other Ghibelline—are radically different; however, since one (Farinata) had been, and the other (Dante) would soon be exiled from that city, they share at least two superficial bonds: their precarious state in exile and their professed love for their noble native city, "quella nobil patrïa." In their original gospel context the words "thy speech doth discover thee" denote a double betrayal, of Christ by Peter who

[25] For a more complete examination of this episode, see my essay, "The Poetics of Citation: Dante's *Divina Commedia* and the Bible," in Albert N. Mancini, Paolo A. Giordano, and Anthony J. Tamburri (eds), *Italiana 1988: Selected Papers from the Proceedings of the Fifth Annual Conference of the American Association of Teachers of Italian, November 18–20, 1988, Monterey, CA*, Rosary College Italian Studies 4 (1990), pp. 1–21.

denies him three times, and of Peter by his speech. By employing an exact Italian translation of these words, Dante may have wished to establish an atmosphere of betrayal and denial, and in the *Inferno* the sin of heresy is presented precisely in terms of death and denial. As deniers of the immortality of the soul, the heretics are appropriately and ironically punished in flaming tombs that reflect the finality, the mortality of their own vision. The visual commentary tradition on this episode in the *Inferno* reflects its grim irony. Tom Phillips, for example, depicts the tombs of the heretics as the "very books in which, denying the afterlife, they signed and sealed their future doom."[26] In his illustration books and flaming sepulchers are one, and they bear epicurean-inspired phrases such as "Carpe diem …" ["Seize the day …"] and "Gather ye rosebuds while ye may," as well as the ironic welcome to newly arrived souls of the heretics who denied the immortality of the soul: "Surprise, Surprise, Surprise."

For Dante translation is not only a textual exercise; it is also the art of transferring the natural landscape into his poem through a few well-chosen geographical references and rendering it vivid and meaningful. For example, in *Purgatory* 4 he alludes to four separate places in Italy in order to convey some sense of the mountain's steepness and the difficulty of the ascent:

> Vassi in Sanleo e discendesi in Noli,
> montasi su in Bismantova e 'n Cacume
> con esso i piè; ma qui convien ch'om voli. (*Purg*. 4:25–7)
> [One can walk to San Leo and descend to Noli, one can mount Bismantova and Cacume with feet alone; but here a man must fly.]

Recognizing these toponyms, readers would immediately visualize the scene and grasp the poet's meaning. Moreover, these four places represent the principal compass points: East (San Leo in the Marche), West (Noli on the coast west of Genoa), North (Bismantova in Emilia), and South (Cacume between Rome and Naples). The physical challenges posed by these arduous places are nothing compared to what the Pilgrim is experiencing here; indeed, no other place on earth is so rugged, and this is reinforced by the sense of spatial totality given by reference to the compass points.

Another example of geographical translation concerns the depiction of the sixth circle of the *Inferno*:

> Sì come ad Arli, ove Rodano stagna,
> sì com' a Pola, presso del Carnaro
> ch' Italia chiude e suoi termini bagna,
> fanno i sepulcri tutt' il loco varo. (*Inf.* 9:112–15)
> [As at Arles where the Rhone slackens its course, and as at Pola, near the Quarnero, which shuts Italy in and bathes her borders, the sepulchers make all the place uneven.]

---

26 Phillips, *Dante's Inferno*, p. 291.

This circle is described as a gigantic cemetery of open and fiery tombs, which house the arch-heretics and their followers, and the scene is likened to the Roman cemeteries at Pola and Arles. This is the first time in the *Comedy* that real geographic places are used as terms of comparison, and this small point gains importance because it underlines the spiritual blindness of the heretics, for whom, on earth, the tomb signified not the beginning, but the end of life. The narrow confines of the red-hot tombs in which their immortal souls will suffer for all eternity are grim, ironic reminders of their limited, earth-centered vision.[27]

Dante also translates the visual arts into his poem. In the canto of the heretics, the self-centered, self-serving, and ultimately self-defeating display of human pride is aptly figured in Farinata, described as a "great soul" ["magnanimo," *Inf.* 10:73], who emerged from the tomb "from the waist upwards" ["da la cintola in sù," *Inf.* 10:33] and "rose upright with chest and brow thrown back as if he had great scorn of Hell" ["s'ergea col petto e con la fronte / com'avesse l'inferno a gran dispitto," *Inf.* 10:35–6]. Farinata certainly is, as Anthony Cassell so brilliantly demonstrated, an infernal perversion or parody of the iconographic types of Noah, the resurrected Christ, and Christ as the Man of Sorrows.[28] This ironic representation is reinforced when we recognize that Farinata's words "la tua loquela ti fa manifesto" (*Inf.* 10:25, as noted earlier) are directed, in this context, toward Dante the Pilgrim who is destined for salvation and, in their original biblical context, toward Peter who would overcome his denial of Christ to attain to eternal glory.

In *Inferno* 34 Dante's depiction of three-headed Lucifer may have been inspired by the mosaic of the Last Judgment in the cupola of the Florentine Baptistery, where Lucifer is depicted seated among the damned with a sinner emerging from his mouth, and from each of Satan's ears, a dragon protrudes holding a sinner in its mouth.[29] Dante's three-faced Lucifer holds Judas in his middle mouth, while from his side mouths the legs of Brutus and Cassius emerge.[30] Dante may have translated this image with significant modifications into the poetic fabric of the

27 For a more detailed study of this point, see my essay, "The Land of the Living and the Land of the Dead: Burial, Entombment, and Cemeteries in Dante's *Divine Comedy*," *Religion & Literature* 31.1 (1999): 49–59.

28 Anthony K. Cassell, *Dante's Fearful Art of Justice* (Toronto, 1984), ch. 2, "Farinata," pp. 15–31.

29 For the possible influence of the cupola mosaics on Dante, see, among others, Ernest Hatch Wilkins, "Dante and the Mosaics in His Bel San Giovanni," in *The Invention of the Sonnet and Other Studies in Italian Literature* (Rome, 1959), pp. 51–60; and my essay, "On Dante and the Visual Arts," in Teodolinda Barolini and H. Wayne Storey (eds), *Dante and the New Millennium* (New York, 2003), pp. 274–92.

30 Lucifer the arch-traitor holds the betrayer of Jesus in his middle mouth, while the betrayers of Julius Caesar are in his side mouths. For a more extensive study of the significance of their positions, see my article, "Dante's Towering Giants: *Inferno* XXXI," *Romance Philology* 27 (1974): 269–85.

Comedy, specifically by making Lucifer a symbolic perversion of the Trinity:[31] Lucifer's three faces, each of a different hue, represent, through opposition, the infernal distortion of the three attributes of the Deity: the yellowish face (= impotence) opposes the Father (= Power), the black face (= ignorance) the Son (= Wisdom), and the red face (= hate) the Holy Spirit (= Love).[32]

Having considered the master hand of Dante the translator, I will now turn my attention to some ways in which the Florentine poet has been translated. In novella CXIV of the *Trecentonovelle* (c. 1392), Franco Sacchetti provides anecdotal evidence of the faulty translation or transmission of the *Comedy*. According to the novella, one day Dante was walking down a street in Florence when he heard a blacksmith pounding on his anvil and singing the verses of the *Comedy*, but in the manner of a popular song ["battendo ferro uno fabbro su la 'ncudine, cantava il Dante come si canta uno cantare"].[33] The blacksmith was making such a hash of his poem, cutting here and adding there, that Dante was greatly offended ["tramestava i versi suoi, smozzicando e appiccando, che parea a Dante ricever di quello grandissima ingiuria"]. Dante entered the blacksmith's shop, took the latter's tools—hammer, pincers, scales, and so on—and threw them out into the street ["piglia Dante il martello e gettalo per la via, piglia le tanaglie e getta per la via, piglia le bilance e getta per la via, e così gittò molti ferramenti"]. To the blacksmith's questions as to what Dante was doing and if he had gone crazy ["Che diavol fate voi? Sète voi impazzato?"], our poet replied in kind, asking: "And you? What do you think you're doing?" ["O tu che fai?"]. Noting that he was merely performing his trade (his *arte*), the blacksmith observed that Dante was ruining his tools by throwing them around ["Fo l'arte mia … e voi guastate le mie masserizie, gittandole per la via"], to which the poet replied: "If you do not want

[31] This has become a commonplace in Dante criticism. See Karl Vossler, *Mediaeval Culture: An Introduction to Dante and His Times* (2 vols, New York, 1958), vol. 2, pp. 298 ff; Luigi Pietrobono, *Il Poema sacro, saggio d'una interpretazione generale della Divina commedia. Inferno* (2 vols, Bologna, 1915), vol. 2, pp. 233–51; Hermann Gmelin, *Die Göttliche Komödie, Kommentar* (3 vols, Stuttgart, 1954–1957), vol. 1, pp. 483–9; and Charles S. Singleton, *Commedia: Elements of Structure*, Dante Studies 1 (Cambridge, MA, 1965), pp. 33–44.

[32] Cf. the inscription over the Gate of Hell: "Giustizia mosse il mio alto fattore; / fecemi la *divina podestate*, / la *somma sapienza e 'l primo amore*" ["Justice moved my high maker: the *divine power* made me, the *supreme wisdom*, and the *primal love*," *Inf.* 3:4–6, emphases mine]. In his commentary on canto 34, Benvenuto da Imola remarks the polar relationship between God and Lucifer in his commentary on vv. 37–45: "Sicut enim Deus est trinus et unus, in quo est summa potentia, summus amor, et summa sapientia; ita in isto est summa impotentia, summum odium, summa ignorantia" ["Just as God is three and one, in whom there is all power, all love, and all wisdom, so in this one (Lucifer) there is all powerlessness, all hatred, all ignorance"] (*Comentum super Dantis Aldhigerij Comoediam*, ed. W.W. Vernon and G.F. Lacaita [5 vols, Florence, 1887], vol. 2, p. 553).

[33] The text of the novella follows Antonio Lanza's edition: Franco Sacchetti, *Il Trecentonovelle* (Florence, 1984), pp. 231–3. The translations are mine.

me to ruin your things, then don't ruin mine" ["Se tu non vuogli che io guasti le cose tue, non guastare le mie"], explaining that the blacksmith is singing his book, but that he is not saying it as he wrote it: "Tu canti il libro [mio] e non lo di' come io lo feci." Dante concludes: "I do not have any other trade, and you are spoiling the one I have" ["io non ho altr'arte, e tu me la guasti"]. Sacchetti concludes the tale as follows: "The smith completely upset and not knowing how to respond, gathered up his things and returned to his work; and whenever he decided to sing in the future, he sang of Tristan and of Lancelot, and left Dante alone ..." ["Il fabbro, gonfiato, non sapendo rispondere, raccoglie le cose e torna al suo lavorío; e se volle cantare, cantò di Tristano e di Lancelotto e lasciò stare il Dante ..."].

Emerging from this tale is the distinction between literature for popular consumption and literature for the intelligentsia. Although he sang the verses badly, the smithy was, nevertheless, acquainted with the verses of the *Comedy*, and this suggests the early diffusion, knowledge, and popularity of Dante's poem among people at various levels of society and serves as well as a demonstration of the faulty "translation" of Dante's poem by ill-informed contemporaries.[34]

Commentators on the poem also provide interesting translations. The episode in *Inferno* 3 where Charon greets the souls and transports them across the Acheron, is glossed by the Ottimo Commento, which declares that not only did Charon give Dante passage across the Acheron, but that he must have had several boats, given that so many souls were arriving in Hell.[35] One manuscript illumination (in London, British Library, MS Yates Thompson 36) may reflect this interpretation in that there appear to be three boats ferrying souls across the river.[36]

The rich visual tradition of the poem offers interesting interpretive challenges. Some illustrations of the *Comedy* seem to ignore the allegorical or metaphorical use of language in the text and provide very literal translations, as, for example, when the monster Geryon[37] is described as swimming upward through the murky

---

34 In this regard see, among others, John Ahern, "Singing the Book: Orality in the Reception of Dante's *Comedy*," in Amilcare A. Iannucci (ed.), *Dante: Contemporary Perspectives* (Toronto, 1997), pp. 214–39.

35 The Ottimo Commento glosses vv. 118–20 of canto 3 as follows: "*Così sen vanno etc.* Su per l'acqua nera di Acheronte; e tanta è la moltitudine che arrivano in Inferno, che anzi che l'una navata sia giunta di là, di qua è accolta l'altra" ["*So they go etc.* On the black water of Acheron; and so great is the crowd that arrives in Hell that before the one boat has reached the other side, another boat has been welcomed on this side"] (*L'Ottimo Commento della Divina Commedia* [Pisa, 1827]).

36 This was suggested by Peter Brieger, "Pictorial Commentaries to the *Commedia*," in Peter Brieger, Millard Meiss, and Charles S. Singleton, *Illuminated Manuscripts of the Divine Comedy* (2 vols, Princeton, 1969), vol. 1, pp. 81–113 at pp. 86–7. There is no apparent link, however, between the Ottimo Commento and the Yates Thompson manuscript. This illustration may also be viewed as representing successive moments in the scene: Charon pilots the boat with Dante and Virgil on board; Charon stands in the boat wielding his oar at the crowd of souls; and Charon's boat arrives on the other shore where three souls debark.

37 See, for example, Vatican City, Biblioteca Apostolica Vaticana, MS Urbinati Lat. 365.

air ["i' vidi per quell'aere grosso e scuro / venir notando una figura in suso," *Inf.* 16:130–31] or when the bloated body of Master Adam,[38] the counterfeiter, is said to have the form of a lute ["Io vidi un, fatto a guisa di lëuto," *Inf.* 30:49]. Some illustrators[39] take quite literally the reference to the strange "bugle" sounded by Malacoda in the final verse (139) of *Inferno* 21: "Ed egli avea del cul fatto trombetta" ["and he had made a trumpet of his arse"]. Similarly, the marvelous opening verses of *Purgatory*, which present metaphorically the raising of the sails of the poet's little ship of genius—"Per correr miglior acque alza le vele / omai la navicella del mio ingegno" (*Purg.* 1:1–2)—are often depicted literally as though Dante and Virgil were piloting a seagoing vessel.[40] The same metaphor occurs in the second canto of *Paradise* where Dante warns those who may attempt to follow him over these uncharted seas in boats unequal to the task: "O voi che siete in piccioletta barca / … tornate a riveder li vostri liti: / non vi mettete in pelago, ché forse, / perdendo me, rimarreste smarriti" ["O you that are in your little bark, … turn back to see again your shores. Do not commit yourselves to the open sea, for perchance, if you lost me, you would remain astray," *Par.* 2:1, 4–6].[41]

One obvious visual "mistranslation" occurs in *Inferno* 13, the wood of the suicides, where Dante is careful to hide all visible traces of the souls. Indeed, the souls have been transformed into trees with no visible human characteristics. They are not "imprisoned" inside hollow trees, rather they *are* trees, and therein lies the horror of the scene, both for Dante the Pilgrim and for us the readers. However, even in his early frescoes in the Strozzi Chapel (Florence, Santa Maria Novella), Nardo di Cione depicts trees with human heads, as do Gustave Doré and William Blake, albeit more dramatically and anthropomorphically. Trees with human faces and branches like arms and legs are, in my view, less true to Dante's conception of the scene and perhaps less effective than certain medieval illuminations that present the strange wood with no human form present.[42]

These examples demonstrate how Dante employs to good effect his "poetics of translation," incorporating elements from a wide variety of sources in the construction of the *Comedy*, and how, in turn, his poem has been translated, for good or for ill, in a number of ways in subsequent centuries. Domenico di Michelino's panel painting (1440) in the Florentine cathedral provides an image of what I would term Dante the translator. This painting shows the poet standing against the double backdrop of Florence and the Universal Order, holding open his book,

---

[38] See, for example, Naples, Biblioteca Nazionale, MS XIII.C.4.

[39] See, for example, Florence, Biblioteca Nazionale Centrale, MS Palat. 313.

[40] See, for example, Perugia, Biblioteca Augusta, MS 81 (formerly B.25), and Florence, Biblioteca Medicea Laurenziana, MS Plut. 40.13.

[41] See, for example, London, British Library, MS Yates Thompson 36, and Florence, Biblioteca Medicea Laurenziana, MS Plut. 40.7.

[42] See, for example, Florence, Biblioteca Medicea Laurenziana, MS Strozziani 152, and London, British Library, MS Yates Thompson 36.

the *Comedy*, and gesturing toward the three realms of the afterlife. Dante appears to be inviting viewers to consider the ways in which he has translated the world of Florence and, more generally, the book of the universe into his poem, encouraging them to read it, to hear its message, and ultimately to see what end may await them. Students, scholars, and ultimately "translators" of his poem are constantly reminded of the importance of these multiple aspects of and approaches to the *Comedy*. For, after all, translation is intended to allow easy and sure movement between the poem and its multiple cultural contexts.

Chapter 7
Traces of the Translators in Late Medieval Italian Vernacularizations

Alison Cornish

In describing the Kane and Donaldson approach to editing a particularly thorny medieval text (*Piers Plowman*), Lee Patterson epitomized the editors' attitude toward the fundamental distinction between scribes and authors:

> The scribes are many, the poet unique; the scribes write the language of common men, the poet composes a language of his own. The poet traces no conventional path but works out for himself the way of genius, and it is the task of his editors to rediscover that way from among the ruins of the manuscripts.[1]

In recent years there has been a tendency to minimize the distinction between authors and scribes as the interventions of the latter have come to be seen not always as errors to be removed in the search for authenticity, but as part and parcel of medieval texts whose very nature is unstable.[2] Translations are no exception to the rule of *mouvance*; on the contrary, they are infinitely updatable. Yet they also carry with them a special concern for authorship, authenticity, and fidelity, however much they may betray their sources from a modern perspective. The goal of vernacular translation is to bring something relatively fixed (a text ultimately by an authority) into something that is still extremely mobile: the nonstandardized,

---

[1] Lee Patterson, "The Logic of Textual Criticism and the Way of Genius: The Kane-Donaldson *Piers Plowman* in Historical Perspective," in Jerome J. McGann (ed.), *Textual Criticism and Literary Interpretation* (Chicago, 1985), pp. 55–91; repr. in Lee Patterson, *Negotiating the Past: The Historical Understanding of Medieval Literature* (Madison, 1987), pp. 77–113 at p. 97. Derek Pearsall describes it as a "sublime notion" of a poem "whose words will always be discerned to be ineffably superior among the mass of scribal variants, and in a sublime notion of the editor as another unique someone who will always be able to discern them" ("Authorial Revision in Some Late-Medieval English Texts," in Alastair J. Minnis and Charlotte Brewer [eds], *Crux and Controversy in Middle English Textual Criticism* [Cambridge, 1992], pp. 39–48 at p. 43). I would like to thank Cambridge University Press for permission to reuse material here from my recent book, *Vernacular Translation in Dante's Italy: Illiterate Literature* (Cambridge, 2011).

[2] See, e.g., Alastair J. Minnis (ed.), *Late-Medieval Religious Texts and Their Transmission: Essays in Honour of A.I. Doyle* (Cambridge, 1994). Paul Zumthor coined the term *mouvance* to describe the inherent instability of medieval vernacular literature in *Essai de poétique mediévale* (Paris, 1972).

nonliterary target language. In terms of Bonaventure's famous definition of the four kinds of makers of books, the *volgarizzatore* is both like a scribe, who should faithfully transmit what someone else says, and like an author, who uses mostly his own words.[3] To use Patterson's language, the author of a vernacular translation in late medieval Italy is likely to be no poet, but neither is he just a scribe. His task, which is by no means mechanical and to be really successful requires no little genius, is to transfer the language of the poet, or the *auctor*, into the language of common men—the *volgare*. And since this language has limited geographical reach and no guarantee of continuity over time, it is something that has to be found again and again by each agent of transmission.[4] The scribes of translated texts participate necessarily in their authorship.

The scribe of a translation becomes himself a translator when, instead of reproducing exactly something that either does not make sense or does not seem sufficiently elegant or idiomatic in his own language, he alters the text in a way that, to his mind at least, renders it more comprehensible and less foreign. For example, in some manuscripts of Brunetto Latini's translation of Cicero's orations, "Gaius" has become "Guido" and "Publius," "Pietro." Such unsophisticated "redressing" is thought to be attributable not to Brunetto himself, but to some lax scribe who thought he was explaining things better.[5] Modernizing interventions on the part of copyists arguably perfect the project of translation, which is after all the immediate purpose of the text they are copying. These scribes are therefore not simply permitted, but are rather, in a sense, *obliged* by the genre to complete the ever-perfectible task of translation—to render it ever more comprehensible, local, vernacular. Copyists of vernacular translations have naturally less reverence for the letter of the translated text they are copying than they would for the original, since it is only a solution advanced by some recent predecessor of theirs, someone essentially of their ilk. The author of the translation being copied was not an *auctor*, after all, but on the contrary had essentially the same status, the same authority,

---

[3] St. Bonaventure of Bagnoregio, *Commentaria in Quatuor Libros Sententiarum Magistri Petri Lombardi, Opera Omnia S. Bonaventurae*, vol. 1 (Quaracchi, 1882), pp. 14–15: "quadruplex est modus faciendi librum. Aliquis enim scribit aliena, nihil addendo vel mutando; et iste mere dicitur *scriptor*. Aliquis scribit aliena, addendo, sed non de suo; et iste *compilator* dicitur. Aliquis scribit et aliena et sua, sed aliena / tamquam principalia, et sua tamquam annexa ad evidentiam; et iste dicitur *commentator*, non *auctor*. Aliquis scribit et sua et aliena, sed sua tanquam principalia, aliena tamquam annexa ad confimationem; et talis debet dici *auctor*." See Alastair J. Minnis, *Medieval Theory of Authorship*, 2nd ed. (Philadelphia, 1988), p. 229; and Albert Ascoli, *Dante and the Making of a Modern Author* (Cambridge, 2008).

[4] Sheldon Pollock, "Cosmopolitan and Vernacular in History," *Public Culture* 12.3 (2000): 591–625, characterized vernacularization as arising from "conscious decisions of writers to reshape the boundaries of their cultural universe by renouncing the larger world for the smaller place" (p. 592).

[5] Francesco Maggini, *I primi volgarizzamenti dei classici latini* (Florence, 1952), p. 23: "grossolano travestimento."

and the same task as the person copying it out. Indeed sometimes it was the same person, who had now changed his mind—producing an authorial variant.[6]

The transcriber of a *volgarizzamento* might well have a better understanding of the past or a better mastery of the language being translated than did the author of the translation whose work he is transcribing. He might, moreover, possess a better copy of the text that was being translated, or another translation either in his own or another language that could influence and contaminate his own rendition. As sites of reworking, *volgarizzamenti* are thus particularly problematic for textual editing, but eloquent with regard to the initiatives of scribes—the anonymous translator-author-editor-compiler-transcribers who were not just copying literature, but *reading* it. The study of the manuscript tradition of *volgarizzamenti* gives a window onto a world of readers, on people trying to make sense of the past with whatever tools they had available.[7]

A good example of such an individual is Lapo di Neri Corsini, the copyist of the oldest extant manuscript of the long Italian version of the *Fait des Romains*, which was already a translation-compilation into French of Sallust, Caesar, Suetonius, and Lucan.[8] Lapo was not a professional scribe, but someone with interests and initiatives of his own, transcribing ultimately for himself. His father was the founder of the Corsini fortunes, active in the silk guild and the Florentine government from about 1277 to 1315. Lapo himself was consul of the Arte della Lana in 1320.[9] While Neri was serving as prior of the commune or as consul to the guild and tending to his large and prosperous textile business, his son, Lapo, was reading and transcribing vernacular translations. Although he noted the date of his transcription of the *Fatti dei Romani* (1313), we know his identity thanks to the sleuthing of the nineteenth-century librarian of the Biblioteca Riccardiana, Salomone Morpurgo, who compared the handwriting with that of another manuscript of *volgarizzamenti* in the Laurentian library to which Lapo signed his name.[10]

---

6 According to Giambattista Speroni, the most recent editor of the *Fiore di Rettorica* (Pavia,1994), the multiplicity of versions does not just arise from energetic copyists and adaptors, but originates with the author himself, who was already changing his mind about how to reorder the text yet again before he had finished his first draft.

7 For a textual editor's view of the complexities and rewards of editing *volgarizzamenti*, see Guglielmo Gorni, *Dante prima della Commedia* (Florence, 2001), p. 183.

8 On the *Fait des Romains*, see especially Jeanette Beer, *A Medieval Caesar* (Geneva, 1976); and Louis-Fernand Flutre, *Li Fait des Romains dans les littératures française et italienne du XIIIe au XVIe siècle* (Paris, 1932).

9 A. Benvenuti Papi, "Corsini, Neri," in Alberto M. Ghisalberti (ed.), *Dizionario biografico degli italiani*, vol. 29 (Rome, 1983), p. 649; Luigi Passerini, *Genealogia e storia della famiglia Corsini* (Florence, 1858), p. 15.

10 For the story, see Rossella Baldini, "Zucchero Bencivenni, 'La santà del corpo.' Volgarizzamento del 'Régime du corps' di Aldobrandino da Siena (a. 1310) nella copia coeva di Lapo di Neri Corsini (Laur. Pl. LXXIII 47)," *Studi di lessicografia italiana* 15 (1998): 21–300 at 29.

Lapo did not know Latin, or even much French, and was therefore literate only in the sense that he read and wrote in the vernacular (technically, an "idiot").[11] He fits Armando Petrucci's profile of the literate person in this "new, mercantile, urban, communal society" who was "free to write apart from any precise social function or constricting juridical obligations," who wrote simply because he was able to do so, and who wrote in the vernacular and in cursive, rather than in Latin and in the scripts that belonged to books as did the medieval "worker-scribe."[12] With the resources he had at his disposal, this scribe was, moreover, engaged in processes of editing and collation that are usually associated with the philological innovations of the humanists.

Lapo's manuscript was so long that it was at some point broken into two, the first part of which has ended up in the Staatsbibliothek in Berlin, the second in the Riccardiana Library in Florence.[13] Like all the surviving witnesses of the so-called long version of the *Fatti*, Lapo's manuscript is contaminated with the much more widely circulating *versio brevis*. In other words, all copyists of the long version also consulted and used the short one.[14] Lapo, moreover, interpolates into the text of the translation that he is copying another, very recent translation of Sallust's *Jugurtha* by Bartolomeo da San Concordio, thereby creating a huge redundancy in the narrative in order, he says, to tell the story in order ("per ordine").[15] At another point he merges the text of the *Fatti* with Bartolomeo's translation of Sallust's *Catiline,* together with elements from the shorter version of the *Fatti*, attempting to stitch it all together with some words of his own. This contamination and corruption of the text is motivated by a

11 An *idiota* is someone who knows his own vernacular, but not Latin. See Silvia Rizzo, *Ricerche sul latino umanistico* (Rome, 2002), p. 18; Jakob Hans Josef Schneider, "Das Wort idiota im mittelalterlichen Latein," in Elisabeth Charlotte Welskopf (ed.), *Untersuchungen ausgewählter altgriechischer sozialer Typenbegriffe und ihr Fortleben in Antike und Mittelalter* (Berlin, 1981), pp. 132–57.

12 Armando Petrucci, "Reading and Writing *Volgare* in Medieval Italy," in his *Writers and Readers in Medieval Italy. Studies in the History of Written Culture*, ed. and trans. Charles M. Radding (New Haven, 1995), pp. 169–235 at p. 178. In "Sul ms. Hamilton 67 di Berlino e sul volgarizzamento della 'IVª Catilinaria' in esso contenuto," *Studi di filologia italiana* 42 (1984): 27–58, Giuliano Staccioli defines Lapo's hand as "notula."

13 The two parts of the manuscript are Berlin, Staatsbibliothek Preußischer Kulturbesitz, MS Hamilton 67, and Florence, Biblioteca Riccardiana, MS 2418. Parodi brought the Hamilton manuscript to Florence and confirmed their relation. See Ernesto G. Parodi, "Le storie di Cesare nella letteratura italiana dei primi secoli," *Studi di Filologia Romanza* 4 (1889): 237–501.

14 The short version, surviving in more than 40 manuscripts, was published by Luciano Banchi as *I Fatti di Cesare* (Bologna, 1863).

15 Hamilton 67, f. 46d: "Ora parleremo e vi conterò la grande ghuerra che' Romani ebero chon Giughurta, re di Numidia, che così va la storia p[er] ordine." Text transcribed in Staccioli, "Sul ms. Hamilton 67," p. 32.

desire to take account of all available translations, as if reduplication rather than selection would get him closer to the truth.[16]

The impression one gets from what we now know about Lapo's manuscript is of someone who did not want to leave anything out, to forget something that might be remembered by his copying it down. In fact for several elements (such as the Sallust portion of the long *Fatti* and the vernacular version of the fourth Catilinarian oration) he is our sole witness. But Lapo's manuscript does not just tell us about him; it is also a material witness to the gradual Italianization of the French text through the subtle interventions of numerous copyists who preceded him.

Like all *volgarizzamenti* of French intermediaries, versions of the *Fatti dei Romani* are full of Gallicisms, that is, words that are just barely translated or are left untranslated from French. David Bénéteau suggested that the continued presence of even simple terms such as "auton" and "iver" might mean that Lapo did not know French very well at all.[17] But in fact the Gallicisms in Lapo's manuscript are fewer than they were in previous versions. Sergio Marroni has been able to demonstrate in his recent collation of Lapo's manuscript with the three other extant copies of the long version a gradual process of elimination of Gallicisms over the course of the text's transmission. In particular he has shown that many of the variants among the manuscripts are explicable not as the reproduction of mechanical errors but as independent responses to French words that must have been present in preceding antigraphs.[18]

Scholars had originally assumed that Lapo's manuscript (H+R) together with copies preserved in the Laurentian library in Florence (L) and the Vatican (V) represented one branch of the long translation's transmission, and the one preserved in the Marciana library in Venice (M) another.[19] As one example among many, for the French text, "Pui saisi li boen destrier *par les resnes*," R has "poscia prese il buono destriere," L has "poi prese il buono destriere," and V has "Antipadre prese lo cavallo," whereas M retains the detail of the reins: "poscia prese *per le redine* lo buono destriere."[20] Yet at the same time there are shared errors and lacunae between M and one or other of the other three that make a clear division between branches less tenable. Of the four manuscripts, M often seems to represent an earlier phase of the tradition, as when for the French word "s'enarbrerent," R has "si levarono," L has "sii levarono," V has "ssi levaro," but

---

16 For well-illustrated examples, see Gianni A. Papini, "I Fatti dei Romani," *Studi di filologia italiana* 31 (1973): 97–155 at 99.

17 David P. Bénéteau, "Per un'edizione critica dei 'Fatti dei Romani,'" *Italianistica* 26 (1997): 401–11.

18 Sergio Marroni, *I fatti dei Romani. Saggio di edizione critica di un volgarizzamento fiorentino del Duecento* (Rome, 2004).

19 Florence, Biblioteca Medicea Laurenziana, MS Acquisti e Doni 72 (L); Vatican City, Biblioteca Apostolica Vaticana, MS Vaticano latino 4808 (V); and Venice, Biblioteca Marciana, MS 6110 (M). See Marroni, pp. 15–22.

20 Marroni, p. 24.

M has "s'inarborarono."[21] In other places it is another one of the four that seems to hold closer to the French, as when for "la noise," R has "le discordie," L has "la riotta," V has "la noia," and M cuts the phrase altogether.

Marroni argues that these four manuscripts were made not by passive copyists, but by active re-elaborators. Collation of hundreds of variants leads him to hypothesize that each copyist of the surviving long versions had consulted not only the short version but also another manuscript of the long one, apart from the one he was copying.[22] It is also possible to see that the surviving witnesses are the end result of a long process of updating Gallicisms (untranslated or barely translated French words) that must have been present in prior versions. This is evident in cases where one of the manuscripts retains a Gallicism from some earlier phase, but the others all have different solutions. For example, for the phrase in the French *Fait*, "fioles de voirres," the variants of "ghuastade di vivorio," "fiole di vetro," and "fogle di noce" are explicable only by something like "uoire" at some stage in the transmission of the translation that would explain both the correct reading of "vetro" and the erroneous ones of "iuoire" and "noier." The misreading of "si vestivano" in R for "se n'estoit" must be from a similar misreading of "v" for "n." "Essillié" is translated variously as "ischaciati," "essilliati," "isbanditi," and "exiliati." Three different readings of the Old French "Thacien," as "Tacien," "Acatien," and "Chatien" also indicate independent efforts at deciphering a French name, not inadvertent scribal corruptions of the same solution.[23]

The reason the variants have failed to clarify the genealogy of the witnesses is that copyists all down the course of the tradition were intervening in the language of the text, in essence perfecting the process of translation from one vernacular idiom to another and thereby becoming co-translators, or coauthors, of the new text as it emerged from their transcriptions. The scribes thus became translators themselves, or *copisti-volgarizzatori* as Marroni calls them, and therefore coauthors of the translation they transcribe. This is a process effected by reading, by readers reading for themselves and comparing readings that they find in sources available to them. The multiple versions of the *Fatti dei Romani* give palpable evidence of a long and gradual process of vernacular appropriation of ancient culture.

Volgarizzamenti are often, on the one hand, anonymous, as is the *Fatti dei Romani*, and as was the author of the original French *Fait des Romains*. Yet these same vernacular versions are almost always associated with the name of an author—a Sallust, a Lucan, a Suetonius, a Livy, or even an Aldobrandino da Siena. So while *volgarizzamenti* come to us through a series of other agents that some scholars have seen fit to equate with authors, their own derivative status vis-à-vis a distant and authoritative author is, if anything, repeatedly underlined. In the colophon of the Laurentian manuscript, where Lapo signed his name, this copyist makes a point of keeping distinct the writerly roles of composition, translation, and transcription:

---

21 Ibid., p. 45.

22 Ibid., p. 39.

23 Ibid., pp. 32, 45–6.

> Qui finiscie lo libro dela fisicha, che-l mastro Aldobrandino conpuose i.lingua franciescha, de la santà del corpo e di ciasqun menbro per sé, traslatato di franciesco in volghare nel MCCCX, di magio, per ser Zuchero Bencivenni notaio, e scritto p[er] me, Lapo di Neri Corsini, popolo sa. Folicie.[24]
> [Here ends the book of medicine, which Master Aldobrandino composed in the French language, on the health of the body and all of its members, translated from French into the vernacular in May, 1310, by the notary, Ser Zucchero Bencivenni, and written (i.e., transcribed) by me, Lapo di Neri Corsini, of the neighborhood of San Felice.]

In his copy of the *Fatti*, Lapo remains faithful to his role as transcriber even when he openly announces his deviation from his model and interpolates other material, which the author he is following left out. At the same time, he almost obsessively repeats phrases such as "Lucano dice" to remind us constantly of the authoritative source behind all of his cutting and pasting.

Although most medieval translators claimed fidelity to their sources, in practice they took great liberties in order to gloss and embellish them, since it was meaning, not the letter that counted. Charles Buridant suggests that this freedom stemmed from their lack of a notion of literary property.[25] Yet the temptation of the medieval transcriber is not so much to claim other people's work as his own as to ascribe to authorities works that he himself cobbled together from a variety of different sources. Elspeth Kennedy wants to describe these enterprising scribes not as authors, but as editors. It is interesting to note that, in her study of the manuscript tradition of such popular "mouvant" texts as the French prose romances of *Lancelot* and *Tristan*, she observes that only in the fifteenth century did French scribes begin to compare "two or more versions, trying to reconcile different readings and picking a sentence now from one MS, now from another."[26] This is also the sort of work that Lapo di Neri Corsini was doing, perhaps in his spare time, perhaps only for himself, in Florence in 1313.

While, as we have seen, in the transmission of the *Fatti*, French terms were gradually eliminated, with Latin texts there seems to have been a movement in two directions. Sometimes Latin terms were left in the original when translators were unsure how to find an idiomatic equivalent, and then such Latinisms would be corrected in later redactions. But there are also occasions in which the vulgarizers, particularly when they went back to retranslate things that had already been translated a first time, would restore the original Latin word or use

---

24 Baldini, "Zucchero Bencivenni," p. 29 (Florence, Biblioteca Medicea Laurenziana, MS Plut. LXXIII 47, f. 105r).

25 Claude Buridant, "*Translatio medievalis*: Théorie et pratique de la traduction médiévale," in *Travaux de linguistique et de littérature XXI* (Strasbourg, 1983), pp. 81–136 at pp. 117–21.

26 Elspeth Kennedy, "The Scribe as Editor," in *Mélanges de langue et de littérature du Moyen Age et de la Renaissance offerts à Jean Frappier*, Publications romanes et françaises CXII (Geneva, 1970), pp. 523–31.

(or coin) a Latinism that works in the vernacular but clearly recalls the foreign term behind it—"repubblica" instead of "comune," for example. Giuliano Tanturli has shown how use of the word "milite" for the Latin "miles" as opposed to "cavaliere" marks the *volgarizzamento* of the Third Decade of Livy as a more sophisticated effort than that of the Fourth Decade, traditionally attributed to Giovanni Boccaccio.[27]

Maria Teresa Casella, following on Giuseppe Billanovich's important discovery that the translations of the Third and Fourth Decades were both based on Petrarch's copy of Livy, believed that Boccaccio worked and reworked, "as in a garden," the vernacular translations of Livy and of Valerius Maximus and its commentary.[28] It is clear that in the complicated tradition of *Valerio Massimo*, a scribe did go back to revise his own earlier translation because there is a proem to that effect at the beginning of the glosses present in two witnesses. This person confesses that when he was asked to put glosses on the translated text, he became aware of how many mistakes he had made in his first attempt to translate it.[29]

This translator's earlier attempt has usually been identified with the most fortunate redaction (surviving in 29 manuscripts and 4 sixteenth-century editions) and hence called the "vulgate," which is full of errors of translation as well as awkward and sometimes impenetrable phrases. In addition to the revised version introduced by the proem quoted above, preserved complete only in a single Florentine manuscript (Florence, Biblioteca Nazionale Centrale, MS Palatino 762), there is a third version preserved in two witnesses, which Concetto Marchesi had first attributed to a later, "unknown and incompetent redactor," but which Adriana Zampieri has demonstrated to be the oldest of all three, blaming its abundance of errors in large part on a poor Latin exemplar. For Zampieri as for

---

27 Giuliano Tanturli, "Volgarizzamenti e ricostruzione dell'antico. I casi della terza e quarta Deca di Livio e di Valerio Massimo, la parte del Boccaccio (a proposito di un'attribuzione)," *Studi medievali* 27 (1986): 811–88.

28 Maria Teresa Casella, *Tra Boccaccio e Petrarca. I volgarizzamenti di Tito Livio e di Valerio Massimo* (Padua, 1982); Giuseppe Billanovich, "Il Boccaccio, il Petrarca e le più antiche traduzioni in italiano delle decadi di Tito Livio," *Giornale storico della letteratura italiana* 130 (1953): 311–37.

29 Florence, Biblioteca Nazionale Centrale, MS Panciatichiano 58, f. 5r, also found in Florence, Biblioteca Nazionale Centrale, MS Palatino 762. Text transcribed in *Un volgarizzamento inedito di Valerio Massimo*, ed. Vanna Lippi Bigazzi (Florence, 1996), p. xxi: "Maximo Valerio … il quale altra volta recai di gramatica in questa volgare lingua, ma però che certi savi religiosi, considerata l'afectione che 'layci portano a questo libro per le narrazioni de' fatti e detti degni di memoria che in esso sono, e considerata la brevitade d'esse storie, che tocca l'autore, la quale ingenera agli uditori sete di più steso stilo, feciono sopra esso, a modo di chiose, certi scritti, onde, pregato di mettere quelle chiose sopra questo testo e spezialmente perché in più parti per la povertà de la mia facultade non sentia quello che li chiosatori sentono, mi conviene di novello ritrarlo a la detta lingua insieme con le chiose necessarie e utili; però non si meravigli chi vedrae diverso questo secondo volgare dal primo."

Casella, similarities between the earliest and latest versions are explained by their persistence in the memory of a single translator, who recalled some of his earliest attempts to translate the text even as he was working on his second revision.[30]

Some manuscripts of the vulgate are accompanied by glosses transcribed in the same hand as the text, indicating that text and gloss were already linked from before the time of transcription. These marginal glosses, which constitute the oldest extant collection of vernacular commentary on Valerius, are thicker in the first books, petering out altogether in the sixth. They have some extended historical and mythological explanations but for the most part are brief definitions and recalls. The witnesses we have of the revised translation, apparently motivated, as we were told in the proem already quoted, by the encounter with the commentary of learned clerics, contain a different set of glosses. Their content makes evident their derivation from the Latin commentary on Valerius Maximus that the Augustinian friar, Dionigi di Borgo San Sepolcro, friend of both Boccaccio and Petrarch, dedicated to Cardinal Giovanni Colonna sometime after 1327. These new vernacular glosses make use of a text of *Valerio Massimo* that is not the same as the vulgate or the revised version, but they survive most fully in two manuscripts that contain the latter, along with the proem announcing a retranslation inspired by the encounter with learned commentators.[31] Tanturli's close study of these manuscripts has yielded a clear stratification present in the glosses even before they were copied down into these two surviving witnesses, already sedimented with traces of scholars, or at least curious readers, at work.

In a layer prior to the accretions of both witnesses, someone was already collating the glosses he was copying with others, as he sometimes makes explicit: "Un'altra chiosa dice che questi è Cato Censorino."[32] He has, moreover, consulted other historical sources, as he indicates in the next sentence: "Ma truovo in Orosyo, libro V°, etc." This is someone observing discrepancies and checking the sources available to him, remarking on different possibilities of translation and interpretation. A word some people translate as "biscanto" ("singing") others translate as "stropiccìo" ("scraping"); some prefer "cose" where others

30 The "vulgate" is the version published in Valerio Massimo, *De' fatti e detti degni di memoria della città di Roma e delle stranie genti*, ed. Roberto De Visiani (Bologna, 1867–1868). Adriana Zampieri, "Una primitiva redazione del volgarizzamento di Valerio Massimo," *Studi sul Boccaccio* 10 (1977–1978): 21–41. This redaction is preserved in two witnesses: Florence, Biblioteca Medicea Laurenziana, MS Ashburn 526 and Florence, Biblioteca Nazionale Centrale, MS Palatino 459. Concetto Marchesi, "Di alcuni volgarizzamenti toscani in codici fiorentini," *Studi romanzi* 5 (1907): 123–236; repr. in Marchesi, *Scritti minori di filologia e di letteratura* (3 vols, Florence, 1978), vol. 1, pp. 343–432 at pp. 391–2.

31 The fuller witnesses of the glosses are Florence, Biblioteca Nazionale Centrale, MSS Panciatichiano 58 and Palatino 762. They also survive in "embryonic" form in Florence, Biblioteca Medicea Laurenziana, MS Acquisti e doni 418 and Vatican, Biblioteca Apostolica Vaticana, MS Ferrajoli 559.

32 Marginal gloss to *Valerio Massimo* 2.10.7 (ed. Tanturli, p. 853).

have "questioni." Those who "keep the letter as it is" interpret the sense of the passage one way; those who understand it differently gloss it differently.[33] These multiple revisions, reworkings, and expansions happened at different moments in the transmission of text and glosses and therefore, as Tanturli soundly concludes, are attributable not to a single person—even one so exceptional as Boccaccio—but to a number of different people.

In the case of the *Fatti dei Romani*, a whole series of intermediate versions could be posited between some first attempt at translating the French text and Lapo's 1313 copy, in the direction of eliminating Gallicisms and rendering the language more fully *volgare*. The "vulgate" text of *Valerio Massimo* similarly smoothes out the raw Latinisms of earlier versions resulting from passive transcription or lack of understanding. Yet the reintroduction of Latinisms in the so-called revised version is not sign of an inability to translate, but an unwillingness to do so.[34] For example, for the Latin phrase "pallium togae subici," the vulgate explains the concept rather than trying to reproduce the words—"sottomettere alla dignitade romana"—whereas the revised version adheres to the literal expression ("sottomettere il mantello alla toga"). Where the vulgate translates "in urbe nostra" simply as "Roma," the revised version stays with the original phrasing ("nela nostra città"); "doctrina" is translated in the vulgate as "scienza" but left simply as it is in the revision. In general, there is a shift between the earlier and later versions from a looser, more readable translation to a stricter, more technical rendition of the Latin.[35]

These layers of variants and reconsidered glosses are witnesses to what Tanturli calls a sedimentation or the "growth rings of a culture." The tradition bears the traces of copyists of a diligence and curiosity similar to that of Lapo di Neri di Corsini, using whatever material they had available, perhaps but not necessarily including knowledge of and access to the Latin original. They consulted other books and sustained a subtle dialogue with other glossators—as when a later commentator criticizes an earlier one: "Alcuno chiosatore, e credo che male, raconta" ["Some glossator, and I think badly, recounts"].[36] The latest glossator of Valerius Maximus actually knows more than Dionigi di Borgo San Sepolcro and

---

33 Marginal gloss to *Valerio Massimo* 1.1.5 (ed. Tanturli, pp. 849, 854): "Questa lettera è da diversi diversamente intesa, che la dove dice 'biscanto' alcuno dice 'stropicciò' e la dove dice 'cose' alcuno dice 'questioni', e chiosano così: che questi due udivano certi minuti piati in alcuno tempio e perché dierono impedimento a l'uficio de' sacerdoti perderono la dignitate dove erano. Chi pone la lettera come è estima che costoro male cantassono e con infamia d'alcuno dio alcune cose basse e vili; di che lo dio indegnato diede per responso che' Romani non avrebbono vittoria sotto il conducimento di costoro due."

34 Zampieri, pp. 47–53. Casella observed the movement from vernacular to a more Latinate syntax in, for example, verbal construction ("quando aringava") or relative clauses ("che li annunciasse") are replaced with present participles ("aringante," "annunziantegli"). Casella, pp. 109–10, 243, 154–60.

35 Marginal gloss to *Valerio Massimo* 2.2.2 (ed. Casella, pp. 154–5; Tanturli, p. 872).

36 Marginal gloss to *Valerio Massimo* 3.2.10 (ed. Tanturli, p. 854).

says so: "Io scrittore non credo la soprascritta chiosa essere vera" ["I, the writer, do not believe the above gloss to be correct"].[37]

As we saw in the transmission of the *Fatti dei Romani*, nothing is more natural in the copying of a *volgarizzamento* than for the copyist to intervene to improve things—either with what he stores in his memory or with what he has stored in front of him in other versions, other glosses, other authorities, other copies of the original text. Symptoms of such contamination and layering are repetitiveness and even contradiction between consecutive glosses. Tanturli sees in these variants not chaos but a progressively more subtle, more historical, more critical understanding of antiquity. There is a concern for getting dates right, for clearing up confusions about people with the same names, and in general filling out the historical context of things Valerius mentions by consulting other authorities and without any hesitation to contradict preceding, even prestigious, commentators.

These observations, together with a similar comparison Tanturli conducted on the *volgarizzamenti* of the Third and Fourth Decades of Livy, suggest that greater understanding makes translation *less* possible, not more, to a point where the reality of the ancient world can be "understood but not translated."[38] Emblematic of this notion of translation that leads ultimately to the abandonment of translation is the one witness of the vernacular Third Decade of Livy, which, when it reaches the point at which the version of the translation it was copying breaks off, continues, in another hand, in Latin.

Volgarizzamenti at this time and place are transmitted not so much by professional scribes who write what and as they are told, but by readers who are interested in the material copying it out for themselves. These reader-writers, although involved in the most derivative kind of work imaginable—copying, translating, glossing, and copying other people's translations and glosses—are ultimately creating something new and are coauthors of that new artifact. The well-taken point of the Rouses that "physical presentation of texts in the manuscripts is determined by readers, rather than authors" is an important distinction when "author" signifies the distant figure, now reduced ultimately to a name, or perhaps a *numen*, hovering in spirit over the literary production and elaboration of a lot of other, mostly anonymous people.[39] This is true where the production of the book is wholly separate from the composition of the author, where books are produced by one set of people (professional scribes) for the needs of others. But in the environment of *volgarizzamento*, the person responsible for the layout of the page and the compilation at the stage visible in surviving witnesses is that book's writer as well as its primary reader. He is, moreover, almost always building upon prior

37 Marginal gloss to *Valerio Massimo* 3.3.2 (ed. Tanturli, p. 875).

38 Tanturli, p. 873.

39 Tanturli, pp. 848–9. Richard H. Rouse and Mary A. Rouse, "*Ordinatio* and *Compilatio* Revisited," in Mark D. Jordan and Kent Emery, Jr. (eds), *Ad Litteram: Authoritative Texts and Their Medieval Readers* (Notre Dame, 1992), pp. 113–34.

acts of writing, ordering, compilation, modernization, trivialization, addition, subtraction, collation, and correction by others.

This lack of respect, one might call it, for the letter of the text, or lack of diligence in passing on the text as one found it, is due to the fact that a *volgarizzamento* is not really a text. That is, it is not the authority; it is not the *littera*. James Zetzel, out of long efforts to produce a critical edition of Cornutus's commentary on Persius, concludes that commentary, because of its natural liability to accretion, reduction, and reuse, cannot be considered a text, in the sense of something originary that could be reconstructed by textual scholarship. *Volgarizzamento* is, essentially, commentary, wherein "preserving the continuing vitality of one text necessarily meant constant alteration of the other."[40] The work of reading is both individual and collective. Translations are readings that accrue to a text and get folded into it by subsequent readers, copyists, and translators. Contamination and re-elaboration of texts can be, and in Italy in this period mostly were, motivated not so much by the creative impulse of compilers, let alone modern authors ambitious to supplant their predecessors. Rather it was often the result of many copyists working indiscriminately, or ecumenically, from whatever versions or combination of versions they had available. All these variants and complicated contaminations in the witnesses are motivated not by the taste for elaboration, as in so many French vernacular adaptations, but in the interest of purity and greater fidelity to the source. *Volgarizzamenti* are witnesses not just of urban reading at a particular moment in Florentine history, but of the evolution of that reading over time.

[40] James E.G. Zetzel, *Marginal Scholarship and Textual Deviance: The Commentum Cornuti and the Early Scholia on Persius* (London, 2005).

PART 4
Translations of Antiquity and of the Romance Tradition

Alison Cornish's work on Lapo dovetails neatly with Jeanette Beer's "Translating Julius Caesar," which surveys the fortunes of the original, anonymous, French *Li Fet des Romains*, a compilation and translation of texts at the core of which is Caesar's *Gallic Wars*, augmented by biographical information on Julius Caesar himself, by Suetonius, Sallust, and Lucan. Beer shows how this text, not least in the way it translates Caesar's "Gaul" as "France," deploys translation as a form of contemporary political engagement, drawing parallels between Caesar's life and the Capetian King, Philip Augustus. Beer notes how the translator blends both classical and medieval sources (including such writers as Augustine, Isidore of Seville, and Geoffrey of Monmouth), repackaging his material encyclopedically to make coherent the classical world to a medieval audience. Especially interesting are the instances of translation of classical material to medieval tastes, as when, Beer shows, Lucan is supplemented with recourse to language familiar from vernacular epic. Beer also suggestively looks at some of the consequences, moral and literary, of the translator's ignorance of the fact that Caesar wrote the *Gallic Wars*, the chief of his sources, authorship of which he credits instead to a certain "Julien." In demonstrating how the translator reworks the past in the interests of a contemporary audience, Beer elucidates something of the *Fet*'s spectacular success across medieval Europe and throughout the Middle Ages.

Also popular throughout the Middle Ages is the classical legend of Orpheus, son of Calliope, Muse of epic poetry, who regains his dead wife Eurydice through the power of song, only to lose her again, and ultimately to be torn apart by women in a Bacchanalian frenzy, which tale offers poets and philosophers the means to self-referential examination of both poetry and music. Russell Stone's "John Lydgate's 'Ugly' Orpheus: Translation and Transformation in the *Fall of Princes*" identifies in the fifteenth-century English writer's work a concern with poetry as vehicle of both truth and (in its ornateness) of falsehood, and examines how Lydgate translates and transforms his sources (Ovid, Boccaccio, and Laurent de Premierfait) to produce an Orpheus at once celebrated as an authoritative maker of songs, but also one disfigured by grief at his loss, and subsequently the misogamous victim of irate women. Having carefully assessed how Lydgate exploits for his own purposes the different stages of the poet's career, Stone concludes with the final redemptive vision of poetry that Apollo offers by stellifying Orpheus's lyre in the night sky, but he has also drawn attention to Lydgate's incongruous association of Orpheus with misogamy and anti-woman rhetoric, suggesting that the later poet is here strategically appropriating Orpheus's authority in order to valorize his own polemic.

In the context of Stone's innovative research, it is worth remembering that Lydgate often troubles his poetry with misogyny at moments of authorial self-invention and intervention, and especially when he measures himself against Chaucer.[1] Lydgate's Orpheus echoes, for example, the language of Chaucer's *Envoy to Bukton*, when he compares marriage to a "chain" by which none would want to be twice bound, and to a "trap" one would be anxious to avoid a second time.[2] The intriguing iconography of MS Harley 1766, as Stone observes, translates the wild Bacchantes into medieval distaff-wielding women (Stone, Figure 9.2); one might add that this stereotypical icon of female power—and is it accident or design that Orpheus's arms, raised in protection against the women's blows, form a mirror-image of the position they earlier adopt to play his harp (Stone, Figure 9.1)?—reinforces the self-reflexive aspect of the poem's anti-woman rhetoric. Manuscript image and poetic echo emphasize together tropes about women that draw attention to questions of translation, tradition, and authority. Perhaps this dual representation of Orpheus is Lydgate's equivalent of Chaucer's simultaneously humble and assertive poetic self-authorizing through the invocation of Dante's Eagle in the *House of Fame*; if Orpheus's stellar lyre proclaims poetry's apotheosis, the *Fall of Princes* also makes room, via its misogamous rhetoric, for a quasi-comical putting into question of the very grounds of authority.

Ana Pairet uses the Iberian fortunes of the Melusine legend to trace translation and genealogy of a different kind, that of romance narrative, in "Intervernacular Translation in the early Decades of Print: Chivalric Romance and the Marvelous in the Spanish *Melusine*." Pairet engages wittily with the Spanish reworkings of the House of Lusignan's conflicted foundation myth romance. She traces the role of the new technology of printing in facilitating the migration and appropriation of fiction across national and linguistic boundaries (and, inter alia, the importance to the romance's popularity across Europe, and to its iconography, of its German versions) in an argument for how the Castilian printed *Melusine* comes to occupy an originary position of its own, as "founding mother of Spanish chivalric romance" (p. 135). Close comparison of the Spanish translations with the French edition, and consideration of an arguably increasingly cavalier attitude to iconography in the use of generic woodcuts, suggest the former are more interested in social issues than in the French text's emphasis on the marvelous; the 1526 edition of the *Historia de la linda Melosina* has naturalized the French version and simultaneously rewritten the ideology of chivalric romance. Pairet's deft situating of the *Melusine* and its literary offspring instantiates a powerful methodology for further research into romance's print history, geographically and across time.

---

[1] See, for example, Nicholas Watson, "Outdoing Chaucer: Lydgate's *Troy Book* and Henryson's *Testament of Cresseid* as Competitive Imitations of *Troilus and Criseyde*," in Karen Pratt (ed.), *Shifts and Transpositions in Medieval Narrative: A Festschrift for Dr. Elspeth Kennedy* (Woodbridge, 1994), pp. 89–108.

[2] *Lenvoy de Chaucer a Bukton*, in *The Riverside Chaucer*, gen. ed. Larry D. Benson, pp. 655–6 (p. 656, ll. 9–10; 22–4). Compare Lydgate, *Fall of Princes*, ed. Henry Bergen (4 vols, Washington, DC, 1923–1927), vol. 1, ll. 5804–38.

Chapter 8
Translating Julius Caesar

Jeanette Beer

Twelve hundred and seventy-one years after Julius Caesar entered Gaul to conquer it for Rome, he reentered Gaul peacefully, thanks to the diligence of an anonymous clerical translator whose encyclopaedic translation *Li Fet des Romains*[1] appeared in 1213. It was the first time the *Commentarii de bello gallico*—or indeed any work of ancient historiography—had appeared in the French vernacular and, on the eve of the battle of Bouvines, the moment was opportune. King Philip, soon to be called "Augustus," was consolidating his authority by political and military means, and the stage was set for another victory of the Capetian dynasty. The translator is not immune to the excitement and reflects the climate of expansionism in a variety of ways. Caesar had begun his description of Gaul with a statement of its tripartite division—"Gallia est omnis divisa in partes tres."[2] The translator inserts before that now-famous introduction a significant introductory comment of his own: "France estoit molt granz au tens Juiles Cesar" ["France was very large in Julius Caesar's time"] (p. 79, l. 1).[3]

The insertion was provocative both by its update of *Gallia* to "France" and by the gratuitous observation that the area in question was once very large—and therefore not coterminous with Philip Augustus's present kingdom. This was just one of several indicators that the translator saw Roman Gaul as a historical justification for Philip's dreams of a larger, unified France. Surprisingly, however, there is no textual evidence to suggest that Philip commissioned the monumental compilation. Nor is there any information about the context in which our anonymous cleric did his work beyond the inescapable fact that he was an inhabitant of Paris and had known the French king from the time of his adolescence.

Concerning Philip he makes several comments, which range from chatty reminiscence to an outburst of political chauvinism deriding the king's enemies: "je tieng por fox et Anglois et Normanz, qui ont fole esperance et quident que Octes li escomeniez, que Diex et seinte Eglise ont degité, doie France envaïr par itel gent (Tyois)" ["I think the English and the Normans are crazy to entertain the foolish hope and belief that Otto the excommunicate whom God and Holy Church have rejected is destined to invade France with the help of such a race (the

---

1 *Li Fet des Romains*, ed. L.-F. Flutre and K. Sneyders de Vogel (2 vols, Paris, 1938). All references will be to this edition.

2 Julius Caesar, *Bellum Gallicum*, ed. Otto Seel (Leipzig, 1968), p. 7, l. 1.

3 This and all translations are my own.

Germans)"] (p. 365, ll. 7–9). Although never shy to join the narrative in the first person, our translator never thinks to give us his name. Unconcerned with personal recognition and, apparently, not beholden to a patron, he is an enigmatic figure.

It has been proposed that he may have translated for a university context,[4] the University of Paris obviously, and he clearly had access to magisterial commentaries from other universities, for example Orléans.[5] Be that as it may, it seems that it was the anonymous translator himself who was struck by the pertinence of Julius Caesar's conquests to current events and was perspicacious enough to see how interesting Rome's conquest of Gaul would be to the present inhabitants of the region.

He does not leave the suggestion of a resemblance between Julius Caesar and Philip implicit, but slips a comparison of the two leaders into a seemingly innocuous context: the way they dressed as young men. Suetonius had mentioned that the young Caesar often appeared in the Senate with his toga too loosely tied.[6] That looseness, in addition to the long-fringed sleeves of his senatorial tunic, suggested to Romans that Caesar was prone to Greek exoticism and effeminacy. Sulla, according to Suetonius, frequently warned the senators to "beware the loosely girt lad" ["ut male praecinctum puerum cauerent"]. The translator renders Sulla's warning correctly and vividly in direct speech as "Gaitiez vos deu valet mal ceint" (p. 18, l. 26). But the same caution, when shifted to a modern context, contains no hint of homosexuality, coming across rather as fatherly—or perhaps grandfatherly—indulgence for prince Philip's sloppy dressing when younger:

> Quant ge lis de Juilles Cesar que Luces Silla l'apeloit le valet mau ceint, si me membre de monseignor Phelipe le roi de France, que l'en pooit bien apeler le valet mau pingnié quant il estoit joenes, car il estoit torjors hericiez. (p. 18, ll. 29–32)
> [When I read of Julius Caesar that Lucius Sulla used to call him "the badly girt lad," it reminds me of my lord Philip the king whom one could certainly have called the "dishevelled varlet" when young because he was always bristlingly untidy.]

Continuing to muse on similarities between Caesar and Philip, the translator moves from his (apparently!) random sartorial reminiscence to more calculated observations:

> Ne il n'a pas mains de sens en lui que il ot en Juilles Cesar, fors seulement de letres, ne n'a pas meins eü affere que Juilles ot; et encontre ce que J<uilles> fu letrez, est li rois sanz malice, car la letreüre aguisa Juilles a meint malice. (p. 18, l. 32; p. 19, l. 2)

---

[4] Bernard Guenée, "La culture historique des nobles: Le succès des *Faits des Romains* (xive–xve siècles)," in Philippe Contamine (ed.), *La noblesse au moyen âge, xie–xve siècles: Essais à la mémoire de Robert Boutruche* (Paris, 1976), pp. 265–7.

[5] Berthe Marti, "Arnulfus and the *Fets des Romains*," *Modern Language Quarterly* 2 (1941): 3–23.

[6] Suetonius, *De Vita Caesarum Libri VIII*, I.45, ed. M. Ihm (2 vols, 1908; repr. Stuttgart, 1978), vol. 1, p. 23, l. 21.

[And he has no less intelligence than Julius Caesar, save for literacy, nor less responsibility than Julius; and against the fact that Julius was lettered, the king is without malice, for literacy incited Julius to frequent malice.]

The highlighting of Philip's "sens" is significant because the prologue of *Li Fet des Romains* had attributed Rome's successes to a trinity of assets, their "sens," their "force," and their "proece" in that order (p. 2, l. 22). If, then, Philip's "sens" is superior to Caesar's and if also, as the translator claims, Philip is *morally* superior to the Roman leader, there is no reason to doubt that the French ruler will achieve even greater successes than the Roman conqueror.

It might be noted, perhaps with a touch of cynicism, that our cleric's ready acceptance of his king's illiteracy maintains a commendable division of labor between unlettered monarchs and lettered clerics who have the *nous* to recognize and promote the relevance of classical history. The text yields little more information on the relationship of the translator to his monarch, but a more important relationship for our purposes is that of the translator to his sources. How did our anonymous cleric meld such a mass of disparate and hitherto untranslated material into a coherent whole?

Of course, the process of compilation was not itself new at this time. From St. Augustine onward, the *speculum* offered a mirror of good conduct for the improvement of its readers, and in the twelfth century *flores historiarum, flores chronicorum*, and *flores temporum* assembled edifying selections of Latin material culled from the past. *Li Fet des Romains* follows their example to the extent that it touts a moral purpose in its prologue, claiming (somewhat vaguely) that there are lessons to be learned from ancient history, "car ou recort des oevres anciennes aprent l'an que l'en doit fere et que l'en doit lessier" [because one finds in the record of the ancients what one should do and what one should avoid] (p. 2, ll. 18–20). But for our learned compiler the *historical* fascination of Caesar's career appears at least to have equaled, if not surpassed, its potential for moral didacticism. Moreover, he seems to have expected that Caesar will have the same fascination for the modern descendants of Caesar's Gallic foes. After all, it was no mean task to assemble all known material about Caesar and arrange it chronologically, let alone translate it in a form that would be reproduced over three centuries.

Methodical conscientiousness is visible from the beginning. First our translator takes two paragraphs of the prologue of Sallust's *Catilina*, personalizing them by adding a paragraph of his own. He then takes a section from Isidore of Seville's *Etymologiae* to explain the unfamiliar terminology of Rome's *cursus honorum*, and translates Suetonius and Sallust in tandem for the early events of Caesar's career in Rome. He borrows relevant parts of Flavius Josephus and Petrus Comestor for events in the East, then returns briefly to Suetonius, before launching into the substantial task of transferring Caesar's *Commentarii de bello gallico* into the vernacular. Almost as substantial is the task of translating the events of Rome's Civil War from Lucan's ten books of the *Bellum civile*. After that the translator returns to Suetonius for Caesar's last days in Rome, having interspersed throughout more than a dozen minor sources, which include the Bible, St. Augustine's *De civitate Dei*, St. Jerome's *De viris illustribus*, Eusebius, the *Alexandri Magni iter ad Paradisum*, Virgil, Ovid, Geoffrey of Monmouth and/or Wace, the *Roman de Thèbes*, and the *Roman d'Alexandre*—not to mention his own comments and invented material, which fill in gaps and bind the material together.

Our cleric is surprising (for a thirteenth-century translator, that is) in that he is not averse to identifying his main sources. Lucan's name occurs 92 times, Suetonius's 26 times, "Celsus('s)" 14 times, and Sallust's 7. Names gave authority to a medieval work, although it is important to note that there is no necessary correlation between the frequency of the name-dropping and the extent of the source's contribution, or a translator's approval of it. Indeed, identifications often serve as a signal that our particular translator is temporarily distancing himself from his source. Such distancing occurs most often with Lucan's purple patches when the sentiments are "over the top" or the source information is unverifiable. In such a context the translator interrupts his translation in mid-sentence with a reminder that "it was Lucan/Sallust who said that": "ce dist Lucans/Sallustes."

For whatever reason, these interruptive identifications are rare during his translation of the *Commentarii*. With Caesar's material, the translator is obviously comfortable and is at his most literal. He collates little, explains little and, in fact, for pages at a time explains not at all. Of course, *all* translation is a type of explanation and in that sense, Caesar is "explained" like the other sources. Unfamiliar words are made familiar wherever possible. *Lutece* is preferred over *Lutetia*, *Helveçois* over *Helvetii*, and suggestively, *France* over *Gallia*. Some Latin names even become French, *Cornelius Phagita* becoming *Cornelius le Mangeur*, and *Marcus Crassus* becoming *Marcus le Cras*, although rebarbative proper names are usually left intact, wherever they occur.

Moving our consideration beyond the lexical to the challenging area of style, there was no vernacular precedent for what *Li Fet des Romains* was attempting, and for that reason our translator's procedures have unique significance because they were formative. Faced with an unusually wide range of stylistic variables in the sources, the translator makes no attempt to reproduce those variables. This may not seem surprising now, in this modern era of bland Google summaries. But it should be remembered that in our learned cleric's day, rhetorical training necessarily included extensive stylistic imitation of the Latin *auctores*. Stylistic variability was therefore a known concept, and a regular practice in Latin.

When working in the vernacular, however, new demands were operative and, since audience understanding was all-important, actual quotation from a Latin source was a dubious enterprise. Thus, Caesar's now-famous phrase *veni, vidi, vici*, clearly unfamiliar in the thirteenth century, required both translation and explanation:

> dist trois paroles en cele procession oiant toz: "Je sui venuz, j'ai veü, j'ai veincu." Par si bries paroles, ce dist <Suetoines>, senefia que il ot eüe cele victoire em poi de tens; car voirementt Pharnax et tuit li Hermine furent de lui veincu en solement .iiij. hores de jor. (p. 711, ll. 21–5)

[in the hearing of all, he spoke[7] three words in this procession: "I came, I saw, I conquered." By such brief words, said Suetonius, he conveyed that he had won this victory in a short space of time; for in truth Pharnaces and all the Armenians were conquered by him in a mere four hours of one day.]

Given audience unfamiliarity with both sources and contexts, nothing but confusion would have been achieved by the imitative reproduction in French of the stylistic individualities of Suetonius, Sallust, Caesar, and—most notably—the declamatory Lucan, whose preferred medium was highly charged rhetorical verse. Stylistic heterogeneity is effective only with an audience that is cognizant and appreciative of it. For an early thirteenth-century French public, stylistic variety was to be sought in vernacular, not rhetorical traditions.

The translator's most innovative move in this regard is his insertion of passages of his own invention into the compilation. The longest of these occurs when the source he is using at the time (Lucan) runs dry and, in a passage redolent of the *chansons de geste*, the translator invites the audience to an imaginative reconstruction of the Battle of Pharsalus with the epic formula: "La veïssiez grant dolor" ["There you would have seen great suffering" (understood: "... if you had been there to view it")]. He even bursts into epic verse![8] His explanation for the expansion is that Lucan has omitted much of the cut-and-thrust of the battle: "il i ot meinte bele joste et meint beau cop feru, dont Lucans ne parole pas" ["there were many fine thrusts and many fine blows which Lucan does not mention"] (p. 522, ll. 11–12). Thus, even here, our translator-turned-author remains conscientious toward the overall goals of his enterprise in that he neatly tags the invented passage as incremental to the source while still managing to justify it. His compilation was, after all, labeled in its prologue "les *gestes* as Romains" (p. 2, l. 21), and his exhilaration at the confrontations of war is unmistakable. In the excitingly expansionist climate of Philip Augustus's reign, here was no namby-pamby cleric!

Another context for his translative expansion is Caesar's dalliance with Cleopatra, although he chooses not to indulge his public with the octosyllabics of the *roman*. If, as the prologue had claimed, the "*gestes* as Romains" were to instruct in doing good and avoiding evil (and Cleopatra indisputably fell into the evil category), there could well be dangers in romancing the fleshpots of Egypt. It was important to handle the erotic episodes of Caesar's life didactically—not neglecting, however, to exploit their titillating potential to the fullest.

---

7 The translator is here in error: the three words were actually a *titulus*, as Suetonius reports: "Pontico triumpho inter pompae fercula trium uerborum praetulit titulum VENI. VIDI.VICI non acta belli significantem sicut ceteris, sed celeriter confecti notam" (*De Vita Caesarum* I.37, vol. 1, p. 18, l. 33; p. 19, l. 3). [In the Pontic triumph among the pieces on display he carried a placard of three words VENI.VIDI.VICI, not signifying the events of the war, as in the others, but the speed of finishing it.]

8 See K. Sneyders de Vogel, "Les Vers dans *Les Faits des Romains*," in *Mélanges de philologie offerts à Jean-Jacques Salverda de Grave* (Groningen, 1933).

The specificity of Lucan's anti-Augustan bias and his sardonic barbs (like his sneer that Cleopatra's palace in Egypt resembled a temple, "Ipse locus templi, quod vix corruptior aetas / Extruat, instar erat")[9] ["The place itself was the size of a temple, such a temple as a corrupt age would hardly rear"]—Caesar was elected Rome's Pontifex Maximus in 64 BC—needed to be tweaked to give them more general appeal. The translator chooses to eliminate all suggestion of religious awe, but transforms and expands the details of Cleopatra's grand palace, whose magnificence "Rome had not yet imported" (*De bello civili* X, l. 110). His lavishly remodeled description with its sards, almondines, and chalecedony, and its statues of ivory, gold, and silver studded with emeralds and topazes now serves as a didactic illustration of woman's dangerous wiles. The very setting exudes temptation and inspires male lust: "Li leus meïsmes estoit covenables a la chose" (p. 625, l. 19), as our cleric reprovingly comments. Thus, although Caesar and Cleopatra spend the night together by Caesar's request, the fault is Cleopatra's because she has made herself irresistible. "Tant l'eschaufa cele nuit et embraça que il li otria quanque ele li quist … nus huem ne se poïst gaitier ne delivrer de li puis que il fust une nuit chaoiz en ses liens" ["That night she so inflamed and so embraced him that he granted whatever she asked for … no man could have protected or freed himself from her once he had fallen into her bondage for a night"] (p. 638, ll. 7–11).

These are just some of the ways in which the translator brings coherence and purpose to his ambitious compilation. Culling encyclopedically from all available sources; translating them with care but never losing sight of his French audience; borrowing explanations for technicalities from glosses or from Isidore; identifying his main sources but supplying markers that reveal his additions or attitudes; and arranging them all in chronological sequence, he manages to meld the disparate materials into a coherent whole.

But there is one serious flaw, one gaping hole in the information available to this translating *maître*, however magisterial. He, like his contemporaries, did not know that Julius Caesar himself wrote the *Commentarii de bello gallico*. The author whom the compiler read and translated with most ease and from whom he rarely distanced himself; the Roman hero with whom he compares Philip Augustus to the advantage of the latter because "literacy only incited Caesar to malice"; the main source, in fact, for his massive compilation is conspicuously absent from the credits. The compilation is rubricked as starring only Sallust, Suetonius, and Lucan: "Ici comencent Li Fet des Romains compilé ensemble de Saluste et de Suetoine et de Lucan."

It was a well-known trinity, respected *auctores* all three, and (crucially!) well-known names even to a layman. But they were not the authors of the biggest chunk of *Li Fet des Romains*. For the Middle Ages, *that* was "Julien," supposed to have authored the *Commentarii* because of a cryptic inscription—the notation

[9] Lucan, *De bello civili* X, ll. 111–12, ed. J.D. Duff, Loeb Classical Library (1928; repr. London, 1969).

perhaps from a *corrector*—"Julius Celsus Constantinus uc legi" at the end of one group of manuscripts.

There were some advantages to the mistaken identity. The "Julien" material was transmitted faithfully, and was untrammeled by the magisterial glosses, dialectical debate, and other accretions that had built up around established *auctores* like Lucan. The translator does feel it necessary to invent some explanation for the omniscient, omnipresent "Julien" who was, he explains, Caesar's constant companion in every campaign. The explanation occurs during Caesar's visit to Britain when he asks the locals about their long midwinter night (*Bellum gallicum* V.13): "nos en demandames assez as païsanz de Bretaigne, dist Juliens qui ce livre fet, car nos i fusmes avec Cesar, n'onques rien ne nos en sorent a dire" (p. 184, ll. 24–6) ["we made extensive inquiries about it from the inhabitants of Britain, said Julian who is writing this book, for we were there with Caesar, and they never managed to tell us anything about it"]. "Julien" was now validated at least by eye-witness authority, even if that did not bestow the literary respect he deserved.

The fictive "Julien" disappears in the eighth book of *Li Fet des Romains*, the book that was supplied by Hirtius in the original *Commentarii de bello gallico*. Hirtius had explained the work as "a supplement to the *Commentaries* of our great Caesar in Gaul" so that Caesar's previous and subsequent writings would fit together properly. It is unclear what the translator made of this explanation, presuming that he saw it. At all events, it is missing in *Li Fet des Romains*, and the transition between books seven and eight in that work is seamless, thanks both to the absence of Hirtius's letter and also because Hirtius had imitated Caesar's style so carefully.

The medieval misconception concerning Caesar's identity was understandable. Caesar had written his so-called jottings (*commentarii*) in the third person, a deliberate ploy to give the appearance of objectivity to his military memoirs as he canvassed for the consulship. The hazards presented by the subterfuge were not syntactic, for, technically speaking, a third-person verb remains a third-person verb and can be rendered as such. But how to translate "attitude"? *Pace* Foucault, ignorance about the author of a text *does* matter, and in the case of the *Commentarii de bello gallico*, ignorance of Caesar's authorship makes it difficult to separate propaganda from reality. If, for example, Caesar reports that Gallic tribes begged him for "his well-known clemency," how does one assess the value of *clementia/mansuetudo*? What were the words uttered and, if they were, were they spoken in flattery by suppliants or were they interpolated by the "merciful" ruler who had a Gallic leader scourged to death and decapitated in front of the troops—presumably *pour encourager les autres*? Can abstractions—"clemency," "generosity," "leniency," and the like—be trusted to serve the same function in translation as they do in the original? In sum, what filter can a translator who is ignorant of his author's identity possibly use to get them right?

Rightly or wrongly, Caesar's generosity is presented in *Li Fet des Romains* as a model for the new age of princes. He was "debonnaires, come cil qui largement despendoit" (p. 45, l. 7) and by speaking "cortoisement" to the Gallic "princes" and offering them "larges dons" (p. 335, ll. 1–5), he fulfilled the courtly ideal of politeness and generosity. This chivalry was the reason, the translator says, that Gaul finally submitted to Caesar, *not* because she was exhausted with conflict, "defessam tot adversis proeliis" (*Bellum gallicum* VIII.49), as Hirtius (surely accurately) explains.[10]

It would be fascinating to know Philip Augustus's reactions to the work in which he figures as a potential Julius Caesar the Second. We do know that *Li Fet des Romains* was owned by various celebrities; that decades later Charles le Téméraire delighted in hearing stories of Rome and particularly enjoyed the *Faits des Romains*; that it traveled with great success to Italy and to Portugal; that a copy was made in Brussels for Edward IV; that it was used with/without acknowledgment by many compilers, for example, Brunetto Latini; and that it was printed in 1490 and 1500 by Antoine Vérard. Quite an achievement for a translator who, ignorant of the identity of his main source, effectively furthers Caesar's values into a new age!

---

[10] For details of the translator's representation of the Gauls, see Jeanette Beer, *A Medieval Caesar* (Geneva, 1976), pp. 73–91 and passim.

Chapter 9
John Lydgate's "Ugly" Orpheus: Translation and Transformation in the *Fall of Princes*

Russell Stone

Among translators and redactors of the English Middle Ages, few can compete with John Lydgate in terms of production. He was a man who, in a manner of speaking, labored throughout his life to translate antiquity within his voluminous writings, and in his modern versions of such imminent classical narratives as those of Thebes and Troy, and indeed within his poetic corpus, Lydgate often reveals his sensibility for the *ars poetica*. He was keenly aware of his debt to writers before him, from Ovid to Chaucer, and of his task to fashion new verses out of the materials of bygone days, not the least because of the efforts in Lancastrian England to perpetuate the English language beyond French and Latin "as a way of consolidating national unity and identity."[1] For Lydgate, the most prodigious writer of this movement, the labor of translating allowed him to revitalize history by making the greatest stories of the classical world, long distorted by creative adaptation, accessible and accurate for his fifteenth-century patrons and audience. Moreover, as I shall argue below, translation in the *Fall of Princes* involved not only the act of rendering words and narratives into his vernacular; it was also an act of appropriation and a means of gaining authority by mingling his voice with that of Orpheus, the most famous poet of antiquity.

John Lydgate, Translator of Antiquity

When Lydgate set about translating his version of the Trojan War in his *Troy Book* of 1412, he began to formulate his theories on this very process of translating the narratives of the ancient world into something enticing for a modern audience. In this, his first major work, he confronted the intimidating task of rendering the most famous siege of antiquity into a book of exemplary deeds and a veritable *speculum principis* for his patron, the future Henry V, while attempting to tell a truthful, legible narrative in verse.[2] The act of translating, Lydgate knew, required him to extract the simple, unadorned nut of history from

---

1 Derek Pearsall, *John Lydgate (1371–1449): A Bio-Bibliography* (Victoria, BC, 1997), p. 19.

2 Lois A. Ebin, *John Lydgate*, Twayne's English Authors Series 407 (Boston, 1985), p. 39.

the embellished, even fallacious shell of poetry; in other words, he had to render into English an accurate version of history (the process of *translatio*) but not add to the confusion wrought by a poetic re-creation of it (the assumption of *auctoritas*). The result is a prologue rife with anxieties and curious conceits, both of which will—to borrow one of Lydgate's favorite metaphors—help to shed light on the *Fall of Princes*. In his invocation for the *Troy Book*, for example, the poet appeals most eloquently to Calliope, the mother of Orpheus, and after Lydgate recalls the wondrous skill of the son (whose music tamed the beasts and the agents of Hades alike),[3] he turns to the mother to aid in his plea for "aureate lycour" for his pen and to

be myn help tenlumyne with this wirk,
Whyche am beset with cloudis dym and dirk
Of ygnoraunce, in making to procede,
To be lusty to hem that schal it rede.
Also in hert I am so ful of drede,
Whan prudent lysters her-to schal take hede,
That in making more skylle can than I,
To whom I preie, ful benignely
Of her goodnesse to haue compassioun
Wher as I erre in my translacion. (*TB* 59–68)

So it is that in his first major work Lydgate introduces the translator as a light-bearer, a representation that would serve him well throughout his career. As a poet of fifteenth-century England, he must produce from his pen an appealing ("lusty") history of Troy, but as a translator, he must present a skillfully executed and truthful record of the past—a record, that is, free of both mistakes and falsehoods.[4] While Lydgate somewhat tritely claims that he works amidst the dark clouds of ignorance, the very task of producing the *Troy Book* provided him with considerable practice in the art and act of translating, and as he confronted the other enormous matters of antiquity, from Thebes to Rome, he gradually saw

[3] In the *Troy Book* [*TB*], 47–53, Lydgate writes that Orpheus's "dites were so mellodyus" that he appeased the Fates, the Furies, and Cerberus in the underworld, and the beasts, fowls, and trees of the world above. This and all subsequent citations from the *Troy Book* refer to *Lydgate's Troy Book*, ed. Henry Bergen (London, 1996).

[4] Lydgate's 'poetic' persona is a tricky matter; as Robert R. Edwards reminds us in his edition of the *Troy Book* (*John Lydgate, Troy Book: Selections* [Kalamazoo, 1998]), Lydgate considered himself to be a translator or 'maker' (an occupation that he announces throughout his works) more than an *auctor* of original creation (p. 3). To be sure, Lydgate found many of his ideas discussed below—including the ability of the written word to preserve famous deeds of the past and the concern with maintaining truthful accounts—in the prologue to Guido de Columnis's *Historia destructionis Troiae* (*Guido de Columnis' Historia destructionis Troiae*, ed. Nathaniel Edward Griffin, Mediaeval Academy of America Publications 26 [Cambridge, MA, 1936]).

the light.[5] Indeed, he recycled time and again the figure of bringing light to obscurity and insisted that, just as authors of old rescued truth and knowledge from ancient deeds "for-dirked of her hewe" and refreshed them so that we contemplate them clear and bright in the "merour only to oure mynde," so modern writers 'illumine' these dimmed narratives with the bright flowers and colors of rhetoric (*TB* 165–8).[6] This illumination with poetic language represents, in essence, the most pragmatic aspect of the "cultural translation" demanded of an archaic, illegible narrative written in another language and intended for a foreign audience.[7]

Yet as Lydgate also knew, this approach to translation could just as soon engender what we might call *poetic license*, a presumption that he considered an unwarranted transformation. "Troy," for example, was a sort of moving picture painted differently (and only sometimes accurately) for centuries, and every writer who retold it had license to appropriate this story and make it his own. As Robert Yeager has written of John Gower's own approach to translation as transformation, "when he read [another poet's work], it was always with a look-out for what he could transform, if we take 'transform' to mean adapt more precisely to edifying use."[8] Lydgate, too, looked for didactic opportunities in his sources, and such an attitude led him to insist upon translation as a search for textual as well as historical accuracy.

His chief hindrances in this search were poets who were also free to riddle that oft-told story with falsehoods and thus undermine its integrity:

For clerkys han this story so depeynt,
That deth nor age, by no maner weye,
The trouthe may not maken for to deye;
Al-be that somme han the trouthe spared
In her writyng, and pleynly not declared
So as it was, nor tolde out faithfully,
But it transformed in her poysy

---

5 Lydgate took up the first in the *Siege of Thebes* and the second in the *Serpent of Division*; he also wrote on the royal lineage and saints of his own national history (e.g., *Verses on the Kings of England* and the *Lives of Saints Edmund and Fremund*).

6 In "Lydgate's Laureate Pose," in Larry Scanlon and James Simpson (eds), *John Lydgate: Poetry, Culture, and Lancastrian England* (Notre Dame, 2006), Robert Meyer-Lee associates Lydgate's concern with presenting a moralistic *speculum principis* with his belief that "poetry … translates the ideal into the human sphere by a process of illumination" (p. 43), and he argues that the poet viewed the process of composing his own poetry in the same terms, as evidenced by the invocation for the *Life of Our Lady*. In this devotional poem on Mary, Lydgate calls for inspiration "tenlumyne this dite."

7 Anne D. Hedeman, *Translating the Past: Laurent de Premierfait and Boccaccio's De casibus* (Los Angeles, 2008), p. 12, explains how Lydgate's predecessor in rendering Boccaccio into a vernacular, Laurent de Premierfait, had already faced the challenges of "a cultural translation from Roman Latin and fourteenth-century Italian mercantile culture to fifteenth-century French courtly culture."

8 Robert Yeager, *John Gower's Poetic: The Search for a New Arion*, Publications of the John Gower Society 2 (Cambridge, 1990), p. 114.

Thorugh veyne fables, whiche of entencioun
They han contrived by false transumpcioun
To hyde trouthe falsely vnder cloude,
And the sothe of malys for to schroude. (*TB* 256–67)

Here, he demarcates the fine line between the text as a means of preservation (a narrative, that is, that both recalls the past and recreates a faithful record of it for future readers) and as a piece of poesy, a new and inaccurate rendering of the past. Once again, Lydgate addresses the danger of hiding, so to speak, the light of truth under a bushel and of abusing rhetoric ("false transumpcioun") to transform, not to translate, truth into fiction, and once again he approaches the task of retelling a story as a visual and imaginative process that requires writers to paint in words ("depeynt") such familiar stories that had been passed down for centuries.[9]

Some 20 years later, these concerns with maintaining truth and decorum in re-envisioning well-known tales were more eloquently expressed in the *Fall of Princes*, which the poet labored over throughout the 1430s.[10] A massive and arduous undertaking, this was nominally an English version of Boccaccio's *De casibus virorum illustrium*, although as Lydgate explains in the prologue, his immediate source was the French writer Laurent de Premierfait, who had translated Boccaccio into his own vernacular at the turn of the century.[11] That it is a translation of a translation (and a project that involved the compilation of several sources into one cohesive narrative) makes the *Fall of Princes* another, even more fertile field for the poet's theories on rewriting ancient narratives, and here Lydgate recalls

---

[9] Even in reminding his readers how they may find in books the story of Thebes as another example of an ancient story rewritten numerous times, he describes the act of reading in visual terms first: anyone may pick up a "recorde of Thebes" and "beholde by gode inspeccioun" the account therein (*TB* 226–8).

[10] As Nigel Mortimer has surveyed in his *John Lydgate's Fall of Princes: Narrative Tragedy in its Literary and Political Contexts* (Oxford, 2005), pp. 1–24, this massive compendium has never enjoyed much scholarly attention or a favorable reception, and Derek Pearsall concludes that the contemporary reception of the *Fall of Princes* was "as a source-book more than as a unified poem" (*John Lydgate* [Charlottesville, 1970], p. 251) (a statement still applicable to many of Lydgate's modern readers).

[11] See the *Fall of Princes* [*FP*] 1–3: "He that whilom dede his diligence / The book of Bochas in Frensh to translate / Out of Latyn, he callid was Laurence." This and all subsequent citations from the *Fall of Princes* refer to *Lydgate's Fall of Princes*, ed. Henry Bergen (Washington, 1923). The first book of Laurent's *Des Cas des noble hommes et femmes* has been edited by Patricia May Gathercole, *Laurent de Premierfait's Des Cas des Nobles Hommes et Femmes, Book 1, translated from Boccaccio*, Studies in the Romance Languages and Literatures 74 (Chapel Hill, 1968), and Boccaccio's *De casibus virorum illustrium* is edited in whole by Vittore Branca (*Tutte le opere di Giovanni Boccaccio*, vol. 9, Milan, 1983). Moreover, Lydgate turned to Ovid's *Metamorphoses* to supplement the stories of mythical characters (including Orpheus) who filed past Boccaccio in his original dream vision, and, finally, Boccaccio's *Genealogie deorum* provided him with a good deal more information on the mythology of Orpheus than the *De casibus virorum illustrium*.

Chaucer's self-identification as a "compilator" in *A Treatise on the Astrolabe*: the translator's task thus stands between the act of writing one language into another and "enditing," or crafting new material from various older sources, a process that "does not preclude the use by a poet of a pattern to guide his creativity."[12] In his own conception of "enditing," Lydgate speaks again of a translator as a craftsman, who manipulates the old text (his source) into something new and better, as a potter might transform an ancient vessel—dangerous territory, as he had explained in the *Troy Book*.[13] Quite often this vessel was outdated or even broken, particularly if the text was obscured by a paucity of words and its meaning unclear, and the translator's task was "to a-menden, correcten, and declare" for the sake of clarity, for his readership deserved plain language and the expansion of ideas that were too brief to comprehend fully (*FP* 86).[14] This notion accorded with Lydgate's belief of shedding light on darkness via poetry, and with the *Fall of Princes*, his old ideas on refashioning and illuminating ancient narratives are a good deal more certain: translation is a creative process, wherein writers visualize in their mind's eye ("ther inward siht") how to render their source texts more appealing (once again "more fressh and lusti to the eie") with the colors of rhetoric (*FP* 17–25).[15]

However, as soon as he reiterates this ideology of translation, familiar from the *Troy Book*, Lydgate turns his attention to the challenges posed by the *Fall of*

---

[12] J.D. Burnley, "Late medieval English translation: types and reflections," in Roger Ellis (ed.), assisted by Jocelyn Price [Wogan-Browne], Stephen Medcalf, and Peter Meredith, *The Medieval Translator: The Theory and Practice of Translation in the Middle Ages*, papers read at a conference held 20–23 August 1987 at the University of Wales Conference Centre, Gregynog Hall (Cambridge, 1989), pp. 37–53 at pp. 38–9.

[13] Lydgate cites Laurent's metaphor in *FP* 8–14. Cf. Laurent, *Des cas*, Prologue II.6: "Et aussi puest un potier casser et rumpre aulcun sien vaissel, combien qu'il soit bien fait, pour lui donner aultre forme qui lui samble meilleur."

[14] The original statement in *Des cas*, Prologue II.2 asserts that the translator is free to "amender ou corriger."

[15] Lydgate's sensibility towards a literary canon of classical and not merely medieval texts clearly evolved between his work on the *Troy Book* and the *Fall of Princes*. As Alain Renoir argues in *The Poetry of John Lydgate* (Cambridge, MA, 1967), the poet's appreciation of Ovid and Virgil had increased considerably by the time he took up the latter project (pp. 68–9). It has been argued that Lydgate's treatment of the ancient world in the *FP* distinguished him from medieval writers and anticipated the attitudes of the Renaissance; e.g., Walter F. Schirmer, in *John Lydgate: A Study in the Culture of the XVth Century*, trans. Ann E. Keep (London, 1961), identifies the poem as "the first work in English to reproduce the heroic ideal of antiquity and to represent the heroes of classical legend and history in a dignified manner, without reinterpreting them in the light of Christian and chivalrous principles" (p. 207). Moreover, the *FP* was commissioned by Humphrey, Duke of Gloucester, whose library of humanistic texts was unparalleled in England, but whose love of Italian humanism and desire to inform the *FP* did not necessarily win over the poet, as argued by Pearsall (*John Lydgate*, pp. 224–5). In *Memory's Library: Medieval Books in Early Modern England* (Chicago, 2006), Jennifer Summit asserts, however, that the poet produced, upon the patron's insistence, a medieval transformation of humanist books on and models of government (pp. 207–31).

Princes and its novel genre of tragedy.[16] While he pledges to follow Boccaccio faithfully and to preserve his Latin sentence (rhetorically speaking, his *res*) and keep the adornment of his own English "stile" to a minimum, in re-telling these tragedies, Lydgate's thoughts move in the opposite direction to those of the *Troy Book*: suggestively washing away the vivid hues of his version of the Trojan War, adorned with all of the rhetorical flourishes and colors at his disposal, he imagines the somber task of translating tragedies in black and white ("Havyng no colours but onli whit and blak") in the *Fall of Princes* (465). Such a passage entrenched entirely in Lydgate's imagination (it is, after all, his vision as a translator, not our vision as readers) distances him from Boccaccio's and Laurent's own approaches to writing the tragedies at hand.

There are, of course, a number of medieval illustrations that portray the author visualizing the scene or subject matter that he is committing to paper, so that the reader views in the act of *lectio* what the writers viewed in the act of *compositio*. In Boccaccio's vision, he explains how he witnesses several *deplorantes exitus*, individuals who "bemoan their deaths" and file past his line of sight (12.4), yet in Lydgate's own imagination, he visualizes (as he explains in the prologue to the *Fall of Princes*) not Fortune and the cast of characters who fill the pages of his translation but words and sentences—the work not of an *auctor* composing a story from scratch, but of a translator carefully choosing what he will write in English and how he will do so. In sum, his metaphor of mending broken vessels, his drawing up of mental blueprints for improving his source texts, and his insistence on rhetorical flowers and colors— vibrant in the *Troy Book* but relegated to the simpler tones of black and white in the *Fall of Princes*—all grant Lydgate a deeply private vision impractical for manuscript illumination. Rather, his task was to illumine these stories in such a way that his audience, too, could re-envision in their own 'inward sights' figures who enjoyed rich traditions of visual representation. Manuscripts of Boccaccio's *De casibus virorum illustrium* and Laurent de Premierfait's translation of it were, for example, often presented with frequent and vivid illustrations, and, as discussed below, the *Fall of Princes* inspired its own pictorial tradition.[17] As I shall argue with his depiction of Orpheus, the legendary Thracian poet whose fall and princely status were well established in the Middle Ages, Lydgate knew—just as he blamed Ovid for writing in poetically "mysty speche" that prevents readers

[16] Boccaccio did not, of course, refer to his *De casibus virorum illustrium* as a collection of "tragedies," but he did adhere to the didactic potential of reading about fallen kings and princes and recognizing "the power of God, one's own fragility, and the unsteadiness of Fortune" ["Dei potentiam, fragilitatem suam, et Fortune lubricum"] and learning that prosperity has its limits ("Prohemium"). In translating Boccaccio, Laurent de Premierfait showed great concern for Fortune and how a wise and virtuous man might extricate himself from its disastrous influence; for his part, Lydgate complicated, rather than resolved, the debate over due suffering for one's sins and the fickleness of Fortune as the causes of tragedies. See Mortimer, pp. 153–218, for a valuable taxonomy of the two translators' views on Fortune.

[17] The tradition of illustrating Boccaccio's text and Laurent's translation is discussed with vibrant representation by Anne D. Hedeman, *Translating the Past*.

from seeing the truth of a story (*TB* 302)—that mental images could be blurry as well and needed to be painted with words in novel and often unexpected manners.

Translating an Ovidian Orpheus

By the time Lydgate composed the *Fall of Princes*, the story of Orpheus had entered the ranks of Troy and Alexander as a subject that had inspired scores of medieval representations.[18] Due to the veritable cottage industry of allegorical commentaries on Ovid, Virgil, and Boethius, the primary sources for the story among medieval writers and commentators, and the development of Orpheus romances, the figure embodied the view of translation as an act of transformation and appropriation.[19] The most egregious such transformation was that of the tragic story into one of blissful reunion—as the *Sir Orfeo*-poet recounts, "Harpours in Bretaine" heard the popular tale and "made [i.e., translated and transformed] her-of a lay of gode likeing."[20] At the core of the classical story remained, however, the moment of crushing sorrow bequeathed to the Middle Ages by these Latin narratives: that having once lost his wife Eurydice to a serpent's bite and having retrieved her from the underworld, the legendary poet lost her again by looking back at her before they had escaped Hades.[21] This momentary, understandable lapse, anticipated by any medieval audience, broke what Ovid termed a *lex*, Pluto's "law" that Orpheus not gaze on his wife until they had reached middle-earth (10.50), and as the crux of the story's tragedy, the seeming peccadillo of Orpheus's gaze signaled his double loss and provided the pathos for

[18] John Block Friedman, "Eurydice, Heurodis, and the Noon-Day Demon," *Speculum* 41 (1966): 22–9, remains an extremely valuable survey of the dissemination of the legend. Kenneth R. Gros-Louis, "Robert Henryson's *Orpheus and Eurydice* and the Orpheus Tradition of the Middle Ages," *Speculum* 41 (1966): 643–6, identifies two traditions of the medieval Orpheus: one scholarly and based on commentaries of ancient works (the allegorical Orpheus), and one in which he was cast as a musician and prophet (the Orpheus of romance narratives).

[19] Indeed, as the Middle Ages continued, such commentaries effectively rivaled, and occasionally even replaced, the primary source texts of Virgil's *Georgics*, Ovid's *Metamorphoses*, and Boethius's *Consolation of Philosophy*. The most popular of these scholarly works was undoubtedly the fourteenth-century *Ovide moralisé*, a massive Christian explication of the *Metamorphoses*. However, this commentary tradition had long thrived, as the twelfth century witnessed a number of influential such works on Ovid; for helpful discussions, see Ralph Hexter, "Medieval Articulations of Ovid's *Metamorphoses*: from Lactantian Segmentation to Arnulfian Allegory," *Mediaevalia* 13 (1987): 63–82; and John Block Friedman, *Orpheus in the Middle Ages* (Syracuse, 2000), p. 147.

[20] *Sir Orfeo*, lines 597–9, in *Middle English Romances: Authoritative Texts, Sources and Backgrounds, Criticism*, ed. Stephen H.A. Shepherd (New York, 1995).

[21] Although Peter Dronke, in "The Return of Eurydice," *Classica et Mediaevalia* 23 (1962): 198–215, examines an archaic tradition, in which Orpheus successfully won and kept Eurydice from the underworld, Virgil's story of permanent separation in the *Georgics* was the first Latin account of Orpheus's backward glance and loss of his wife.

many a representation of the brooding widower-poet. Indeed, this devastating loss of Eurydice cast such a pall over portrayals of Orpheus that it effectively created two distinct icons: the pre-Hades Orpheus, well known for his musical authority and ability to charm the beasts, trees, and the natural world at large, and the post-Hades Orpheus, recognizable by his face marred by mourning and despair.

Lydgate used, of course, both of these icons. As we have seen, he recalled Orpheus the peerless poet in his invocation to the *Troy Book*, as he sought to establish his own voice as an English translator in verse, but in the *Fall of Princes*, he engaged with a broader, Ovidian conception of the legendary figure. Here, Lydgate encountered an Orpheus no longer famed merely for his harping and the loss of his wife, but one endowed with a vaster *auctoritas* that generated no little controversy among medieval writers. After, that is, Ovid relates how Orpheus loses his wife by the backward glance, he grants the figure a shared authority within the *Metamorphoses*: Orpheus, feeding on his grief, fills the epic's tenth book with songs of love's labors lost, and when Ovid resumes his duties as narrator, he relates that the poet spurns the love of women, and as an "author," he "translates" his love to boys instead, and scorned Bacchantes thereafter dismember him in their frenzied rites.[22] This provided medieval writers with a dual paradigm for tragedy (in that Orpheus, despite his musical authority, lost both his wife and his own life) and for poetry itself (in that he used this authority both to captivate flora and fauna and to sing the tales of such famous lovers as Venus and Adonis). However, Orpheus's roles as an author and translator were expunged from Lydgate's primary medieval source, Laurent's translation of the *De casibus virorum illustrium*. Boccaccio, followed by Laurent in his French telling, simply chose to rewrite, rather than translate, this aspect of the account: in their versions, Orpheus establishes *his* Bacchic rites (not those of the vengeful Bacchantes, as in Ovid), and he forbids women from participating during their times of menstruation, and for that, they tear him asunder.[23] However, Lydgate, fearful of such transformation, departed

---

[22] Ovid, *Metamorphoses* 10.79–85: "Orpheus had wholly fled the love of women—either because it had ended badly for him, or because he had sworn that he would do so—but a desire to be joined to the poet still possessed many women, and many were repulsed and aggrieved. Indeed, he was the first author among the Thracians of transferring love to young boys and of plucking their first flowers and life's fleeting spring this side of youth" ["omnenque refugerat Orpheus / femineam Venerem, seu quod male cesserat illi, / sive fidem dederat; multas tamen ardor habebat / iungere se vati: multae doluere repulsae. / ille etiam Thracum populis fuit auctor amorem / in teneros transferre mares citraque iuventam / aetatis breve ver et primos carpere flores"]. This and all subsequent quotations from the *Metamorphoses* are taken from *Ovid's Metamorphoses, Books 1–5*, ed. William S. Anderson (Norman, 1997). See 11.1–66 for the raving Bacchantes.

[23] Boccaccio, *Genealogie deorum gentilium* (5.12): "Orpheus first established the Bacchic rites, and at Thrace he ordered the choruses of Maenads (that is, menstruating women) to remove themselves from the company of men during that time, since this was not only abominable, but also pernicious to men. Some time later, when the women found out about this plan and thought that it was intended to reveal their foulness to men, they conspired against Orpheus, killed him unawares with spades, and threw his head in the river

from the liberties of his sources on this point and turned instead to the motives found in Ovid's *Metamorphoses*, wherein the Bacchantes decry Orpheus as *nostri contemptor*, contemptuous of their sex, and plot his murder and dismember his body (11.7). For his part, Lydgate would preserve Ovid's idea (the *res*) of an Orpheus who composes and sings songs of "boys loved by gods and girls stricken with forbidden lust" (10.152–4) but he would rewrite the words (the *verba*) of these songs, as well as Orpheus's translation of love to his own sex. In so doing, he maintained the comedic tones of Boccaccio and Laurent's jabs at women, but he also strove to conclude the story with a rather Ovidian image befitting the tragedy of such a famous figure.[24]

When Lydgate's Orpheus first appears in the *Fall of Princes*, there can be little doubt that the English poet is constructing such a tragedy and that he recalls his earlier theories on translation—first to visualize the changes one can execute on an older text, then to improve it by expanding and re-fashioning it into something more pleasurable to the reader's eye. In fact, the first words that Lydgate employs to describe Orpheus impose entirely visual cues. Not unlike the scene in London, British Library, MS Harley 621, f. 217r, in which Boccaccio is depicted, for example, surveying the characters of his narrative that Laurent has translated, Lydgate describes the procession of figures viewed by the Italian poet:

> And whan Mirra from Bochas was withdrawe …
> Cam Orpheus, ful oughli on to see,
> Sone off Appollo and off Calliope,
> And appered with a ful doolful face,
> Whilom brouht foorth and iborn in Trace. (*FP* 1.5776–89)

Neither Boccacio nor Laurent make mention of Orpheus's physical person, but for Lydgate, the legendary poet's appearance provides both a means of introduction and of painting in the reader's mind the very image of tragedy—ugliness and the grief visible on Orpheus's face, the physical signifiers for a man disfigured (or metamorphosized) by tragedy.[25] He may begin as an attractive man, but he will meet his end with this corporeal (and then later, non-corporeal) transformation.

Hebrus" ["Orpheum primo Bachi sacra comperisse, et ea iussit apud Traces choris Menadum, id est mulierum patientium menstruum, ut illas illo tempore auferret a commixtione virorum, cum non solum abominabile sit, sed etiam perniciosum viri. Quod cum mulieres post tempus advertissent, et existimassent hoc adinventum ad turpitudinem earum viris detegendam, in Orpheum coniuravere, illumque nil tale suspicantem interfecere ligonibus, et in Hebrum fluvium deiecere"]. This and all subsequent quotations are taken from Boccaccio's *Genealogie deorum gentilium libri*, ed. Vincenzo Romano (2 vols, Bari, 1951). Cf. Laurent, *De cas* 12.59.

24 For Lydgate's attempt to translate Laurent's text into something more Ovidian—with a focus on individual transgression and a more expansive use of elegies, or complaints—see Maura Nolan, "'Now wo, now gladnesse': Ovidianism in the *Fall of Princes*," *ELH* 71.3 (2004): 531–58.

25 In Boccaccio, *De casibus* 1.12.5, Orpheus appearing "weeping wretchedly" ["perdite deflens"] for the loss of Eurydice and his murder by the Bacchantes; Laurent, *Des cas* 12.59, simply translates this as "desespereement plouroit."

Moreover, the stark juxtaposition of Orpheus's visage and his reportedly extraordinary authority in music and eloquence serves to underscore his fall, or *casus*, which Lydgate visually identifies in his prologue as a moment when one sees "Ioie vndir cloude, prosperite in the shade" and generically defines as a story that "Gynneth with ioie, [and] eendith with aduersite" (*FP* 1.24 and 5.3121). As Orpheus enters the *Fall of Princes*, then, he is an icon of tragedy, a man instantly and equally recognizable for his grief and his poetic prowess and as much for his ugly face as the harp in his hand.

From the outset, Lydgate insists on this harp as the "instrument" of tragedy—an idea he found in the Orphic songs of the *Metamorphoses*—and uses it as another easily identifiable, visual cue to associate the poet's ugly appearance with his sorrow over Eurydice. It becomes, in Lydgate's narrative, a means of reflecting on Orpheus's once prosperous but ultimately woeful past: as Ovid wrote and Lydgate reiterates, this harp was the common device of Orpheus's joy and grief, for with its dulcet tones ("soote touchis sharpe") he charmed the world around him, won Eurydice from the constraints of Hades, and played his torment on it when he lost his wife again (*FP* 1.5790–96). In London, British Library, MS Harley 1766, a copy of *The Fall of Princes* dating to just after Lydgate's day (c. 1450–1460), the harp is portrayed as an instrument of courtship as well. In the first of two drawings (Figure 9.1), Orpheus appears at the height of happiness, certainly not yet ugly, and using his harp to woo Eurydice, as he has done with beasts, trees, and streams. Here, he sits contentedly with his beloved, in the midst of longing glances and songs of love, and while it is his inability to deny himself such a glance that will soon hasten the story towards its tragic conclusion, the songs and the music will persist. If, that is, one sees Orpheus here in a brief (and perhaps unfamiliar) moment of happiness with his wife, then one also equates this scene with the figurative apex of Fortune's Wheel. The poet will soon be cast down, and while he will lose his wife, he will keep his harp. Anyone familiar with the story of Orpheus would not expect this scene of courtship and love poetry to last for long, and for Lydgate, this made all the difference in retelling this tragedy and refashioning it in an unexpected and idiosyncratic manner.

In these songs, Ovid had found a means of intertwining his own poetic voice with that of Orpheus, who sings in the *Metamorphoses* a book's worth of lovers' tragedies after experiencing his own, and Lydgate, well aware of these Ovidian-Orphic songs, will follow suit. However, it is at this point that he begins as well to undermine the pathos of the story and, we might say, shed some new light on an ancient narrative. Although a contemporary audience would have naturally expected a lamentable tale of a famously doomed couple, Lydgate here executes not a word-for-word translation of Ovidian disaster but a figurative *translatio* of a noble figure who could be conventionally appropriated for a collection of tragedies (a "fall of princes") and innovatively for critical, even farcical attitudes towards women and marriage. In his mind, for example, Orpheus is a lucky man, not a victim, and in Lydgate's first commentary on the widower's loss of Eurydice by looking back at her and breaking Pluto's *lex*, he concludes:

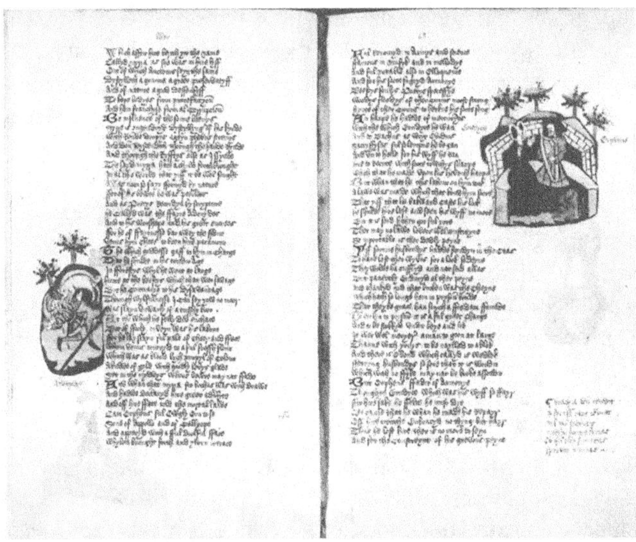

Fig. 9.1 Orpheus and Eurydice. (London, British Library, MS Harley 1766, ff. 75v-76r.)

> Yiff summe husbondis hadde stonden in the cas
> Ta lost her wyues for a look sodeyne,
> Thei wolde haue suffred and nat seid allas,
> But pacientli endured al ther peyne,
> And thanked God, that broken was the cheyne
> Which hath so longe hem in prisoun bounde,
> That thei be grace han such a fredam founde. (*FP* 1.5804–10)[26]

This joke seemingly creates an irreparable gap between Lydgate, the translator of and now facetious commentator on Orpheus's story, and Orpheus himself, whose own writings and songs will soon fill Lydgate's narrative space. After centuries' worth of tradition, one must presume that the widower will sing elegies and songs of lament, yet Lydgate insists on undercutting nearly all sense of mournfulness in the loss of Eurydice by seizing the opportunity for a long polemic against marriage.

Such eccentric treatment of a famously emotive tale of loss and lament is certainly not due to an ignorance of his source texts. Indeed, Lydgate proves himself capable of faithfully translating the more mournful scenes from the *Metamorphoses*, such as when Orpheus, after looking back at Eurydice, reaches

---

[26] Still, Patricia May Gathercole finds that Lydgate's sentiments against women are milder than those of both Boccaccio and Laurent ("Lydgate's *Fall of Princes and the French Version of Boccaccio's De casibus*," in F. Simone [ed.], *Miscellanea di studi e richerche sul Quattrocento francese* [Turin, 1967], pp. 165–78 at p. 171).

out for her but grasps nothing but air, then finds himself outside of the gates of the underworld haunted by her memory.[27] Yet the Orpheus that Lydgate translates from Ovid and the version that he rewrites for his own agenda stand in sure opposition; the one remains dumbstruck by "the green memorie, the tendre remembraunce" of his wife, while the other snidely remarks that "who hath onys infernal peynys seyn, / Will neuer his thankis come in the snare ageyn" (*FP* 1.5826–31). Still, at this very moment when Ovid allots the widower his own book of songs of ill-advised love and tragic transformations, Lydgate also gives voice to Orpheus—what these opposing versions of the legendary character sing, however, reveals just how malleable the tragedy of Orpheus and the *Metamorphoses* were in Lydgate's hands.

In the Roman narrative, wherein the story is firmly rooted in the conventions of elegy, the moment when the grieving Orpheus yields to his memories of Eurydice is crucial for Ovid, who earned, after all, considerable notoriety as an elegist. As his Orpheus sings of love and grief, he reminds his listeners how the memory of his lost beloved brings excruciating pain, and when he ultimately displaces his grief by indulging in physical affairs—in translating, that is, his love to boys—and calling to mind the tragedies of famous lovers, he is effectively traversing the elegiac experience of Ovid's earlier writings. In the *Metamorphoses*, however, Orpheus at last exceeds the limitations of the genre upon his death. Here, Ovid grants the story an uncharacteristically cheerful postscript, although later redactors of the story would neglect this fact and focus instead on Orpheus's sorrow and murder, the fundamental elements of his tragedy permanently cast in text and image. Often ignored in medieval translations and appropriations is what Ovid wrote *after* the Bacchantes dismember Orpheus: his head and lyre murmur ineffectual poetry, described by Ovid as *flebile nescio quid*, "something doleful, I don't know what" (11.50–53). The elegiac experience literally floats away, and the lover has instead achieved what every good elegist desires, his beloved in perpetuity: as the river above washes the body parts downstream, Orpheus reaches the underworld, where he reunites with her, and "they wander with their steps aligned, now Orpheus follows his wife walking ahead of him, now he goes ahead and safely looks back at his Eurydice" (11.64–6).

Such an image of domestic contentment attracted neither Boccaccio nor Laurent (nor, of course, Lydgate, who firmly imprints his stance against marriage in the story), but the English poet, at least, demonstrates a keen awareness of Ovid's narrative, and as *his* Orpheus sits haunted by the memory of Eurydice, Lydgate begins to turn the Ovidian template of elegy on its ear. The Orpheus of the *Fall of Princes* remains a poet and *auctor*, but rather than perpetuating elegy, he is transformed into a writer against the genre and against marriage. In singing not about disastrous love affairs but about the dangers of marriage, Lydgate's Orpheus becomes, in short, Lydgate himself:

27 See, e.g., "whan he made his repair, / Off hir in trouthe enbracid nothyng but hair" (*FP* 1.5821–2), which is a faithful translation of "[Eurydicen] prendere certans / nil nisi cedentes infelix [Orpheus] adripit auras" (*Metamorphoses* 10.58–9).

This Orpheus gaff counseil ful notable
To husbondis that han endurid peyne,
To such as been prudent and tretable:
Oon hell is dreedful, mor pereilous be tweyne;
And who is onys boundyn in a cheyne,
And may escapen out off daunger blyue—
Yiff he resorte, God let hym neuer thryue! (*FP* 1.5832–8)[28]

Surrounded by a riveted audience of husbands, this Orpheus creates, in essence, a homocentric society as he does in Ovid, but without the complication (for the Bacchantes and medieval commentators) of physical love. Moreover, Orpheus's warnings against marriage are not that far removed from his warnings about disastrous love affairs in Ovid, and Lydgate is, in fact, translating both the idea and the authority of Orpheus's poetry from his Roman source. At the same time, he is joining a long tradition of playing Orpheus and expressing one's agenda under the aegis of his poetry, which was an established authorial conceit and act of appropriation that served as another means of translation, a sort of *translatio imperii* for writers.[29]

As we have seen, when Lydgate invoked Calliope to fill his pen with 'golden liquid' to write the *Troy Book*, he expressed, for example, his desire to compose as well as Orpheus, tamer of beasts and the father of harmony. So, too, in the *Fall of Princes*, when Lydgate turns to the women angered at Orpheus's advice against marriage, the words with which he describes this advice recall the terminology from his prologue and his theories on translation and rhetoric:

On this sentence women war vengable,
And to his writyng ful contrarious,
Seide his counseil was not comendable.
At the feste thei halwed to Bachus,
Thei fill echon vpon this Orpheus;
And, for alle his rethoriques suete,
Thei slouh, allas, this laureat poete. (*FP* 1.5839–45)

[28] In *Music, Body, and Desire in Medieval Culture: Hildegard of Bingen to Chaucer* (Stanford, 2001), Bruce Holsinger discusses the possible underlying agenda of this unexpected argument against marriage (pp. 337–8): Humphrey, the Duke of Gloucester and the patron of the *Fall of Princes*, was a man who had initiated a lengthy debate over the legitimacy of marriage to a woman already in wedlock. Amidst great scandal, Gloucester lost, so to speak, one wife and had his affair with another woman awkwardly brought to light. Lydgate is assumed, in this argument, to have played Orpheus and to have altered his familiar songs in order to issue counsel to his patron once mired in controversy.

[29] For centuries, as examined at length by Friedman, *Orpheus in the Middle Ages*, pp. 164–8, aspiring poets had used classical versions of the legend to practice the *ars poetica* and appropriate the voice of Orpheus for their own compositions.

Given how Lydgate invoked the authority of Orpheus in the prologue of the *Troy Book*, this designation of him as a poet laureate should come as no surprise. The English writer clearly saw in the legendary poet an authoritative vehicle by which to deliver his snide anti-matrimonial advice and an opportunity to merge his own *vox poetica* with the most exalted voice from the ancient world. The Orpheus legend uniquely offered, of course, such an occasion: Robert Henryson, another poet who manipulated the legend—once it had been, as Lydgate would have appreciated, excavated from "vnder the cloke of poesie"—did so to give voice to his moral judgments and allegorical interpretation.[30]

Yet the designation of poet laureate is all the more important with regard to the manner in which Lydgate—a translator of antiquity and a poet who "brought into English a mode of authorial self-representation that serves as the grounds of laureate performance"—concludes his Orpheus story.[31] He did not, to be sure, follow tradition, although the artist of British Library MS Harley 1766, the copy of the *Fall of Princes* produced right about the time of Lydgate's death, would have it otherwise. Here, the second and final image of Orpheus portrays the aftermath commonly associated with his rejection of women (Figure 9.2). Although the artist has performed his own translation in rendering the traditional murder weapons (sticks and stones) into medieval distaffs, his narrative in pictures is ultimately traditional and expected by those familiar with the story: he first depicts Orpheus courting one woman (his beloved Eurydice) and then paying the penalty for rejecting other ones (the Bacchantes) after losing her in the underworld. While medieval audiences would have primarily associated Orpheus with the loss of his wife and his songs of sorrow, they surely would have recalled, too, his gruesome demise. In this final illustration of Orpheus in the Harley manuscript and its portrayal of his usual end, they would have seen, then, precisely what they have expected.

In the verses just below this drawing, however, Lydgate explains *his* final image of Orpheus and the moment when he appropriates Ovid's primary agenda of singing of figures transmogrified into *nova corpora*, new bodies, just as he rewrites the fate of this ancient Orpheus. Rejecting the Roman poet's rather cheerful ending of lovers reunited in the underworld, Lydgate invites his audience to look skyward and see a memorial for and 'translation' not of love, but of poetry, not of ugliness, but of something spectacular:

---

[30] Henryson, who appended an allegorical reading of the tragic ending of "Orpheus and Eurydice" as man's relapse into lust and sensuality, relied on the commentary of Boethius by Nicholas Trevet. In his telling (*The Poems of Robert Henryson*, ed. Denton Fox [Oxford, 1981]), Trevet's work was also cast as an act of the translation of 'misleading' poetry: "Quhilk in the self, suppose [Boethius's *Consolation*, Book 3, Metrum 12] fenyeit be, / And hid vnder the cloke of poesie, / Yit maister Trewit, doctour Nicholas … applyis it to gude moralitee, / Rycht full of frute and seriositee" (419–24).

[31] Meyer-Lee, "Lydgate's Laureate Pose," p. 37.

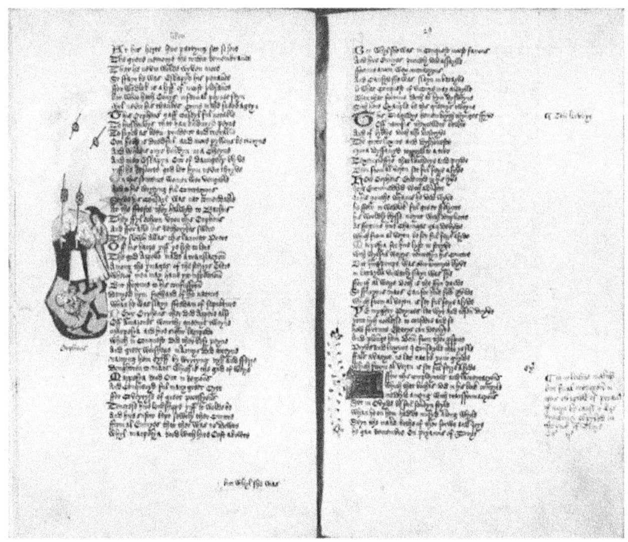

Fig. 9.2 The Death of Orpheus. (London, British Library, MS Harley 1766, ff. 76v-77r.)

> And off his harpe yiff ye list to lere,
> The god Appollo maad a translacioun
> Among the ymages off the sterris cleere,
> Wheroff men may haue yit inspeccioun. (*FP* 1.5846–9)[32]

In this parting directive, his request is to look beyond the expected, as it appears, for example, in British Library MS Harley 1766 and view instead the new, heavenly 'image' that is both Ovidian and non-Ovidian. Indeed, it is a Lydgatian image, not 'misty' like the *Metamorphoses* and the poetic narratives of old, but a clearly visible beacon of what the English writer desired most in translating, light and illumination, and a new icon with which his audience might associate Orpheus in their imaginations. Orpheus's songs of love have been lost in translation, but the instrument of his poetry has gained perpetuity via transformation, curiously absent in the *Metamorphoses* but granted in the *Fall of Princes*.

---

[32] This translates Boccaccio, *De casibus* 5.12, who reports that Orpheus's "lyre was taken up into the heavens and placed among other celestial images" ["Lyra … in celum assumpta et inter alias celestes ymagines locata est"]. In "Arthur's Stellification in the *Fall of Princes*," *Philological Quarterly* 57 (1978): 155–71, Richard A. Dwyer discusses another curious moment of stellification in the *Fall of Princes*, that of Arthur, whom Lydgate portrays as a "sun" among men and whose constellation concludes his story in book 5.

Chapter 10
Intervernacular Translation in the Early Decades of Print: Chivalric Romance and the Marvelous in the Spanish *Melusine* (1489–1526)

Ana Pairet

While medieval translations of texts from the Arabic, Greco-Roman, and Hebrew traditions have received sustained critical attention, vernacular transtextuality remains largely uncharted territory. One way to assess the production and reception of translations between vernacular languages in late medieval Europe is to study the effects that early printing and the nascent book trade had on practices of textual transmission. What kinds of works were translated into other vernaculars during the first decades of print? What genres were singled out for translation and to what purpose? How did the new print medium and its economics contribute to and shape the rhetoric and poetics of intervernacular translation? This essay will focus on chivalric romance, a genre that reinvented itself with the advent of print. Indeed, early editions of fourteenth- and fifteenth-century French prose romances met with such popularity in their native tongue that many appeared in translation—into English, Dutch, Flemish, or Spanish—within a few short years of their first printings in Geneva or Lyons. This remarkably swift migration of chivalric fictions across linguistic and geographic boundaries prompts us to ask how political and literary cultures coalesced around the practice and business of translation at the close of the fifteenth century.

To investigate the chains of transmission of chivalric fiction in the incunabular period I will single out here the editorial trajectory of *Melusine*, the first romance known to have been printed in French (1478). The fourteenth-century source text tells the story of an outcast knight, Raymondin, who marries the fairy Melusine after giving his word that each Saturday he will abstain from gazing upon his spouse. Melusine founds the fortress of Lusignan and bears ten male children, only to vanish when her husband goes against her visual prohibition and discovers that during her weekly disappearance Melusine turns into a hybrid creature, half-woman, half-snake. Weaving together myth and history through the motif of metamorphosis, the story of the flawed founding mother provides an etiological myth to account for the rise and decline of the House of Lusignan, an obscure lineage that came to rule Jerusalem and Cyprus.[1] It is my contention that by examining the linguistic, discursive, and iconographical transformations of *Melusine* in early print culture, one can ascertain the particular weight of ideology on practices of translation. Of particular interest in this respect are the two early Spanish versions of the romance printed in Toulouse (1489) and Seville (1526). My approach will emphasize the lexical and discursive choices and presentational strategies—including prefaces and first-person interventions—that Spanish adaptors used to recast, in a new politico-cultural framework, chivalric exemplarity.

The textual history of "la noble histoire de Lusignen," as *Melusine* is called in the *explicit* of Paris, BnF, MSS fr. 1482 and 1484,[2] is complicated by the coexistence of two rival romances, one in prose, the other in verse. Composed during the Hundred Years War, the two narratives stood at opposite ends of the political spectrum. Jean d'Arras's prose version was commissioned in 1393 by Jean, Duke of Berry, who wanted to assert his authority over the fortress of Lusignan, the last English stronghold in the Poitou region of West-Central France. After May 1400, Coudrette produced a rhymed version for Jean de Parthenay, who was one of the fiercest opponents of Valois rule. Throughout Europe, the notoriety of Coudrette's later version would surpass that of Jean d'Arras's own, thanks to its German-language prosification in 1456 by Thüring von Ringoltingen, which assured its lasting influence in Northern Europe.[3] As early as 1467 this German prose version made its way into print, and no fewer than three illustrated German-language editions of *Melusine* appeared between 1474 and 1478 alone, stimulating a spate of translations across Europe and exerting a lasting impact on the work's iconography.

Was this unqualified success of early German editions of *Melusine* then the root cause of French-language printers' rediscovery of Jean d'Arras's original prose version, which had been completed at the turn of the preceding century? The woodcuts of the first French edition of *Melusine* suggest as much, as these are directly copied after those used by Bernhard Richel in his richly illustrated edition of Thüring's adaptation, printed in Basel c. 1474. The *editio princeps* of the French text appeared in Geneva under the imprint of Adam Steinschaber in August 1478, the very year that Genevan presses first began production. Indeed, this in-folio qualifies as one of the very first illustrated books in French, a title to which the

1 While the eldest branch of the Lusignan was extinct from 1308, the younger branch came to rule Jerusalem (1187) and Cyprus (1192). The history of Melusine's sons fictionalizes the matrimonial alliances that led some of the Lusignan to rule over ephemeral Latin kingdoms in the Mediterranean and Middle East.

2 *Mélusine ou La Noble Histoire de Lusignan*, ed. Jean-Jacques Vincensini (Paris, 2003), pp. 44–5.

3 *L'Histoire de la Belle Mélusine de Jean d'Arras: Reproduction en fac-similé de l'édition de Genève imprimée par A. Steinschaber en 1478*, ed. Wilhelm-Joseph Meyer (Paris, 1924), pp. 11–12.

Mirouer de la rédemption de l'umain lignage, produced in Lyons on August 26 of the same year, also aspires.[4]

In Northern and Central Europe, any printed translations of Jean d'Arras's prose romance thus appeared after those of Coudrette's verse narrative. But Jean d'Arras's *Melusine* did see one important medieval translation in the nascent culture of print. In 1489 Juan Parix, first active in Heidelberg, and Estevan Cleblat published in Toulouse a *Historia de la linda Melosina* "compiled after the truthful chronicles of France." The popularity of the Poitou legend in the kingdoms of Aragon and Castile is attested by the writing of a second, derived version, "revised, corrected, and transposed into elegant style," that appeared in Seville in 1526 off the presses of Jacobo and Juan Cromberger, two brothers whose booklist featured the greatest titles of chivalric literature. We are also aware of the existence of a Valencian version of 1512, although no copies are extant.[5]

The translation of *Melusine* partakes in a long tradition of peninsular translations of French romances, a tradition preserved in medieval manuscripts and early editions. Romances of Antiquity and Arthurian prose romances of the Vulgate and Post-Vulgate cycles were translated in the course of the thirteenth and fourteenth centuries.[6] Epic poems of the Carolingian cycle or idyllic narratives like *Paris et Vienne* were also adapted for a peninsular readership. When the Castilian *Melusine* was published at the close of the fifteenth century, interest in chivalry was burgeoning, as suggested by a growing body of doctrinal literature. Moreover, as the Iberian Peninsula underwent significant political and territorial reorganization a new model of monarchic chivalry, wherein feudal bonds played a lesser role, was drawn up and codified.[7] During the closing decades of the century, Spain notably saw the union of the crowns of Castile and Aragon (1469), the end of the *Reconquista* (1492), and the beginnings of the opening onto the Atlantic world. That chivalry as a military institution had become all but obsolete after the

[4] The German translation of *Speculum humanae salvationis* was printed in Basel in 1476 by Richel, who was also responsible for the first illustrated *Melusine* in German (c. 1474). The parallel migration of woodcuts that illustrated these two texts seems to confirm the leading role played by iconography for the distribution of Jean d'Arras's romance in the early decades of print in France.

[5] Alan D. Deyermond, "*La historia de la linda Melosina*: Two Spanish Versions of a French Romance," in Alan D. Deyermond (ed.), *Medieval Hispanic Studies Presented to Rita Hamilton* (London, 1976), p. 62.

[6] On early Spanish translations and adaptations of the Arthurian Vulgate and Post-Vulgate cycles, see William J. Entwistle, *The Arthurian Legend in the Literatures of the Spanish Peninsula* (New York, 1975), and Harvey L. Sharrer, *A Critical Bibliography of Spanish Arthurian Material* (London, 1977). In studying the French models of sixteenth-century *libros de caballerías*, Sylvia Roubaud-Bénichou, *Le roman de chevalerie en Espagne: entre Arthur et Don Quichotte* (Paris, 2000), examines Spanish adaptations of romances of Antiquity and Arthurian prose cycles but does not consider early printed materials.

[7] Jesús D. Rodríguez Velasco, *El Debate sobre la caballería en el siglo XV: la tractadística caballeresca en su marco europeo* (Salamanca, 1996), pp. 380–82.

French army's defeat at Agincourt in 1415 makes this rebirth of chivalry in Spain all the more remarkable.[8] Conflicting visions of warfare came to the fore during the joint military campaign that led to the conquest of Granada (1481–1492), but chivalric customs such as singular battles would survive for at least another 50 years.[9] The Catholic Kings' revival of *Reconquista* ideals did much to keep the chivalric ethos alive not only in the Iberian Peninsula but also in the New World.

The first printing presses on the peninsula were active in Seville beginning in 1476, shortly before the Inquisition was instituted in that same city. The early years of print in Spain gave new impetus to translations from the French. Close examination of texts printed in the vernacular evinces the leading role played by translations in literary culture from 1488 onward. The majority of romances that appeared before Montalvo's landmark *Amadis de Gaula* (1508) were in fact either fresh translations from the French or adaptations of extant manuscript translations of French works. Nearly all of these romances were adopted for the purposes of the book trade: as such, contemporaries were able to witness the birth of a new industry in which translators played more than a bit part, directly assisting in the production process. It appears as a result that this extensive body of translations filled a generic gap, responding to the needs of readers who coveted fictions able to foment an exemplary and nostalgic representation of chivalric ideals.

This flow of translations did not abate after the runaway editorial triumph of *Amadis de Gaula*, which spurred multiple sequels and imitations. *Olivier de Castille*, to give one example, was published at least three times in the two years following the first printing of Montalvo's celebrated book. In 1526, nearly 50 years after the first Spanish edition of *Historia de la linda Melosina*, the Cromberger brothers' booklist still included a number of romances translated from the French, such as *Oliveros de Castilla* (1510), *Partinuplés* (1519), or *La historia de la linda Magelona* (1519). The Crombergers rarely deigned to produce bona fide first editions, preferring instead to print quality editions of works that had already met the test of time and of the market, as Clive Griffin's study demonstrates.[10] The fact that prestigious printers who were able to draw on a rich and varied inventory elected to adapt the Poitou legend for contemporary tastes confirms the lasting interest that the Castilian *Melusine* had exerted in the course of three decades. In this regard, it is not an exaggeration to describe the *Historia de la linda Melosina* as the founding mother of Spanish chivalric romance.[11]

8 While distinct from fifteenth-century doctrinal literature, which codified a model of chivalry inspired by Ancient Rome, chivalric romances were read as exemplary and conveyed some doctrinal elements as well (Rodríguez Velasco, *El Debate*, pp. 25–7).

9 Fernando González de León, "Soldados Pláticos and Caballeros: The Social Dimensions of Ethics in the Early Modern Spanish Army," in David J.B. Trim (ed.), *The Chivalric Ethos and the Development of Military Professionalism* (Leiden, 2003), pp. 235–68 at p. 237.

10 Clive Griffin, *The Crombergers of Seville: The History of a Printing and Merchant Dynasty* (Oxford, 1988).

11 *Melusine* is one of the two earliest chivalric romances printed in Castilian, along with the translation of *Livre de Clamades et de Clermonde*, the first known edition of which, *Historia del noble cavallero Clamades*, dates to 1521.

Through what methods, then, was the work of translation accomplished? The two Spanish versions of Jean d'Arras's prose romance include many instances of *abbreviatio*, as well as extended examples of descriptive and discursive amplification.[12] So prevalent in the 1526 edition are both contraction and amplification that scholars Alan Deyermond, who first brought attention to the two versions of the Spanish *Melosina*, and Ivy Corfis, who in 1986 edited them side by side, have presented them as independent translations. Nonetheless, Donatella Gagliardi has argued persuasively that the two versions in fact share a number of renderings and misreadings that cannot be explained other than by the use of a common source; the 1526 version, she concludes, is at least partially derived from the 1489 edition.[13] Miguel Ángel Frontón Simón, who produced a critical edition of the 1526 romance in an unpublished dissertation from 1996, likewise considers the Sevillian imprint to be a rewriting of the Spanish *editio princeps*. Textual rewriting could have occurred as early as 1512, whereas the renewal of the iconography is probably the work of the Cromberger brothers. If that is indeed the case, then the 1489 translation and its 1526 adaptation provide fine examples of what can be described as aesthetic and ideological recasting.

It is useful in this context to highlight those modifications such as abridgment, topical amplification, or nonstandard lexical choice that reveal the ideological agenda of Castilian adaptations. In particular, the Spanish translators' treatment of two narrative motifs seems to reshape substantially the construction of alterity: first, in the encounter between Melusine's father Elinas and the fairy Presine; second, through the evocation of the marvelous signs that grace the faces of Melusine's sons. Comparison of textual evidence from Steinschaber's 1478 French edition and the two Castilian translations shows that the encounter between Elinas and Presine undergoes significant rewriting. Among several omissions in the Spanish translations is the comparison of Presine's song with that of the sirens ("que oncques sereine ne chanta si melodieusement ne si doulcement"), which in the medieval tradition was associated with deadly seduction. Amplifications and additions, underscored in the text below, are no less revealing:

Geneva 1478

> Lors s'en arresta tout esbahi de la beaulté qu'il appercevoit en celle dame qui tousjours chantoit si melodieusement que oncques seraine ne chanta si melodieusement ne si doulcement; et ainsi il s'arresta tant pour la beaulté de la dame que pour sa doulce voix et son chant, et se mucha le mieulx qu'il peut dessoubz les feulles des arbres, affin que la dame ne l'apperceut, et oublia toute la chasse et la soif qu'il avoit par avant, et commença à penser

[12] Miguel Ángel Frontón Simón, "*La historia de la Linda Melosina*: edición y estudio de los textos españoles," PhD dissertation, Universidad Complutense de Madrid, 2002, pp. 168–82.

[13] Donatella Gagliardi, "*La historia de la linda Melosina*: una o due versioni castigliane del romanzo di Jean d'Arras?" *Medioevo romanzo* 22.1 (1998): 116–41 at 137.

au chant et à la beaulté de la dame, tellement qu'il fut ravy et ne sceut se il estoit jour ou nuyt, et ne sçavoit s'il dormoit ou veilloit.

... Adonc le roy Thiaus fut si abusé qu'il ne luy souvenoit de nulle chose du monde, fors tant seullement qu'il oyoit et veoit ladicte dame.[14]

Toulouse 1489

E asy todo maravillado, pasmandosse por la hermosura que vio en aquella que tan melodiosomente cantaua, estuvo pues quedo, asy por considerar su hermosura como por oyr su muy dulçe voz e armonja. E asy estaua mejor que podia de las ojas de los arbores cubierto por que ella, por su vista, de cantar no ceçasse. E tanto era en su dulçor e musica dulçe elevado que la caça e cavallo, fasta la propria tierra e de que viujria, se olujdava. E aun lo que mas fuerte era que el canto suplio la fuerça de la sed que ende lo avia traydo. E asy como de cauo su vista hechaua de cada costado en la linda figura, e no menos a oyrla era de tanta atençion, que de tarde o mañana, dia o n[o]che, para se rretornar no pensava ... E asy de todo lo que hazer deuja olujdado, solo a la vista e oyr se atendia.[15]

Seville 1526

... quedo tan marauillado y tanto afuera de todos sus sentidos que no pudo passar adelante para mejor conocella y por gozar de la dulce armonia de su canto que sospechaua, siendo visto o sentido, cessaria. E assi andando con [el] pensamiento reboluiendo entre si quien podria traer por alli tan adornnada donzella, assi en belleza como en tan grande riqueza como sobre ella traya, pues assi cubierto de las ramas y fojas de aquellas arboles que alli eran, lo mejor que pudo porque no pudiesse ser visto, en tal manera se transporto en el dulce canto de aquella donzella y apostura de su gesto que ya ni se acordaua donde estaua ni menos de la caça, ni menos de la causa porque alli viniera. Ni se acordaua de su tierra. Ni se acordaua de si mismo. Ni pensava en otra cosa que en contemplar y oyr aquella donzella que apenas creya ser vmana por las gracias que en ella veya.[16]

The two Castilian versions explicitly link Elinas's voyeurism to the pleasure provoked by the seductive song. In the 1489 translation, synonymous doubling ("maravillado" and "pasmandosse") extends the semantic possibilities of the

---

[14] All references to the French *editio princeps* are from Charles D. Brunet's edition, *Jean d'Arras. Melusine. Nouvelle édition conforme à celle de 1478* (Paris, 1854). I have also consulted Meyer's facsimile edition. Frontón Simón's analysis of common variants in the Spanish *editio princeps* and the Lyonnais imprint produced by Guillaume Le Roy c. 1486 (his edition, pp. 158–61) sustains Isidro J. Rivera's hypothesis that the source of the Spanish translation may have been the editions printed c. 1485–1486, in "*The Historia de la linda Melosina* and the Construction of Romance in Late Medieval Castile," *MLN* 112.2 (1997): 131–46 at 137. The genealogy of the three first Lyonnais editions (c. 1479–c. 1486) remains to be established.

[15] *Historia de la Linda Melosina: Edition, Study, and Notes*, ed. Ivy A. Corfis (Madison, 1986), pp. 4–6.

[16] Ed. Corfis, p. 5.

French adjective "esbahi." The Crombergers's reworking of 1526 highlights by contrast the physiology of the marvelous ("afuera de sus sentidos") as it follows in free indirect style the king's train of thought. Whereas the translation of 1489 resorts to periphrasis ("en aquella que tan melodiosomente cantava") to avoid mention of the lady's true identity, the text of 1526 opts on two occasions for the connoted term "donzella" or maiden, insisting on the fact that "she was so graceful that she almost did not seem human." While erasing the marvelous elements of the encounter with the fairy, the two versions underscore the social threat of king Elinas's enchantment, as suggested by the anaphora "ni se acordaua" in the Sevillian edition, which associates memory ("caça"/"causa"), social identity ("tierra"), and selfhood ("de si mismo").

A second set of examples appears in the treatment of the birthmarks of Melusine's children. The romance itself is constructed around the antithesis between the hidden, metamorphic body of the founding mother who transforms into a hybrid creature each Saturday, on the one hand, and the monstrous bodies of her sons on the other. Of Melusine's ten children, only the last two do not have a physical abnormality.[17] The disfigurements of five children affect organs of perception:[18] Guy, for instance, has one eye set higher than the other, Renaud is a cyclops, and Horrible possesses three eyes; three of the sons have animal features (a lion's claw, a boar's tooth, a patch of moleskin). These disfigurations are permanent metonymic marks of the fairy mother, a concrete translation of her ontological and bodily hybridity. Except in the case of Horrible, whom Melusine will order to be killed, physical abnormalities do not correlate with moral flaws. Rather, as Jean-Jacques Vincensini puts it, they function as "qualifying wounds" that mark the fairy's sons as exceptional warriors.[19] Anthoine, for instance, proudly displays a lion's claw on his cheek, a mark that turns into a sign (*señal*) in the Spanish translations:

Geneva 1478

> Et apres porta Melusine le quart enfant et s'en délivra à terme, et eut nom Anthoine. Nul plus bel enfant ne fut veu; mais au naistre il apporta en la joue ung grif de lyon, de quoy moult furent ceulz qui le virent esbahys.[20]

Toulouse 1489

> [E] dende un año, pario Melosina su quarto hijo syn algun peligro e dieronle nonbre Antonjo. E no avia tan hermoso njño en toda su tierra. Et avia en la qujxada una señal como vna pata de leon, de lo qual eran todos muy maravillados.[21]

---

17 Peggy McCracken, *The Curse of Eve, the Wound of the Hero* (Philadelphia, 2003), p. 82.

18 Ed. Vincensini, pp. 38–9.

19 Ed. Vincensini, p. 40.

20 Ed. Brunet, p. 117.

21 Ed. Corfis, p. 50.

Seville 1526

> Aueys de saber que dende a vn año, pario Melosina u quarto hijo, al qual pusieron nombre Anthonio. Y era muy hermoso y tenia en la vna quexada vna señal como vna pata de leon, de lo qual eran todos muy maravillados.[22]

Anthonio proudly bears on his cheek not a lion claw ("ung grif de lyon") but a "señal," which has the double meaning of "sign" or "mark," that resembles it. Here the work of translation transforms the metonymic mark of the fairy mother into a heraldic device. Similar comparisons tame the zoomorphic features of the Lusignan clan, including the boar's tooth of Melusine's firstborn ("como un colmillo de puerco montés") and the patch of moleskin displayed by the monk Froimundo, described as a spot in the first translation ("una taca") but as a sign ("señal") in the rewriting of 1526. The transformation of animal features into distinctive birthmarks stands among the most striking examples of the chivalric transposition of the marvelous theme in the *Historia de la linda Melosina.* Dispelling the threat embedded in alterity may have been a necessity during a period of intense persecution against *conversos*.[23] The reinterpretation of the Melusinian bestiary turns marvelous ambiguity into socialized attributes, constructing a sanitized male Christian body in its place.

This process of linguistic and ideological transposition in printed editions must be considered in relation to the visual translation the editions' woodcuts provided. It is beyond doubt that an unusually rich iconography was responsible for *Melusine*'s success across Europe. The first three Lyonnais editions of c. 1480 and c. 1485–1487 simply reused the woodcuts that had served for the German *editio princeps*; some of these same images were later used in the first Castilian edition.[24] The fact that in the latter several figures are inverted right/left or left/right confirms the hypothesis that *Melusine*'s woodblocks were recycled, with wear and tear requiring that some fresh blocks be cut after the model of those used for the first two Lyons editions.

Melusine's linguistic and thematic transformations thus appear to lie in tension with the relative stability of its iconographic program. If the woodcuts of the first German printing, which, we recall, presented Thüring's prose translation of

---

[22] Ed. Corfis, p. 51.

[23] I am indebted to Ryan Szpiech for his comments on references to birthmarks in anti-Jewish fifteenth-century polemics.

[24] On Melusine's iconography, see in particular Laurence Harf-Lancner, "L'illustration du *Roman de Mélusine* de Jean d'Arras dans les éditions du XVe et du XVIe siècle," *Le livre et l'image en France au XVIe siècle*, special issue of *Cahiers V.L. Saulnier* 6 (1989): 29–55; and "La serpente et le sanglier: les manuscrits enluminés des deux romans français de Mélusine," *Le Moyen Âge* 101 (1995): 65–87. Critics who have studied *Melusine*'s Spanish editions (Eisenberg, Corfis, Romero Tobar, Frontón-Simón) concur with M.-Louis Polain, *Catalogue des livres imprimés au quinzième siècle des Bibliothèques de Belgique*, vol. 2 (Brussels, 1932), according to whom the woodcuts are derived from the Lyonnais editions of Guillaume Le Roy and Ortuin-Schenck (p. 634).

Coudrette's verse adaptation, were simply reused in the first three Lyons editions as well as in the Spanish *editio princeps*, the images featured in Steinschaber's Genevan printing of 1478 do not to our knowledge reappear elsewhere. In the Crombergers's edition of 1526, importantly, all that remains is a series of generic woodcuts representing key moments in chivalric life. In keeping with the iconographic practices of the period, these illustrations are interspersed in a text whose content they make no effort to mirror. Indeed, most of these images had previously served the iconographic program of other chivalric novels, such as the Spanish translation of *Olivier de Castille* produced by the Crombergers in 1510.[25] The recycling of stereotyped images for the Spanish *Melusine* further contributes to the dilution of the romance's marvelous elements by effacing the singular characteristics of its protagonists.

To be sure, practical factors such as sheer availability of materials must have influenced the decision of printers across Europe to reuse the woodcuts popularized by the German language prosification. From the Basel German-language edition printed c. 1474 to the Spanish *editio princeps* of 1489, marvelous figures shape the narrative's course, downplaying the role of chivalric ideology. The place and singularity of the image nonetheless recedes significantly during the first third of the sixteenth century in Parisian editions as well as in the 1526 Spanish imprint. Here, the marvelous components of Jean d'Arras's romance are progressively blunted, to such an extent that the Cromberger brothers can present the work as a manual of chivalry of sorts.

What specific role does translation proper play in the process of adaptation? To what extent did the Castilian versions of *Melusine* make known their status as intervernacular translations? Both versions reproduce Jean d'Arras's narrative first person and refer to the Duke of Berry's patronage ("el señor del componedor de dicha ystoria"). Yet where the edition of 1489 bills itself as the adaptation of a text composed in French, the 1526 Sevillian imprint makes no explicit mention of its source.

The earlier edition keeps closely to the French author's narrative voice, from which it departs only at a few key moments. For instance, in the prologue's final section the Spanish translator reproduces Jean d'Arras's reference to his sources ("Segun mas verdaderamente pude coger en las coronjcas e libros de Francia" ["as I could truthfully gather in the chronicles and books of France"]), only to add that the work was commissioned by the printer "maestre Juan Parix"[26] so that the story might also become known ("manifestada") in the Kingdom of Spain. Once he begins the story proper, the translator intervenes only in two instances. In the first, situated at the point where the French author recounts the marvelous appearances of the Fairy Palestine, the translator evokes the oral report of Aragonese witnesses, who include the king himself. Since it is not the translator's design to pass for the

25 Leonardo Romero Tobar, "Ediciones en castellano de la *Melusina* de Jean d'Arras," in *Homenaje a Justo García Morales* (Madrid, 1987), pp. 1005–20 at p. 1013.

26 Ed. Corfis, p. 4.

king's personal interlocutor, he distances himself from "the person who composed the present story in French." In the romance's epilogue, he reprises Jean d'Arras's modesty topos, excusing himself for the quality of his translation: "E avn que no sea la ovra trasladada como pertenesce" ["though the work was not translated as well as it should have been"]. The *explicit*, which supplies the printers' names, recalls that the work at hand is indeed the fruit of translation:

> Fenesçe la ystoria de Melosina empremjda en Tholosa por los honorables e discretos maestros, Juan Paris e Estevan Cleblat, alemanes, que con gran diligençia la hizieron pasar de françes en castellano.
> [Here ends the story of Melosina printed in Toulouse by the honorable and discerning German masters Juan Paris and Estevan Cleblat, who diligently translated it from French into Spanish.]

The approach of the later Spanish edition is quite distinct, for even as it vaunts various improvements to the Melusine legend and reutilizes the modesty topos ("Y aun que no se la obra transladada como pertenece"), the edition of 1526 will make no reference to its vernacular source. The prologue and colophon, which supply only the name of the printers, give no clues as to the work's authorship, even as its rubrics promise a reconfigured and embellished story ("emendada y puesta por elegante estilo"). And if the anonymous adaptor makes note of the patronage supplied by Jean Duke of Berry, he chooses to dedicate the text to an unnamed Spanish Princess. Consequently, little if anything allowed the sixteenth-century reader to distinguish the *Historia de la linda Melosina* from other Spanish-born romances whose plots unfold in a foreign country or semi-fictional land, as in *Amadis de Gaula*.

Paratextual transformation, visual and linguistic transposition, and cultural adaptation attest to the vitality of *Melusine* in the early years of print. The fairy's corporeal metamorphoses in the marvelous tale seem to prefigure the metamorphoses of chivalric fiction itself, a genre that met with astonishingly wide popularity in early modern Europe. As such, the trajectory of the work—from Jean d'Arras and Coudrette to Thüring von Ringoltingen and the anonymous Spanish translators; from Poitou to Basel and Geneva, Lyons, Seville, and further afield—provides a precious example of the reception and ideological transformation of medieval romance, upon which the Renaissance would bestow a new exemplarity. The transformations of chivalric discourse and rewriting of the marvelous tale through intervernacular translation point to the ways in which ideology and the economics of the marketplace impact the work of translation itself, and as such invite further study.

PART 5
Translations and Religious and Political Institutions

If the trope of translation as linguistic hospitality suggests a general cultural openness, the essays in this section remind one that the *hostis*, originally in Latin the "guest," the "stranger," can also be the "enemy," for they sharply focus attention on translation's fundamental importance in shaping and reflecting religious institutional attitudes and political ambitions, and the tensions that can exist between different politicized, ideologically driven, constituencies. Boris Todorov, in "Monks and History: Byzantine Chronicles in Church Slavic," shows how monastic translations of universal histories constitute rather more than the simple transferral of information from one language into another. In the fourteenth century, the translation in the Balkans of Byzantine chronicles produced by George Hamartolos, Symeon the Logothete, John Zonaras, and Constantine Manasses was to prove foundational to a Church Slavic-driven reconceptualization of history and its purposes. If the broader dissemination of this aspect of Byzantine learning can be seen as part of a general Byzantine enculturation of the Balkans, argues Todorov, it can equally demonstrate an eagerness to rework the emphases of another culture for new audiences and to new objectives. Todorov's informative account demonstrates both how the translation of history is inextricably linked to the political importance of monastic institutions in the Balkans, and how the diminution of that political influence over time made the universal histories matter for spiritual contemplation, rather than active instruments of the monasteries' dynamic cultural and political engagement with current events.

Réka Forrai's eloquent introduction to her paper on "Greek at the Papal Court during the Middle Ages" makes clear how one line of investigation uncovers gaps and lacunae in broader areas of cultural knowledge; to ask about the extent to which the papal court was cognizant of Greek culture in the Middle Ages, defining itself by and against it, is to open up the wider question of its intellectual climate *tout court*. Her paper draws on evidence from the rule of Pope Gregory I (590–604), whose relations with Byzantine Church and state were complex at best, to the late thirteenth century, before Clement's removal of the papal court to Avignon in 1309. Forrai sketches the fraught interaction of spiritual and political concerns that informs relations between Greek and Roman cultural worlds throughout this period. Asking three central questions, concerning papal interest in sponsoring translation, the nature of Greco-Roman theological debate, and the possibility of reconstructing papal library holdings, Forrai identifies a papal desire to appropriate Greek culture and to establish the papal court (in competition with other political centers) as the mediator of Greek culture for the rest of Western Christendom. In drawing out the web of cultural translation of which, as she observes, textual translation is but one element, Forrai also, however, wisely warns against too homogenized a view of papal influence across time, and in indicating the richness of the material that awaits further exploration, shows how the literary evidence cannot be divorced from the social and political circumstances that produced it.

Forrai's essay mentions the Dominican Humbert of Romans's promotion of translation as a "spiritual weapon," whether against Jew, Arab, or Greek; Ryan Szpiech, in "Translation, Transcription, and Transliteration in the Polemics of Raymond Martini, OP," takes up a thread of this Dominican narrative in considering Martini's career primarily in terms of his willingness to recognize non-Christian sources as authorities, but as part of his own polemical enterprise against Judaism and Islam. Martini translates and glosses Hebrew and Arabic in a way consonant with his own ideological and theological interests, using translation as a tool of appropriation and aggression. Most intriguing is Martini's growing faith in the power of the materially realized original language, over and above intelligibility, in the context of his polemic, which leads him to (for example) transliterate into Hebrew characters and quotations from the Qur'ān as part of an anti-Jewish argument he intends to be read or heard by Hebrew speakers. Szpiech considers how Martini thus imaginatively anticipates and creates the intellectual experiences of his supposed opponents, yet how, at the same time, the novel material means that he adopts to authoritative mastery confront him all the more starkly with the ambiguities of his own translation strategies, which serve to undermine those claims to authority.

Chapter 11
Monks and History: Byzantine Chronicles in Church Slavic

Boris A. Todorov

Universal chronicles held an important place among texts available to South Slavic readers during the Late Middle Ages and the Ottoman period.[1] They were of similar format, covering the history of mankind from the Creation to approximately the time of the original author. Some paid more attention to the period after the Christianization of the Roman Empire, others devoted space to biblical events and ancient history. While none was originally composed in Church Slavic, the genre grew visibly popular in the fourteenth century when four different Byzantine chronicles were translated from Greek: those by George Hamartolos, Symeon the Logothete, John Zonaras, and Constantine Manasses. This was part of a larger trend of creating original works, or translating Greek theological, canonical, and hagiographical texts, within the Bulgarian and Serbian space: one stimulated by the growth or revival of royal power among Serbs and Bulgarians and by the tangible South Slavic presence in the monastic culture of the Balkans during the century preceding the Ottoman conquest. The Serbs' and Bulgarians' productivity offers insights into many questions of cultural transmission, perception of difference, and appropriation of external cultural patterns. Translating Greek texts in particular was a channel through which the values of a universal empire with a rich religious tradition and a diverse secular culture were made accessible to the South Slavs whose social and institutional structures relied on much more limited vocabulary and practice.

Acquiring Byzantine knowledge can be interpreted in terms both of cultural achievement and of subjection to a pervading Byzantinization. Specifically the universal chronicles seem to betray the process of Byzantinization inasmuch as Bulgarian and Serbian readers would by default accept a Byzantine perspective on the past of mankind, including their own place in it; yet the opposite view, which associates a chronicle focusing largely on the Roman past, such as the one

[1] The research for this paper would not have been possible without the generous assistance of the staff of the Hilandar Research Library at Ohio State University, Columbus, Ohio, especially that of its director, Predrag Matejić. I am grateful to the brothers of the Hilandar Monastery, on Mount Athos, for their kind permission to use the microfilm copies of their manuscript collection available in Columbus, as well as to Robert Romanchuk and the anonymous reviewer of the manuscript for Ashgate for their useful comments and suggestions.

by Zonaras, with the imperial claims of the Serbian Tsar Stefan Dušan (r. 1337–1355), is to be considered as well.[2] Regarding the very problem of translation, which is the focus of the present collection, we may accept that these two possible views of the Byzantine chronicles' place in the cultural and political life of the South Slavs bespeak two rather opposite understandings of the act of translation itself. In the first case, translating from Greek to Church Slavic is nothing but making accessible a given text to readers unfamiliar with the original language; it denotes integration and assimilation, and largely ignores the tensions between the original Greek and the Church Slavic versions of a particular text. In the second, we have an act of ideological proportions—a representation of power inscribed in the Church Slavic text which has mastered the Greek original and transferred it from one imperial discourse into another, together with imperial insignia, titles, administrative practices, and so on. Both perspectives are valid, yet should be adjusted. Below we will see evidence that translations were not thought of as transparent reproductions of an original made accessible once for all, but as limited and opaque, requiring the reader's quest for the original meaning. Similarly, appropriating the historical discourse was an important ideological act, yet less so against the background of Roman-Byzantine imperial tradition than in the context of Christian piety. The superposition of intellectual quest and piety substantiate a third dimension of the act of translation: the passing of the historical narrative from a primarily public, worldly sphere of life where knowledge of the past justifies and helps interpret decision-making and action into the sphere of the spiritual—the confines of the monastery where the reader has chosen to stay away from the world and engages in a life of contemplation. This third dimension touches upon the broad issue of the place of the chronicle in medieval culture in general, well beyond the temporal and spatial scope of the present paper.

The following pages present some clues contained in the Church Slavic texts, just as in the physical outlook of the manuscripts carrying them, as to how medieval translators, copyists, and readers formulated their interest in history and understood the implications of translation. In seeking new ways of explaining the place of translated historical narrative in the written culture of late medieval Slavs, the paper dissociates the Slavic from the Greek readers of the chronicles and points to some visible differences in the expectations of one reading audience and another. It further dissociates the lay sponsors from the translators, copyists, and majority of readers who were primarily monks or secular clergy (in the Eastern Orthodox churches, ideally bishops come from the monastic clergy). And it concludes with observations on the practical function of a translated Byzantine chronicle in a post-Byzantine world.

The chronology of the Church Slavic translations of Byzantine universal chronicles follows a sequence quite different to that of the original works.

---

[2] Vladimir Kačanovskij, "Iz srbsko-slovjenskoga prievoda bizantinskoga ljetopisa Joanna Zonare," *Starine* 14 (1882): 125–72 at 125; and Sima M. Ćirković, *The Serbs* (Malden, MA, 2004), p. 65.

The oldest Slavic text seems to be that of John Zonaras's *Historical epitome* (*Epitomē historiōn*).[3] It must have been produced before 1344 as seen in the conflicting interpolations by various Slavic scribes. John Zonaras used the refoundation of Constantinople in 330 to deride prognostication by telling the story of an astrologer who predicted that the city would stand for precisely 696 years. According to Büttner-Wobst's edition,[4] Zonaras did not make calculations, but in 1170 a Greek copyist must have written down that 840 years had elapsed since 330. This number 840 made it into the Slavic translation and appears in several manuscripts: Athos 433 (Mount Athos, Hilandar Monastery, SMS 433), dated 1525–1530; Vienna 126 (Vienna, Austrian National Library [ÖNB], Cod. Slav. 126), dated 1534; and the abridged version from 1408, in Moscow 415 (Moscow, State Historical Museum [GIM], MS Eparkh. 415).[5] However, a later scribe deleted the number as redundant and inserted the year 6852 (1343/4) when he worked—the correction appears in St. Petersburg 24.4.34 (St. Petersburg, Library of the Academy of Science [BAN], MS 24.4.34), from the first half of the sixteenth century, and in Moscow 1191 (Moscow, Russian State Library [RGB], MS Undol'skii 1191), dated 1603.[6]

Next in line was the *Chronicle* (*Synopsis historikē*) by Constantine Manasses.[7] The two earliest extant Slavic copies were both commissioned by the Bulgarian Tsar Ivan Alexander (r. 1331–1371), in 1345 and 1348 respectively (Moscow 38 [Moscow, State Historical Museum (GIM), MS Sinod. 38] and Vatican 2 [Vatican City, Biblioteca Apostolica Vaticana, Cod. Vatic. Slav. 2]), and because of the Middle Bulgarian linguistic features we may safely assume that the original translation from the Greek took place at about that time in or around the Bulgarian capital Turnovo.[8] The third work in question was the later Church Slavic translation of the *Chronicle* of George Hamartolos, known as the *Letovnik*,[9] of which the

[3] Henceforth *Zonaras*. The complete Greek text can be found in *Ioannis Zonarae epitomae historiarum libri XVIII*, ed. Moritz Pinder and Theodor Büttner-Wobst (3 vols, Bonn, 1841–1897); the partial Greek text in *Ioannis Zonarae epitome historiarum*, ed. Ludwig August Dindorf (3 vols, Leipzig 1868–1875); and the partial Church Slavic text in *Die byzantinische Geschichte bei Joannes Zonaras in slavischer Übersetzung*, ed. Angelica Jacobs (Munich, 1970). Quotations from this text will be taken from Dindorf and cited parenthetically by volume and page numbers.

[4] Pinder and Büttner-Wobst, vol. 3, p. 15.

[5] Reproduced in *Paralipomen Zonarin*, ed. Osip Bodianskii (Moscow, 1847).

[6] Jacobs, p. 115.

[7] Henceforth *Manasses*. The Greek text is to be found in *Constantini Manassis Breviarium chonicum*, ed. Odysseus Lampsidis (2 vols, Athens, 1996); Church Slavic text in *Die slavische Manasses-Chronik* [1922], ed. Joan Bogdan, German intro. J. Schröpfer (Munich, 1966).

[8] A facsimile edition of Vatican 2 is in: *Letopista na Konstantin Manasi. Fototipno izdanie na Vatikanskiia prepis na srednobulgarskiia prevod*, ed. Ivan Dujčev (Sofia, 1963).

[9] Henceforth *Letovnik*. The Greek text is to be found in *Georgii Monachi Chronicon*, ed. Carolus de Boor (2 vols, Leipzig, 1904).

oldest extant copy is dated to the 1360s (Athos 381 [Mount Athos, Hilandar Monastery, SMS 381]), while the latest was the translation of the *Chronicle* by Symeon the Logothete.[10] The Greek original of the *Logothete* covered the history of the Byzantine Empire until 948, but the Slavic version added to it unabridged a portion of *Zonaras* continuing as far as 1068, in an independent translation. The Slavic *Logothete* most probably predated the several copies of the *Letovnik* from the 1380s that contain two passages from it regarding the Creation and the Cherubim (Moscow 148 [Moscow, State Historical Museum, MS Sin. 148]: ff. 428v-430v; Vienna 10 [Vienna, Austrian National Library (ÖNB), Cod. Slav. 10]: ff. 215v-217v).

The probable chronology of the Church Slavic translations, therefore, is *Zonaras*, *Manasses*, *Letovnik*, *Logothete*. Their Greek originals were composed in rather opposite sequence. George Hamartolos wrote his universal chronicle in the second half of the ninth century,[11] bringing its content to the year 842. His work was later augmented with material from other chronicles, especially the *Logothete*. Precisely such a version made it into Church Slavic. Symeon the Logothete wrote in the early second half of the tenth century, during the independent reign of Constantine VII (r. 948–959), or soon after, covering events much more concisely than Hamartolos, from the Creation to the year 948. John Zonaras, an erudite canonist and theologian, composed his *Epitomē historiōn* during the earlier half of Manuel I Komnenos's reign (1143–1180) in the monastery on the isle of St. Glykeria. His comprehensive account of Jewish, Roman, and Byzantine history is unique for its interest in the Republican period.[12] Roughly contemporary is Constantine Manasses's *Synopsis historikē*, composed in the political verse used by court orators, which was recited in the presence of Eirene Komnene, widow of Manuel I's brother Andronikos, around the year 1150. It covers the period from the Creation to the end of the reign of Nikephoros Botaniates (1078–1081).

The seemingly random rediscovery of Byzantine universal chronicles by the South Slavs during the fourteenth century reflects both the poor transmission of texts and the search for historical reading more adaptable to the needs of readers. That transmission was poor is easy to see: the translator-compiler of the Slavic *Logothete* apparently had no access to the already existing Slavic *Zonaras* and approached the Greek text independently; similarly, the *Letovnik* suggests that scribes in the Balkans were unaware of the much older Church Slavic translation

---

[10] Henceforth *Logothete*. The Greek text is to be found in *Symeonis Magistri et Logothetae Chronicon*, ed. Staffan Wahlgren (2 vols, Berlin, 2006); Church Slavic text in *Slavianskii perevod Khroniki Simeona Logofeta*, ed. Viacheslav I. Sreznevskii (St. Petersburg, 1905; repr. London, 1971). Quotations from this text will be taken from Wahlgren and cited parenthetically by page number.

[11] Athanasios Markopoulos, "Sumvolē stē chronologēsē tou Geōrgiou Monachou," *Summeikta* 6 (1985): 223–31.

[12] Ruth Macrides and Paul Magdalino, "The Fourth Kingdom and the Rhetoric of Hellenism," in Paul Magdalino (ed.), *The Perception of the Past in Twelfth-Century Europe* (London, 1992), pp. 117–56.

of *Hamartolos*, the *Vremennik*, produced in the tenth or early eleventh century, either in Bulgaria or in Kievan Rus', and still in circulation among the Eastern Slavs during the fourteenth century.[13] But even more importantly, Slavic readers did not share their Greek-speaking neighbors' expectations of what a historical narrative should contain.

The best example to this effect is the fate of *Zonaras* in Church Slavic. The editing of the text and the selection of the material suggest that Slavic readers were not interested in everything that the Byzantine author offered to his own Greek-speaking audience. John Zonaras came with the most sophisticated and comprehensive of Byzantine universal chronicles, supplementing older authors with his own account of the century he lived in. In his *prooimion*, the author spoke with the voices of anonymous friends complaining that ancient historians spent useless time discussing battles and public speeches that the readers had neither time nor interest to follow:

> Τοὺς μὲν οὖν τοιαῦτα ἔλεγον τὰ τῶν ἱστοριῶν ἐκδεδωκέναι συγγράμματα, πεπλατυσμένα δηλαδὴ καὶ πρὸς τὸ φιλοτιμότερον ἀποκλίνοντα, τοὺς δὲ ἀντιθέτως ἐκείνοις διατεθῆναι περὶ τὴν τῶν ἱστοριῶν συγγραφήν, βραχυρρημοσύνῃ χρησαμένους, κἀντεῦθεν περὶ τὰ καίρια ζημιοῦντας τοὺς περὶ τὰ [...] συγγράμματα, ἅτε καὶ αὐτὰς τὰς καιριωτέρας τῶν πράξεων τῶν ἱστορουμένων παραλελοιπότας ἀνδρῶν, ἐνίας μέντοι καὶ ἐξυμνεῖσθαι δικαίας, βράχιστα δέ τινα περὶ ἐκείνων εἰπόντας, καὶ ταῦτα μήτε τὸ ἦθος ἐκείνων ἢ τὴν φύσιν παραδηλοῦντα καὶ τὴν προαίρεσιν, μήθ' ὅπως τῶν βασιλευσάντων ἕκαστος τῆς βασιλείας ἐκράτησε, μήθ' ὅστις ἦν πρὸ ταύτης, μήτ' ἐκ τίνων ἐγένετο. (1: 3–4)
> [They (the friends) said that some (historians) were offering universal histories quite clearly too big and degenerating into a show of ambition, while others were arranging the historical accounts exactly the opposite way, using scant words, even when this disarmed (...) the vital questions; and that, even while praising their just deeds, they were neglecting the most significant actions of the historical figures, recounting them only in short, describing neither the character of those men, nor their physical appearance and career, nor how each one of the kings obtained the kingdom, nor what he had been before that, nor of what parents he was born.]

Zonaras promised the reader to construct an easily accessible narrative that focused on the reigns of kings and connected the "historical figure" to the events of his time. Such an approach seems natural, especially when one takes into account the invisible eschatological background of Byzantine written culture—Christians implicitly sought to decipher signs announcing the Antichrist and were suspicious of their rulers. Besides the sequence of kings, Byzantines were furthermore conscious of the sequence of kingdoms, the prophetical power of which was

[13] Text is to be found in *Kniga vremennyia i obraznyia Georgiia mnikha: Khronika Georgiia Amartola v drevnem slavianorusskom perevode. Tekst, issledovanie, slovar'*, ed. Vasilii I. Istrin (3 vols, Petrograd, 1920–1930).

revealed in Daniel's vision of the four beasts—a powerful model supporting what Gerhard Podskalsky labeled "imperial eschatology."[14] History had to confirm to Byzantine readers that their empire was, indeed, the last kingdom as predicted in eschatological prophecies like the seventh-century Syriac *Revelation of Methodios of Pathara*,[15] or as formulated in the enigmatic tenth-century *Life of St. Andrew of Salos*.[16] Slavic readers of history, including the Bulgarian tsar, were equally eager to count the kingdoms in the spirit of Daniel's prophecy, as we see in the marginalia added to the Slavic *Manasses*: "hence it is clear that the Assyrians, the Chaldeans, the Persians and the Medes were all just one of the kingdoms on earth."[17] The owners of a sixteenth-century Moldovan copy of the Slavic *Manasses* addressed history and eschatology together, since the codex contained excerpts from eschatological texts as well, including the *Apocalypse of Pseudo-Methodios* and the apocalyptic prophecy from the *Life of St. Andrew of Salos* (Bucharest 649 [Bucharest, Romanian Academy, MS Slav. 649]: ff. 18v-19r, 64r-102v).

John Zonaras shared a view of the four kingdoms different from those of Christian apologists like Hippolytus of Rome who identified them with the Assyrians, the Persians, the Macedonians, and the Romans. He built on the assumption that the true kingdom came from God and that it had been first substantiated with the elevation of Saul; therefore, the four kingdoms in time were actually those of the Jews, the Persians, the Greeks (Macedonians), and the Romans. Such a division of universal history was in fact invented at least several decades earlier as witnessed in Oxford 60 (Oxford, Bodleian Library, MS Holkhamensis gr. 60), dated 1118, which contains a compilation of George Hamartolos and Symeon the Logothete. In the margins of the manuscript, we see marks counting down the kings, starting with Saul. On two occasions, ff. 125v and 134r, cinnabar (red ink) titles mark the beginning of the Persian, and then of the Greek kings.

Still, eschatology was not the primary reason for Zonaras's ambition to replace the existing universal chronicles with his own. In his *prooimion*, he attacked not only historians of politics and wars, but also historians who "addressed sermons at [the heretics], as if those were still alive" (1: 2). George Hamartolos seems to be the clearest target of such accusations. Zonaras believed his future readers needed material accessible enough for them to obtain practical wisdom and ethical instruction ("γνωμολόγειν καὶ ἠθικευέσθαι") (1: 3). The focus of such instruction was the person of the political man making good or bad decisions according to his virtues. The actions of rulers were a way to know what God had reserved

14 Gerhard Podskalsky, *Byzantinische Reichseschatologie. Die Periodisierung der Weltgeschichte in den vier Grossreichen (Daniel 2 und 7) und dem Tausendjährigen Friedensreiche (Apok. 20). Eine Motivgeschichtliche Untersuchung* (Munich, 1972).

15 *Die Apokalypse des Pseudo-Methodius. Die ältesten griechischen und lateinischen Übersetzungen*, ed. Willem J. Aerts, and George A.A. Kortekaas (2 vols, Leuven, 1998).

16 Lennart Rydén, "The Andreas Salo Apocalypse: Greek Text, Translation, and Commentary," *Dumbarton Oaks Papers* 28 (1974): 197–261.

17 Bogdan, p. 22.

for everyone. This is what Zonaras's friends allegedly asked for, claiming they wanted to learn "about God and what he gave to each" ("πρὸς τοῦ θεοῦ καὶ τούτου ἀνταπόδομα") (1: 2).

Zonaras was addressing a Greek-speaking audience for whom historical readings were part of a larger field of learning focused on rhetoric and dialectic. His future Slavic readers had little access to such education and for them universal histories were even more the sources of practical wisdom and ethical instruction. During the next few centuries, some of them carefully went through the pages of the various copies and put indicators against passages important to memorize, such as the famous sentence by Caesar, "Veni—vidi—vici" (Athos 433: f. 228r, Vienna 126: f. 283v). In other cases, *Zonaras* was used as authority in correcting the alternative chronicles. A careful reader of the *Letovnik* wrote regarding the fall of Judaea: "Zonaras said that, after Jesse, the Jews had been ruled by judges for five hundred years, and then by kings, for five hundred and thirty-two years, seven months and ten days" (Athos 17 [Mount Athos, Panteleimon Monastery, SMS 17]: f. 73r). A late copy of the Slavic *Manasses* functioned both as a "mirror of princes" and as a textbook in rhetoric when scribes or later readers indicated in the margin such passages as described the shifting fate of rulers, or made show of ornate speech (see Bucharest 649: f. 169r). Yet the limitations of the Slavic reader showed in the translator's misunderstanding of features of the social life in Constantinople, like the circus factions,[18] or using complex verbal constructions in order to recreate Zonaras's summary of Roman political history.[19]

Slavic readers and scribes were conscious of the linguistic barrier separating them from the immediate understanding of the Greek original. John Zonaras had viewed the reading of history as an interactive process, referring to his readers as "οἱ τῷ συγγράμματα ἐντευχομένοι," literally "people conversing with the text" (1: 6). The fifteenth- and sixteenth-century South Slavic scribes or readers did converse with the text through numerous marginal notes. Sometimes a hand would add information that helped readers to better understand the narrative. Bucharest 321 (Bucharest, Romanian Academy, MS Slav. 321), a *Zonaras* from the second quarter of the fifteenth century, contains a note from after 1526. The inline text points out that the Temple was burned twice, first by the Babylonians and then by Titus, on the same day of the same month. The reader added, correctly, that the Ottoman capture of Belgrade, in 1521, and the battle of Mohács, in 1526, which brought the Ottoman conquest of Hungary, took place on the same day and month as well (f. 139v). In other cases, scribes would copy earlier marginalia serving as a primitive index. Vienna 126 and Athos 433 contain numerous such notes enumerating the different reigns, but also point out important events omitted in the chapter titles. At times this principle of interaction with the text reflected precisely the realization of Slavic readers and copyists that they were dealing with translations. An angry marginal note in the Bucharest *Zonaras* scolds an

18 Compare Pinder and Büttner-Wobst, vol. 3, p. 398 to Jacobs, p. 208.

19 Compare Dindorf, vol. 2, pp. 84–5 to Athos 433, ff. 188v-189r.

earlier copyist for inventing the story that the Black Sea took its name from a king-monk (*črъnecъ*, literally "dressed in black"). The note, which also appears in the *Paralipomen Zonarin*, an abridged version of the chronicle, explains that this nonsense could have been avoided had the copyist looked into the Greek original, which said "Red Sea" (the Church Slavic for "black" and "red" are practically identical).[20]

This angry editor clearly worked in a scriptorium that owned a copy of the Greek *Zonaras*. It is perhaps his criticism that inspired the Hilandar scribe Grigorije, who produced the 1408 copy serving as base for the *Paralipomen Zonarin*, to discuss the problem of textual integrity. Grigorije boasted that he never undertook the copying of a manuscript before he had read and understood all of it. Because some "uncouth peasants" ("grubye poselęny") had worked on the text before him, he was filled with doubts regarding numerous passages; he wanted to check the translated *Zonaras* against the Greek original ("ōbrazy knigy po grečeskomou"), but since there was no copy at Hilandar, nor was there anything by Xenophon, Herodotus, or the other historians Zonaras had cited, Grigorije had to confine himself to George Hamartolos.[21] The frustrated copyist could not edit the text substantially, yet he used the opportunity to warn against the tendency of Slavic scribes to abridge:

> Jave sutь množaiši ōt iže našego nakazanię glagolju slovenьskago pisanïę izvykšix. i v pročitanïix i prěpisovanïix jaže nedomyslimo těmъ i ne pō těxъ vyčenïju, ōt nedostatьčьstva. nedostatočno vьměnęjout po rečennomu […], nь nedostoitь sice vьmęnęti xoteštemu pravě razsuditi razumenïa.[22]
> [Many from our educational background, I mean those using Slavic, out of their own limitation, have grown accustomed, whenever—reading or writing—they come upon something beyond their apprehension, or not according to what they are used to, to not follow closely what has been said (…), yet it is undeserved that they should thus limit him who wants to understand the idea clearly.]

This tendency is to be explained the same way as the misunderstandings with the Red Sea or the circus factions: by the inevitably limited perspective of translators and copyists working in monastic scriptoria. The limited precise data regarding the identity and location of South Slavic copyists confirms that in the fourteenth century, even in a relatively urbanized center like the Bulgarian capital Turnovo, the copyists were either monks or priests working in the scriptoria of the palace church, of the numerous other churches around town or in the monasteries within the city and in its proximity.[23] Even when a book was commissioned by a lay sponsor, the copyists were envisioning a reading audience with similar intellectual interests as the clergy. Universal history could perhaps be a genre more open to

---

20 Bucharest 321, f. 198v, and Bodianskii, p. 69.

21 Bodianskii, pp. 2–3.

22 Ibid., p. 4.

23 Vassil Gjuzelev, *Bulgarien zwischen Orient und Okzident: Die Grundlagen seiner geistigen Kultur vom 13. bis 15. Jahrhundert* (Vienna, 1993), pp. 192–4.

lay interest and lay perspective, particularly in the case of the Slavic *Manasses*, which reproduced a text originally meant for the entertainment of the Byzantine court. Bulgarian Tsar Ivan Alexander commissioned a richly illuminated copy and probably encouraged additions to the text that fitted well the Bulgarian courtly culture of the period, including a romance-style story of the Trojan War, whose central character, Paris-Alexander, happened to be the namesake of the tsar. Yet clear distinction between courtly and pious literature was impossible: the other copy of *Manasses* sponsored by the same tsar was included in a collection of short instructive and apologetic texts eventually making it to the Hilandar monastery where it was reproduced in the seventeenth century.[24]

Another member of the royalty to sponsor the copying of a universal chronicle was the Serbian Prince Stefan Lazarević (r. 1389–1427) who commissioned the copy of *Zonaras* that Grigorije of Hilandar produced in 1408. Grigorije wrote on behalf of Stefan Lazarević:

> Się ubo ne prostě i jako priluči, se isputue, ašte i bagrenïceju ōděanь, i o ōruženostvi pekyse veliky samodrъžьсь srъpskyi despōt stefanь, nь žělo ōpasně i vъnimatelně jakože ašte ō těx eдiněx popečenïe iměl by točiju, i těx sladostiju upivšese togo douši, nesytno račenïe kъ six stežanïju polagaetъ, ne po drevnemu ōnomu ptolemeu iže mnōgočislie knižnoe vъ udivenïju, tъčïju i člьvъčьscě xvalě, a ne kь polzy douševněi napisavšemu, nь eže těx premudrostiju ukrasiti nravy i slovesa, i těx blagodatiju doušu prosvěštati. i kъ bogopozvaniju privlačiti.[25]
> [These (historical writings) the great Serbian autokrator Despot Stefan, even if vested in purple and occupied with the deeds of arms, did not examine superficially, but rather carefully and intently, as if he had no other responsibility but them, and after his soul had been saturated with their sweetness, he displayed his insatiable desire to study them, not like that ancient Ptolemy who had composed a multitude of books not for the benefit of the soul but for the sake of impressing others and receiving human praise, but so that he might adorn his own manners and discourse with their wisdom, and that he might lavishly instruct the soul and lead it to those called upon by God.]

There are two voices speaking in this passage. One is that of Stefan, who allegedly came upon the Slavic *Zonaras*, read it, and ordered a copy for himself. It is overtaken, however, by the voice of the copyist, who reasons out what the benefits of reading history might be. John Zonaras himself had followed a centuries-long tradition of seeing history as a teacher of the political man who wants to make the difference between good and bad government and decision-making. For Grigorije, the reader was engaging upon a pious quest leading to the enlightenment of "being called upon" (*bogopozvanie*) or, in case there was a misreading, of "knowing God" (*bogopoznanie*).

---

[24] I. Dujčev and M.A. Salmina, *Srednebolgarskii perevod khroniki Konstantina Manassii v slavianskikh literaturakh* (Sofia, 1988), p. 75.

[25] Bodianskii, p. 1.

Grigorije's dismissive attitude regarding the "uncouth peasants" and his untypical boasting about the depth of his intellectual education point toward the essential function the universal chronicle played as reading for monks. Approaching history was a solitary occupation and an endeavor of the mind surpassing the educational background and the intellectual abilities of most members of the monastic community. The reader had to converse, perhaps struggle, with the text and obtain his instruction directly from it. The matter of universal history did not belong to a larger context that could offer insights into the meaning of events. The cultural background of South Slavic monks kept them apart from the political and social realities of the Roman and early Byzantine world. After the Ottoman conquest of the Balkans, this distance was further enforced, since now even the contemporary political context lay well beyond the discursive frames of monastic intellectual culture.

Yet it was precisely monks, enjoying a virtual monopoly over the production of books in the South Slavic space, that established the framework of historical discourse. The selection of the translated material reflected their views of what was beneficial and what superfluous. In dealing with the enormous work of Zonaras, the translator reproduced in its entirety only the parts narrating biblical history—all the more useful, since during the fourteenth century there still existed no integral text of the Old Testament in Church Slavic. South Slavic copyists faithfully preserved Zonaras's own principle of arranging the entire material according to precisely numbered and listed reigns. Moscow 1191, Athos 433, and the presumably lost Belgrade 47 (Belgrade, Library of the Serbian Orthodox Church, MS Theological School 47) contain a list of the reigns at the end; Vienna 126 has such lists both at the beginning and the end, in addition to the careful cinnabar marginal notes throughout the body of the text; even a strongly abridged version contains a similar list.[26] Yet this was almost ironic, since the original Slavic selection omitted a great many Roman and Byzantine emperors. The last article, under the title of reign 76, was about Leo the Armenian who chronologically preceded Theophilos, reign 70. The scribe of Vienna 126 realized the mistake and warned the reader with a cinnabar note on f. 2r, yet did not even try to readjust the sequence. Slavic monks were not interested in the precise number or sequence of emperors and often preferred that same universal chronicle that Zonaras had derided: the one by George Hamartolos.

It is generally difficult to trace open competition between *Zonaras* and *Letovnik*. We may assume that at least one major South Slavic monastic institution, Hilandar on Mount Athos, did not have a copy of *Zonaras* toward the end of the fourteenth century, regardless of the fact that the work had been available in Church Slavic decades earlier: in the introduction to the *Paralipomen Zonarin*, Grigorije claims that when Stefan Lazarević sent the work to be copied at the monastery, the scribe could not find the text in the library when he wanted to correct his poor original.

---

26 Piotr A. Lavrov, "Iugoslavianskaia peredelka Zonary," *Vizantiiskii vremennik* 3.4 (1897): 452–60 at 452–3.

All the help Grigorije could find came from the "most wise chronicler George the Monk."[27] The Hilandar monks produced at least two copies of the *Letovnik*, the one preserved today in the monastery and Moscow 148. The Hilandar copy was frequently used, and in 1619 a monk by the name of Longin (Athos 381: f. 1v) had to replace or paste together several missing or ruined folios. Interest in the text shows in the later manuscripts as well. Bucharest 330 (Bucharest, Romanian Academy, MS Slav. 330), from the last quarter of the fifteenth century, is a compilation including numerous articles on church canons regarding priestly and monastic status, or marital and sexual misbehavior; it further includes concise interpretation of the Great Schism (with the Catholic Church), as well as apocryphal wisdom addressing questions such as "why there are no epidemics in the desert, even among pagans" (f. 160v). The *Letovnik*, which occupies the second half of the heavy volume, apparently sits well in a collection of useful readings that could be adapted to the needs of a city church or monastery alike. In a different case, the arrangement of the page where long titles in cinnabar frame paragraph-long passages, as in the sixteenth-century Bucharest 320 (Bucharest, Romanian Academy, MS Slav. 320), reveal the likely use of the chronicle as a textbook divided into hundreds of fragments easy to identify and address separately. Unlike the typical structuring of *Zonaras* into imperial reigns, this particular *Letovnik* breaks the reigns of emperors into smaller narratives dedicated to a particular event (an earthquake, a military campaign) or a particular scandal involving the clergy and secular authorities (such as the disgrace of Patriarch Photios, 187–90).

What George Hamartolos offered more than John Zonaras, or Constantine Manasses, was detail regarding ecclesiastical history and the polemic against heresies—the very features Zonaras found superfluous. Zonaras wrote at a time when Byzantium was still enjoying relative stability; his audience was a prosperous and well-learned urban aristocracy, proud in its educational background and eager to rediscover the glories of Antiquity. When the monks of Hilandar were producing their copies of the *Letovnik*, the Balkans were under the sway of Ottoman military power and local Christian communities anxiously looked for strategies to confront Islam. The growing interest in a historical narrative that loudly defended the true faith against heresies of older times coincided with the heightened sensibility regarding orthodoxy typical of late Byzantine political and religious culture.

Looking for a historical narrative that offered theologically acceptable formulas regarding biblical events explains the place of the *Logothete* among the translated chronicles. The work did not enjoy wide diffusion, yet it was not a random choice. The unidentified Greek original of the Slavic *Logothete* remains the most comprehensive exemplar of the work within the entire stemma of its transmission. That the anonymous Bulgarian translator found an original with the integral text—when the large majority of Greek manuscripts were compilations containing fragments intermingled with excerpts from other works[28]—suggests

27 Bodianskii, p. 3.

28 Wahlgren, p. 43.

a deliberate search. Furthermore, the Slavic *Logothete* is much more reliable in reproducing the Greek, including the part taken from *Zonaras*.

The reliability of the *Logothete* shows best in the introductory passages dealing with the Creation. They enjoyed such popularity that copyists transferred them to the *Letovnik* where they played the role of a textual convoy for centuries. The very first lines of the chronicle say:

> Θεὸς ὁ ἄχρονος τόνδε τὸν κόσμον μὴ πρότερον ὑφεστῶτα ἐν χρόνῳ παράγων ἐποίησεν ἐν ἀρχῇ οὐρανὸν καὶ γὴν. συνυπέστη δὲ τῇ γῇ τό τε ὕδωρ καὶ τὸ πῦρ· καὶ τοῦτο τεκμήριον ἐναργὲς τό ἐκ λίθου μὲν καὶ σιδήρου ὄντων ἐκ γῆς πῦρ ἄφθονον ἐξάλλεσθαι, ἐκ πηγῶν τε καὶ φρεάτων ὕδωρ πλούσιον ἀναδίδοσθαι. ταύτης γὰρ ἐκ μὴ ὄντων ὑποστάσης δῆλον, ὅτι καὶ τὰ ἐν αὐτῇ. (5)
> [The timeless God, bringing into time this world which had not existed before, made in the beginning heaven and earth. For water and fire are sediments of the earth. And here is the clear proof, (namely that) fire proceeds abundantly from stone and iron which are of the earth, (while) water is given abundantly away by springs and wells. For it becomes clear that the sediment is out of those things that are not, and that they are in it.][29]

This original way of explaining the Creation actually refers to the Trinitarian view of the three hypostases of God, none of which was created. The Greek used deliberately the verb *synypestē*, of the same root as *hypostasis*, to exemplify the noncausal creation of the elements: water and fire proceed from the earth, yet are not created by it, just as the Holy Spirit proceeds from the Father, yet is not created by Him. The narrative of history was being embedded within an acceptable theological discourse—perhaps just a detail from the point of view of Symeon the Logothete himself, but a fact of growing importance for the reading communities of late medieval Slavic monks.

For such readers, universal histories were becoming a solitary exercise with exclusively spiritual benefits. These may be deduced from the colophon in Moscow 148, one of the Hilandar-made copies of the *Letovnik*, commissioned by one Radovan in 1386. This colophon, practically identical to the one in Athos 381, is unusually long and, considering its faithful reproduction in two other codices, may be seen as an expression of a properly "Hilandar" perspective on the value and usefulness of the work. The scribe who finished the manuscript anticipated the rejoicing of the sponsor Radovan in reading about kings of old, and then copiously wrote down the names of the scribes involved in the production of the manuscript, together with that of the hegumen of the monastery. Yet, more importantly, the mysterious scribe dedicated an entire page to praise the Lord Jesus Christ in terms similar to the *arengae* medieval rulers included in their pious donations:

---

29 Sreznevskii, p. 1: "Bogъ bezlětnyi, sъ mirь ne syi prežde vъ lěto prived, sъtvorivъ načęlo nebu i zemli. izdaati že zemli vodǫ i ōgnь. i semu znamenïe javě, eže ōt kamenïi ubo i želěza sǫnštem ōt zemlǫ ōgnь nezavistno isxoditi, ōt istōčnika že i rъvenikь vodǫ bogatno izdaati. Sei bō ōt nesǫštïix ʋpostasi iavě, jako i sǫštïimь vъ nei vъsěmь."

> Prorьki poslalь jesi xriste prorešti iže kь namь prišьstvije tvoje. Apostoli že propovědati tvoja veličija […] taže mučьniky svetyje javilь jesi. iže vsa uměti vьměniše. Da tebe jedinogo priōbrěštutь. radosti aggьlōmь i čьlovьkōm […] i ješte že i prěpodobnyix ōtьcь sьbori množьstva. iže prosijaše vь vsemь mirě jako světila […] im že ne bě dostoinь vьsь mirъ. iže ni spisavša različnaja žitija i povědanija jaže prežde zakona i blagodati. i vь zakoně i po blagodati …. (Moscow 148: ff. 433r-434v)
>
> [You have sent prophets, Christ, so that they prophesy to us Your coming, and apostles, so that they preach (to us) about Your greatness (…) and further You showed to us the holy martyrs who turned everything upside down in order to find You, the only one, the joy of angels and men (…) and even further, You summoned the multitude of the blessed fathers who shone like stars throughout the world (…) and for whom this world was of no worth. Of all these things different *vitae* and stories have taught us, about the things before the Law and the Grace, and in the Law, and according to Grace, etc.]

Praising the merciful deeds of the Lord, particularly in conclusion to a historical reading, all too naturally substantiates the monastic view of universal history. The historical process is nothing but a confirmation of the truthful incarnation of the Lord, everything important that has happened in history either predicting or confirming the coming of Christ; and the deeds of kings are worth knowing insomuch as they give meaning to the feats of martyrs and hermits. In a period of greater and greater distancing between the monastic institutions in the Balkans and the non-Christian administration of the Ottoman Empire, the matter of history was becoming a closed narrative, composed once for all, and with no connection to the living reality of ongoing events. Conversing with historical books, struggling with the corruptible text, was a spiritual exercise similar in its essence to the coenobitic rule or the anchoritic discipline. Reading the narrative of the universal chronicle was one more way for the monk to reach a state of contemplation of the Divine Creation, as it had unfolded over the course of time.

Chapter 12
Greek at the Papal Court During the Middle Ages

Réka Forrai

> Una storia degli studi greci alla Curia Romana durante il medio evo non è ancora stata scritta.
>
> —Robert Weiss[1]

> The intellectual history of the medieval papacy has yet to be written.
>
> —Thomas F.X. Noble[2]

Introduction

Robert Weiss's observation has not lost its validity in the past 30 years: there is an almost complete lack of studies on papal involvement in Greek learning in the Latin West. While Weiss's statement has inspired the following pages, Thomas Noble's remark points to an even larger hiatus: this preliminary study therefore must locate a phenomenon in a landscape not yet fully charted.[3]

Rome's crucial role as mediator between East as West throughout the Middle Ages and beyond has been often noted.[4] But so far no systematic study has been made on the papacy's share in this mediation. The present paper does not claim to fill this gap; it will rather indicate some possible directions for future research. A variety of sources, some of them unpublished, still await careful investigation: papal letters and papal biographies, dedication letters and translations proper, and council acts, to name a few.

---

1 *Medieval and Humanist Greek* (Padova, 1977), p. 193.

2 Noble, "The Intellectual Culture of the Early Medieval Papacy," in *Roma nel'alto Medioevo*, Settimane di Studi del Centro Italiano di Studi sull'Alto Medioevo 48 (2 vols, Spoleto, 2001), vol. 1, pp. 179–213 at p. 179.

3 This article summarizes the preliminary findings of my ongoing postdoctoral research. The initial steps of this project were supported by a Dumbarton Oaks Summer Fellowship (2008) and a Mellon Foundation Fellowship at the American Academy of Rome (2008–2009).

4 See most recently: Paolo Chiesa, "Traduzioni e traduttori a Roma nell'alto medioevo," in *Roma fra Oriente e Occidente*, Settimane di Studi del Centro Italiano di Studi sull'Alto Medioevo 49 (Spoleto, 2002), pp. 455–92.

Lack of interest in this aspect of medieval culture originates in the Humanist view of an unappealingly dark Middle Ages. Bartholomew Platina's account of the life of Pope Nicholas V stressed that under his patronage Greek and Latin letters finally regained some of their splendor, after a neglect of 600 years.[5] It is the span of this half a millenium *in tenebris* that I plan to examine, with the premise that Platina's dark image is a false one. On the contrary, "the greatest medieval sponsor of academic search for knowledge was the Roman Christian Church."[6] There was more Greek at the courts of medieval pontiffs than the Humanists noticed. Admittedly, one finds Greek at the papal court when looking at things other than those that interested Platina and his Humanist contemporaries: instead of classical Greek historiography, one finds its Late Antique (and Christian) counterpart; instead of Plato, the *opera omnia* of Aristotle. Moreover, preoccupation with other languages, and the impact of other cultures on Latin Christianity (or, equally importantly, the impact of Latin Christianity on other cultures—that is, missionary activity) can be detected everywhere from the letters of Gregory the Great to the decrees of the Council of Vienne (1312).

In standard historiography, the story of the medieval papacy is generally held to extend roughly from Gregory the Great to Boniface VIII, with an extended epilogue in Avignon. While the end of my investigation will be marked by the pontifical court's move to Avignon, an entirely different geopolitical entity, I have chosen the pontificate of Gregory the Great as an initial chronological signpost due not only to Gregory the Great's formative role in the "invention" of the Middle Ages but also to his attitude toward Greek: a combination of reverence and contempt (resembling somewhat that of Cato) that is typical of the the Medieval West.

Papal history is mostly told in terms of "rise and fall" narratives. For the purposes of this essay, it is important to emphasize that the "rise" of the medieval papacy is generally conceived as a gradual detachment from the Byzantine Empire, and thus, is characterized by the phenomenon of "Westernization" and by growing distance from the East, not only politically but also in matters ecclesiastical, dogmatic, and cultural. The Byzantine Church was viewed with mixed feelings by the West: it was at once the source of countless heresies and also the repository of many of Christianity's spiritual treasures. The Byzantine Empire was also a contemporary rival political entity. The overlapping of these concerns often resulted in an ambivalent attitude as regards the acceptance, reception, or acquisition and appropriation of elements pertaining to "Greekness." However, this parting of the ways, though rich in animosities, positively influenced the

---

5 "litterae Graecae et Latinae, quae sexcentis iam antea annis in situ et tenebris iacuerant, tum demum splendorem aliquem adeptae sint." *Liber de vita Christi ac omnium pontificum*, ed. Giacinto Gaida, Rerum italicarum scriptores 3/1 (Città di Castello, 1932), p. 338.

6 B.B. Price, "Patronage of Science," in Thomas F. Glick, Steven J. Livesey, and Faith Wallis (eds), *Medieval Science, Technology and Medicine: An Encyclopedia* (London, 2005), p. 386.

interest in Greek learning. Conflict generates communication and communication is impossible without certain linguistic and cultural skills.

At the Second Council of Lyon (1272), Humbert of Romans (c. 1200–1277), earlier Master General of the Dominican Order, was asked to put together a dossier discussing the three main issues to be addressed by the council: namely, crusading, church union, and ecclesiastical reforms. In his *Opusculum Tripartitum* (II.17), under the heading *Que sunt utilia et necessaria ad istius negotii executionem et consumationem* (referring to the union of the Greek and Latin churches), he emphasized the need for knowledge of Greek and for translations of Greek texts. On a long and hierarchically ordered list of suggested remedies for the Schism, learning Greek came first. Humbertus considered translation a spiritual weapon (*arma spiritualia*) to be used by the Church for fighting the enemy, whether Arab, Jew, or Greek.

For this reason, one cannot speak about Greek learning and translation solely in terms of the transmission of texts. Scholars have observed of the Arabic-Latin and the Greek-Arabic translation movements that they were "the result of a clash between two worlds, both embodying universal claims to political and ideological dominance."[7] The same can be said, I argue, of the Greek-Latin translation movements. At the papal court, Greek and Greekness meant several things in relation to Latin and Latinness: an ancient and a contemporary political entity at the same time, "a site of contention and difference as well as value and authority."[8] Patronizing, and at the same time controlling, the flow of Greek writings was of primary interest for the papacy. "The story of knowing Greek is also the story of building of scholarly and institutional walls around Greek knowledge."[9] Texts were used strategically to build up cultural identity: appropriation of items of the Greek legacy via translation reflects, in fact, a rivalry with the political entity of Byzantium. In the same manner, claiming the role of mediator between Latin and Greek culture exclusively for the papacy reflects its anxiety for cultural control in Western Christian literary production. Translations from Greek to Latin were used as spiritual weapons not only in the rivalry with Byzantium but also in competition with other Latin political and cultural entities, such as the major royal courts of Europe. As Thomas Noble puts it, "Perhaps in the end the question of the knowledge of Greek in papal Rome, or anywhere else in the early medieval West, is either a false question, or else a question falsely put. It might be better to speak in terms consonant with Augustine's image of spoiling the Egyptians, that is,

---

[7] Mohammed Abbattouny, Jürgen Renn, and Paul Weinig, "Transmission and Transformation: The Translation Movements in the Medieval East and West in Comparative Perspective," *Science in Context* 14.1 (2001): 1–12 at 6.

[8] Simon Goldhill, *Who Needs Greek? Contests in the Cultural History of Hellenism* (Cambridge, 2002), p. 296.

[9] Goldhill, *Who Needs Greek?* p. 8.

the Greeks."[10] The metaphor of spoliation perfectly captures the strategy for resolving the problem caused by this double approach of Western Latin medieval culture toward Greek. The image was evoked by the translators themselves: Rufinus refers to himself as *magna sibi Graeciae spolia deferentem*.[11] This was likewise the approach of the ninth century papal librarian, Anastasius Bibliothecarius, who would sometimes claim that his translations are retroversions of Greek translations of texts originally composed in Latin. Indeed, his entire translation project might be described as despoiling the treasures of the Greeks. Anastasius's main concern was repatriation of cultural values: for him, Greek lore represented a kind of bounty that would enable the West to celebrate the superiority of Latin Christian culture over Greek.

This "despoiling" also frequently had immediate and practical value beyond just the archiving of treasures. Over centuries, the papacy saw empires rise and fall, and the appropriation of Greek culture often played a major role in arguments supporting any type of *translatio imperii*. Pope Sylvester II (999–1003) wanted to see the Ottonian dynasty flourish. Before ascending the papal throne, Gerbert of Aurillac was invited to be the tutor of the future emperor Otto III. He accepted the task, saying: "I don't know what more evidence of the divine there can be than that a man, Greek by birth, Roman by empire, as if by hereditary right seeks to recapture for himself the treasures of Greek and Roman wisdom."[12]

Otto had a Greek mother, Empress Theophanu. But if we look at the way Sylvester II used the terms "Greek" and "Roman" in the service of a *translatio imperii*, it becomes obvious that there was more in the "Ottonian Hellenism"[13] than just literary interest in his mother's culture.

How can such a complex and long history be told? While it would be impossible to postulate a linear and unchanging papal policy, it is certainly meaningful to analyze the mechanisms of different cultural-political strategies and to chart the dynamics of a constant preoccupation, including its main motivations and directions. In the following pages, I will point out three possible lines of investigation that would highlight some facets of papal involvement in Greek

---

[10] Thomas F.X. Noble, "The Declining Knowledge of Greek in Eighth- and Ninth-Century Papal Rome," *Byzantinische Zeitschrift* 78 (1985): 56–62 at 62.

[11] *Tyrannii Rufini Opera*, ed. Manlio Simonetti, Corpus Christianorum Series Latina 20 (Turnhout, 1961), p. 281.

[12] *The Letters of Gerbert, with His Papal Privileges as Sylvester II*, trans. H.P. Lattin (New York, 1961), pp. 296–7. Or, as he put it in another letter to the emperor:

> I shall set forth briefly my conclusions on this question lest Greece shall boast of herself alone both in imperial philosophy and in Roman power. Ours, ours is the Roman Empire. [...] Our august emperor of the Romans art thou, Caesar, who, sprung from the noblest blood of the Greeks, surpass the Greeks in empire and govern the Romans by hereditary right, but both you surpass in genius and eloquence. (*Letters of Gerbert*, trans. Lattin, p. 298)

[13] Walter Berschin, *Greek Letters and the Latin Middle Ages. From Jerome to Nicholas of Cusa*, revised and expanded edition, trans. Jerold C. Frakes (Washington, DC, 1988), pp. 184–5.

learning in the West, namely the active, the performative, and the receptive stages of this process: patronage of translators, religious debates with the Greeks, and Greek holdings in the papal library.

Patronage of Translators

The patronage of translators and the translation activity in general is indicative of the active phase of transmission. Whether as commissioners or dedicatees, from Late Antiquity onward, popes figure in many translators' prologues. Translators' connections to the papal court varied widely: some were papal officials, some diplomats engaged also in interpreting—sometimes even popes themselves were active translators. Both long- and short-term collaborations occurred, either in the form of epistolary contact or of actual physical presence at the curia.

Any enumeration of such instances can, of course, go back much further than the papacy of Gregory I, to Jerome's correspondence with Pope Damasus and their shared concern for codifying the canon of biblical texts in Latin. The list continues with Dionysius Exiguus, who worked for Popes Hormisdas and John I to produce translations of important synodal decrees and canons. Rusticus, editor and translator of several council acts, was actually the nephew of Pope Vigilius, and his travel companion to Constantinople. Two popes in the late sixth century, Pelagius I and John III, themselves translated the *Apophtegmata patrum*. According to the *Liber Pontificalis*, Pope Leo II at the end of the seventh century had the acts of the sixth ecumenical council translated. Bonifatius Consiliarius, translator of the miracles of Saints Cyrus and John, seems to have been a Roman cleric connected to the court of Benedict II in the seventh century. In the eighth century, Pope Zacharias himself translated Saint Gregory's dialogues, though in the opposite direction, from Latin to Greek. Anastasius Bibliothecarius, the most prolific translator of the Carolingian period, was the close collaborator of three ninth-century popes: Nicholas I, Hadrian II, and John VIII. Arguably the two most important figures of twelfth- and thirteenth-century translation movements, Burgundio of Pisa and William of Moerbeke, both had important connections at the pontifical court: Burgundio dedicated one of his Chrysostomus translations to Pope Eugen III, while William was penitentiary of Pope Clement IV, completing much of his Latin Aristotle while at the papal court at Viterbo. Aside from these well-known instances, traces of Roman connections can also be hypothesized for anonymous literary productions.[14]

However impressive this far from complete list might look, a mere enumeration of names of popes and translators certainly does not in itself imply the existence of conscious papal cultural policies. But upon closer examination, the fate of a text can illuminate the cultural policies of a whole period. One can observe literary canons emerging, traditions being established, invented, and contested.

---

[14] Carmela Vircillo-Franklin, *The Latin Dossier of Anastasius the Persian: Hagiographic Translations and Transformations* (Toronto, 2004).

Religious Debates with the Greeks

Confrontations illustrate the performative aspect of the transmission process. Apologetic literature targeting various heretical tendencies in Byzantine theology is a clear mirror of the growing and increasingly selective knowledge of Greek patristic thought among the upper echelons of the Western clergy. Sustained confrontation with the Eastern dogmatic tradition gave birth to various literary genres, from the florilegia to the so-called *Contra errores Graecorum*, all with the same aim: to defeat the Greeks on their own ground. In this regard, among the most important textual source groups are the conciliar acts and related documents, especially the ecumenical ones, which tend to produce a substantial amount of patristic lore.

The earliest instances of such documents are already surprisingly well-informed dossiers.[15] While seventh- and eighth-century Roman florilegia were most likely prepared with the help of the Greek monks in the city, Western clerics later became involved in the process. On October 23, 867, Pope Nicholas I requested the assistance of Hincmar and all other Frankish bishops, who were asked to combat the errors of the Greeks by writing treatises refuting them.[16] By showing that Greeks not only question the Romans, but, by extension, Western Christian practices in general, he involved the Frankish clergy in the conflict. We do not know how many of the bishops responded to Nicholas's call to arms: the surviving sources (Aeneas, Bishop of Paris's *Liber adversus Graecos* and Ratramnus of Corbie's *Contra Graecorum errores*) may represent all or part of the response. Aeneas's and Ratramnus's contributions are for the most part compilations from all sorts of sources, Latin and Greek, as if to stress their ability to combat Greek heresy with Greek authority, and to demonstrate that the Greek Fathers were on their side.

In 1177, Hugh Etherianus sent his work defending the theory of the procession of the Holy Spirit, *De sancto et immortali Deo*, to Pope Alexander III. Composed at the request of Emperor Manuel, dedicated both to the pope and to the patriarch of Antioch, prepared in both Latin and Greek, it is a fascinating product of twelfth-century political and theological conflicts. It is not much more than a patristic compilation, but it is an excellent example of a Latin arguing against the Greeks with firsthand knowledge of Greek patristic theology. It later served as inspiration for the first mendicant *Contra errores Graecorum*, which in turn triggered a whole series of such writings, culminating in Aquinas's *Contra errores Graecorum* dedicated to Pope Urban IV.[17]

---

[15] A. Alexakis, *Codex Parisinus Graecus 1115 and Its Archetype*, Dumbarton Oaks Studies 34 (Washington, DC, 1996).

[16] Kevin Kennedy, "The Permanence of an Idea: Three Ninth Century Frankish Ecclesiastics and the Authority of the Roman See," in H. Mordek (ed.), *Aus Kirche und Reich: Studien zu Theologie, Politik und Recht im Mittelalter. Festschrift für Friedrich Kempf zu seinem 75. Geburtstag und fünfzigjährigen Doktorjubiläum* (Sigmaringen, 1983), pp. 105–16.

[17] A. Dondaine, "Contra Errores Graecorum: Premiers écrits polémiques des domincains d'Orient," *Archivium Fratrum Praedicatorum* 21 (1951): 320–446.

Greek Holdings in the Papal Library

The examination of books, library holdings, and the different ways this knowledge was kept and organized will shed light on the reception of Greek originals as well as their translated variants. Bernhard Bischoff, discussing feasible methodologies for a possible reconstruction of the early papal library, suggested two approaches: critical research based entirely on palaeographical evidence, and imaginative solutions relying on references from various other types of resources.[18] Building a case on more equivocal evidence than palaeographical data might be risky, but it is certainly necessary when, as was the case at the pontifical court, the library was not a static depository of books. We must imagine a heavy traffic of manuscripts coming and going, being loaned, given away as presents, requested, and copied. The very first surviving catalogue of the papal library dates from 1295, and lists 23 Greek volumes. By 1311, the collection had been enriched with a further ten Greek volumes. The history of the papal library before its transfer to the Vatican has never been told, mainly because of the scarcity of evidence for periods such as the seventh to ninth centuries.[19] As for its location, we know that by the seventh century at the latest both the library and the archives were moved to the Lateran palace; but we know nothing about its organization, its function, and above all, its holdings.

However, we can get a rough estimate of the dimensions and the character of a library without tracking down the original volumes it contained by speaking about "texts" rather than "manuscripts" held by the library. To reconstruct the Greek holdings of the Vatican library, one good starting point would be the literary activity of translators. Were they enriching the library by bringing in new texts, or were their translations motivated by texts already held by the library? These are questions worth asking: the list of translations is a resource that, even if does not allow a complete reconstruction, is at least indicative of the profile of the Greek collection of a "virtual" or "ideal" papal library.

Such results, combined with other data, can get us closer to the full picture. Recently, for example, Alexander Alexakis has argued that the papal library's Greek holdings were more extensive than scholars have supposed: according to him, the archetype of *Parisinus Graecus 1115*, a florilegium of Greek ecclesiastical and theological texts, was produced by the papal scriptorium, and moreover, this compilation implied the presence of the complete volumes of its sources on the pontifical bookshelves.[20] Pope Paul I in the eighth century sent a whole set of Greek books to Pipin III. Eugen III, patron of Burgundio of Pisa, initiated the

---

[18] Bernhard Bischoff, *Manuscripts and Libraries in the Age of Charlemagne*, trans. M. Gorman (Cambridge, 1994), p. 56.

[19] For later periods, see A. Paravicini Bagliani "Le bibliotheche curiali duecentesche" and M.-H. Jullien de Pommerol, "La bibliothèque de Boniface VIII," in Giuseppe Lombardi and Donatella Nebbiai dalla Guarda (eds), *Libri, lettori e biblioteche dell'Italia medievale (secoli ix–xv). Fonti, testi, utilizzazione del libro* (Roma, 2000), pp. 263–75 and 487–505.

[20] Alexakis, *Codex Parisinus Graecus 1115 and Its Archetype*.

quest for Greek manuscripts of the homilies of Chrysostom on Matthew, to be then translated by Burgundio: he requested a copy from Aimery, patriarch of Antioch, who replied to the demand, and thus provided the original on which Burgundio's Latin is based. Simon of Genoa, physician of Pope Nicholas IV and possibly also of Boniface VIII, lists at the beginning of his *Clavis sanationis* a bibliography of Greek medical works upon which he had based his medical glossary. It testifies to a precious collection of rare ancient Greek medical books, the provenance of which has yet to be carefully investigated. For example, the copy of the Ophtalmikos of Demosthenes he consulted is probably directly connected to the copy Pope Sylvester II requested from the abbot of Bobbio.[21] Scholars still cannot reach a consensus regarding the provenance of another important set of ancient Greek manuscripts, namely the collection of philosophical works found in the catalogues drawn up during the reign of Boniface, though it is certain that some of them formed the basis for the translations of William of Moerbeke.[22]

Conclusion

As this rapid overview illustrates, to neglect pontifical participation in the spread of Greek learning in medieval Europe would be to overlook an influential and powerful agency. I therefore think that a comprehensive examination of all evidence testifying to the presence of Greek at the papal court from the early seventh to the late thirteenth century is essential to our understanding of Greek in the West. Far from claiming a universal monopoly for the papacy in process of transmission, I claim that only by detailed study of *all* aspects of the presence of Greek in the Latin Middle Ages can we arrive at a fuller picture without running into the danger of gross generalizations.

What exactly was the role of the pontifical court in the medieval Greek-Latin cultural exchange? It is undeniable that popes, as patrons or as dedicatees, often lurk behind the most important translation achievements—not to mention the special cases in which they themselves are engaged in such activities. Literary systems are parts of social systems, and it is therefore justifiable to approach translation projects as ideological apparatuses serving the development of cultural identities. The canon of translated works from one language into another is rarely the result of the translator's individual literary taste. Institutions and their current political and cultural interests have immense influence on the formation of such a canon. One such extremely influential institution was the medieval papacy. It was, moreover (in contrast with royal or princely courts, where such preoccupations are sporadic), the only curia with a more constant attentiveness to this question.

---

21 A. Paravicini Bagliani, *Medicina e scienze della natura alla corte dei Papi nel Duecento* (Spoleto, 1991), pp. 249–50.

22 Paravicini Bagliani, *Medicina e scienze della natura*, pp. 170–75, 411–54; Marwan Rashed, "Nicolas d'Otrante, Guillaume de Moerbeke et la 'Collection Philosophique,'" *Studi medievali* 43 (2002): 693–717.

Nevertheless, while treating the papacy as an institution, one must leave room both for translators' initiatives and individual papal contributions to this process. In the case of William of Moerbeke, for example, it is meaningless to substitute the now discredited legend of his translating *ad instantiam fratris Thomae* (that is, Aquinas)[23] with an *ad instantiam papae*; but at the same time it must be stressed that the papal court at Viterbo, where Moerbeke completed many of his translations of Aristotle, not only is a physical space where the translator accidentally happened to be, but also reveals a great deal about the sociocultural context of the transmission process.

The history of medieval Greek-Latin translation is deeply marked by the papacy's changing policies toward the Greeks. Multiple motivations, from doctrinal sensitivity to intellectual curiosity should be considered, since such preoccupations spring up or die out for various reasons: sometimes they are governed by political agendas, sometimes by religious controversies, and sometimes, indeed, by the intellectual orientations of the popes, or simply by the cultural atmosphere at court. I hope I have shown that there is a pattern worth investigating here, and a history worth telling. Studying this impact can result in interesting findings concerning the relationship between intellectuals and different power zones throughout the medieval centuries and concerning the way pontifical policies were shaping the cultural identity of Latin Christendom. The outcome of such investigation can, I believe, greatly contribute to a more profound and nuanced understanding of the presence of Greek learning in medieval Europe.

---

[23] See Carlos Steel, "Guillaume de Moerbeke et Saint Thomas," in J. Brams and W. Vanhamel (eds), *Guillaume de Moerbeke: recueil d'études à l'occasion du 700e anniversaire de sa mort (1286)* (Leuven, 1989), pp. 57–82.

Chapter 13
Translation, Transcription, and Transliteration in the Polemics of Raymond Martini, O.P.[1]

Ryan Szpiech

The authority associated with a medieval *auctor* was not usually the product of just one particular text but often depended on the authenticity of the whole corpus of texts attributed to that *auctor*'s name. The *auctor* was seen as an authority because he embodied *auctoritas*, the wisdom to speak well, the authority to speak truly, and the believability to be trusted as a source. According to A.J. Minnis, *auctoritas* requires two things: intrinsic worth and authenticity. To have intrinsic worth meant that what one wrote did not contradict Christian doctrine; to have authenticity linked an *auctor* with a true and ancient source.[2] In polemical writing, the concept of *auctoritas,* traditionally based solely on biblical *testimonia*, began in the twelfth century to expand noticeably with the introduction of secular texts of philosophy that initiated a shift to argument that was based on *ratione et auctoritate*, on reason and authoritative textual proof. By the second half of the thirteenth century, this expansion of the concept of *auctoritas* in polemical writing, which itself can be understood as part of a broader shift in the meaning of the medieval *auctor* in light of new Aristotelian ideas about the "effective cause" of a text,[3] came to involve the invocation as textual *auctoritates* those texts considered authoritative by Jews and Muslims, but not Christians, such as the Talmud, Qur'ān,[4] Midrashic exegesis, and collections of Muslim traditions about the sayings of Muḥammad

---

[1] This research is part of a collaborative project entitled "The Intellectual and Material Legacies of Late Medieval Sephardic Judaism: An Interdisciplinary Approach," directed by Dr. Esperanza Alfonso (CSIC). I wish to thank the European Research Council for its support of this project with a four-year Starting Grant and to thank Dr. Alfonso for her ongoing coordination as Principal Investigator of the project. I also wish to thank Edward Casey for his editorial corrections.

[2] Alastair Minnis, *Medieval Theory of Authorship*, 2nd ed. (Philadelphia, 1988), pp. 10–12. Minnis develops the ideas of M.-D. Chenu, "Auctor, Actor, Autor," *Bulletin du Cange: Archivum Latinitatis Medii Aevi* 2 (1927): 81–6; and idem, *Toward Understanding St. Thomas*, trans. A.-M. Landry and D. Hugues (Chicago, 1964), pp. 129–32.

[3] Minnis, pp. 28–39.

[4] Transliteration of Hebrew and Arabic has loosely followed the norms established by the *Journal of Semitic Studies* with simplified Hebrew vowels.

known as *ḥadīth*.[5] This use of non-Christian texts as *auctoritates* evidenced the growing desire by Christian polemicists for authenticity, garnered at the expense of intrinsic worth.

This use of non-Christian texts as *auctoritates* became a labor dominated by the Dominican order, newly founded in 1215 for combating the heretics of Provence but quickly adapted to other anti-heretical struggles. The Dominicans embraced language study as a key part of their modus operandi virtually from their inception: the first Master General after Dominic himself, Jordan de Saxony, stated in 1236 that friars ought to learn the languages of those to whom they preached.[6] Less than two decades later, Master Humbert of Romans specified that this should include Arabic and Hebrew.[7] Dominican efforts were organized in Murcia in 1266 to teach Hebrew and Arabic, as well as in Barcelona (1275, Hebrew), Valencia (1280, Arabic), and Játiva (1302, Hebrew and Arabic).[8] Such efforts can also be connected to the emphasis on rhetorical effectiveness in preaching by Raymond of Peñafort, Master General after

---

5 On this "expansion" of *auctoritas* in polemical writing, see Gilbert Dahan, *Les intellectuels chrétiens et les juifs au Moyen Âge* (Paris, 1990), pp. 440–76; and Ryan Szpiech, *Conversion and Narrative: Reading and Religious Authority in Medieval Polemic* (Philadelphia, 2013), pp. 69–74. The discussion that follows has benefited greatly from Dahan's analysis of *auctoritas* in Martini's work and from Brigitte Miriam Bedos-Rezak's conceptualization of the intersection of *auctoritas* and authenticity in Christian anti-Jewish polemic, "Les juifs et l'écrit dans la mentalité eschatologique du Moyen Âge chrétien occidental (France 1000–1200)," *Annales. Histoire, Sciences Sociales* 49 (1994): 1049–63.

6 "Monemus quod in omnibus provinciis et conventibus fratres linguas addiscant illorum quibus sunt propingui [*sic*]" [We order that in all provinces and convents, Friars learn the languages of those around them]. *Acta Capitulorum Generalium Ordinis Praedicatorum ab anno 1220 usque ad annum [1844]*, ed. Benedictus Maria Reichert (Rome, 1898–1904), p. 9.

7 "Curandum est ut aliqui Fratres idonei insudent in locis idoneis ad linguam arabicam, hebraicam, graecam et barbaras addiscendas" ["It should be seen to that some suitable Friars labor (lit. "sweat") in suitable places in learning Arabic, Hebrew, Greek, and foreign tongues"]. Humbert of Romans, *Opera de Vita Regulari*, ed. J.J. Berthier (2 vols, Rome, 1888–1889), vol. 2, pp. 187–8.

8 On the history of such movements, see José María Coll, "Escuelas de Lenguas Orientales en los siglos XIII y XIV," *Analecta Sacra Tarraconensia* 17 (1944): 115–38; 18 (1945): 59–89; 19 (1946): 217–40, at 17: 121–4 and 18: 76–7; and Robin Vose, *Dominicans, Muslims, and Jews in the Medieval Crown of Aragon* (Cambridge, 2009). Such efforts, which can only loosely be called "schools" and represent the efforts of a few very small groups, were contemporaneous with those of Catalan polemicist and savant Ramon Llull, who helped establish chairs in Semitic languages at several universities. Llull, after himself learning Arabic with his Muslim slave for nine years, successfully petitioned king Jaume I of Aragon to support the foundation of the Monastery of Miramar in Mallorca in 1276, where Franciscans could study both Hebrew and Arabic. He went on in 1311 to petition the Pope's help at the Council of Vienne at which two chairs each in Arabic, Hebrew, and Aramaic were ordered to be established at universities in Bologna, Oxford, Paris, Salamanca, and the Papal Court. On this history, see Sebastián Garcías Palou, *El Miramar de Ramon Llull* (Palma de Mallorca, 1977), pp. 19–36.

Jordan, following directly in the tradition of Pope Gregory the Great.[9] The writing of the Aragonese polyglot Raymond Martini (Ramon Martí, d. after 1284), well-known for its impressive manipulation of non-Christian sources, fits within this trend of Dominican attention to Hebrew and Arabic and, more importantly, within the larger process of the transformation of *auctoritas* that accompanied it.

This essay examines the evolution of Martini's approach to language over the course of his career as a Dominican from the 1250s to the 1280s, specifically looking at his use of translation, transliteration, and transcription as part of his understanding of "authentic" textual authorities.[10] As Martini focused more exclusively on anti-Jewish rather than anti-Muslim polemic, languages and translation played an ever more important role in his writing. As language came to constitute an essential part of his polemical arsenal against Jews in a way that it had not in his anti-Muslim polemic, Martini grew more concerned with the imagined Jewish responses to his arguments. In response to this anxiety, he developed an increasingly careful and punctilious methodology that corresponded to his mounting anxiety over the authenticity of his sources. As his career progressed, Martini strove to approximate to what he saw as the most authentic and familiar form of his cited authorities, first through translation, then through transliteration, and finally through transcription of original languages and alphabets. I propose that Martini's use of language formed part of a new rhetoric of authenticity in Christian apologetics in which writers aimed to move ever closer to an elusive affirmation of theological identity through the terms of non-Christian difference. In this, the theological expression of Christian identity came to find its most apposite vocabulary in foreignness, and authority increasingly depended, in its justification of that identity, on an appeal to alterity. At the same time, a comparison of Martini's evolving use of sources shows how his appeal to authenticity was constantly in tension with his own interpretive choices in the process of transcribing and translating his sources.

Before looking at Martini's works, a word on terminology is in order. In this essay, "translation" is used to describe Martini's practice of interpreting and rewriting his source citations in a language other than the original (usually this meant translation from Hebrew or Arabic to Latin, but sometimes Hebrew and Arabic were also languages of translation). This practice is to be distinguished from "transliteration," in which Martini includes representations of sounds or phrases from Arabic or Hebrew sources in Latin characters (or in one case, Hebrew in Arabic characters). Both of these practices are distinguished here from "transcription" of original material in Hebrew and Arabic passages in their most common form (in the

---

[9] Peñafort stated in his highly influential *Summa de Paenitentia*, "Debent, sicut ait Gregorius, tam iudaei quam sarraceni auctoritatibus, rationibus et blandimentis, potius quam asperitatibus, ad fidem christianam de novo suscipiendam provocari" ["Jews as well as Muslims should, as Gregory (the Great) says, be provoked to take up … the Christian faith with authorities, reasons, and blandishments rather than asperities"] (ed. Xaverio Ochoa and Aloisio Diez [Rome, 1976], p. 309).

[10] See Bedos-Rezak, pp. 1061–3, for other examples of the same phenomenon.

Hebrew or Arabic alphabets). As we will see below, Martini makes use of all three techniques to varying degrees, often transcribing a passage in Hebrew or Arabic and then translating it into Latin (or translating a Latin passage into Hebrew), within which he sometimes intersperses examples of transliterated sounds or words.

Over the course of Martini's polemical career, which spanned the time between his entrance in the Dominican order (approximately in the late 1230s) until his death sometime after 1284, he composed a spate of polemical and apologetic works that included refutations of Judaism and Islam on the basis of non-Christian texts. His first works, *Explanatio simboli apostolorum* [*Explanation of the Apostles Creed*], composed around 1256/7, and *De Seta Machometi* [*On the Sect of Muḥammad*],[11] of unknown date but probably from the same period, draw in various places from the Qur'ān, *ḥadīth*, and Arabic philosophers such as Avicenna, al-Ghazālī, and Averroes. While the *Explanatio* principally contains an apologetic, theological discussion of the foundations of Christian belief into which Martini blended a polemical attack on Islam, the *De Seta* focuses exclusively on anti-Islamic argument and includes an *ad hominem* attack on Muḥammad and his status as prophet.[12] Martini is also often credited with a lengthy Arabic-Latin lexical list known as the *Vocabulista in Arabico*, probably composed in the same years, although this attribution continues to be debated and will not be considered in detail here.[13]

Despite their different focuses, the *Explanatio* and the *De Seta* contain many similarities and even share some identical passages. Both aim their polemical apparatus against Islam rather than Judaism, making use of citations from Islamic sources to buttress their arguments. More importantly, however, both works cite Islamic sources in Latin translation only, and in some cases they notably change or abbreviate the original text. For example, if we compare the well-known "Light Verse" from the "Surah of Light" (Qur'ān 24:35) with the terse rendition of it in the *Explanatio*, we see how Martini reduces it almost beyond recognition, stating,

---

11 J. March, "Ramon Martí y la seva *Explanatio simboli Apostolorum*," *Annuari de l'Institut d'Estudis Catalans* (1908): 443–96 at 462; and *De Seta Machometi o de origine, progressu, et fine Machometi et quadruplici reprobatione prophetiae eius*, ed. and trans. Josep Hernado i Delgado, *Acta historica et archaeologica medievalia* 4 (1983): 9–51.

12 This work repeats many of the Qur'ānic citations of the *Explanatio* and expands upon them, adding more references as well to the *Sīra*, an eighth-century work of biographical lore about Muḥammad by the author Ibn Isḥāq, and the *ḥadīth* collections such as the *Ṣaḥīḥ* of al-Bukhārī and that of Muslim Ibn al-Ḥajjāj.

13 On the *Vocabulista*, see the edition by Celestino Schiaparelli (Florence, 1871), and the studies by David Griffin, "Los Mozarabismos del 'Vocabulista' atribuído a Ramón Martí," *Al-Andalus* 23 (1958): 251–338; 24 (1959): 85–124, 333–80; 25 (1960): 93–170; and Federico Corriente, *El léxico árabe andalusí según el "Vocabulista in Arabico"* (Madrid, 1989); Federico Corriente, "Notas de lexicología hispanoárabe. I. Nuevos romancismos en Aben Quzmán y crítica de los propuestos. II. Los romancismos del 'Vocabulista in Arabico': addenda et corrigenda," *Vox Romanica* 39 (1980): 183–210; and Federico Corriente, "Notas de lexicología hispanoárabe. III. Los romancismos del Vocabulista. IV. Nuevos berberismos del hispanoárabe," *Awrāq* 4 (1981): 5–30.

"Dicit in c. *Luminis*, quod Deus est lumen celorum et terre, et similitudo luminis eius sicut lampas olei incensa lumine" ["It says in the chapter *Light*, that God is the light of the heavens and earth, and the likeness of his light (is) like an oil lamp flaming brightly"].[14] As this passage continues, we see that Martini not only condenses his sources but sometimes also alters the original sense in subtle but significant ways. He continues (citing the "Surah of Abraham," Qur'ān 14:25): "Item in C. *Abraam*: Dicit Deus, secundum credulitatem eorum. Inducit Deus similitudines hominibus ad hoc, ut recordentur" ["In the chapter *Abraham*: God, according to their (mode of) belief, said, 'God brings forth likenesses/similes to humankind in this (context), in order that they may remember'"] (462).[15] The original text reads, by contrast, "Allah sets forth *parables* (*amthāl*) for men, in order that they *be admonished / made to remember* (*yatadhakarūna*)." He translates the ubiquitous Qur'ānic word *amthāl*, meaning in both places "parables" or "analogies," in its literal meaning as "similitudines" ("likenesses" or "similes") rather than "exempla" (as given in the *Vocabulista*) or "parabolae" (in the Gospels and in the *Pugio*).[16] Likewise, Martini's literal rendering of the final verb removes the explicitly admonitory sense of the verse by making men simply "remember" rather than be "made to remember." Although these changes seem slight, they shift the focus of the verse to better fit Martini's discussion of the Trinity according to Augustine's own image of the "analogy" (*similitudo*) of fire and its multiple properties.[17] Such changes are, in fact, part of a pattern of translation in Martini's early works, and may reflect the influence of the Arabic anti-Islamic polemic

[14] J. March, "Ramon Martí," p. 462.

[15] The text reads "recondentur," which is clearly a scribal error.

[16] In the *Vocabulista in Arabico* (which, even if we do not concede it is Martini's work, does shed light on contemporary usage and translation), *mathal/amthāl* are given as "exemplum/exempla" and "proverbium/proverbia" (pp. 177 and 541). *Similitudo*, by contrast, is the translation of *Ŝibh* (p. 123). For an example of medieval Arabic translation of the Gospels, see Bernard Levin, *Die griechisch-arabische Evangelien-Übersetzung: Vat. Borg. ar. 95 und Ber. orient. oct. 1108* (Uppsala, 1938). A very clear example of his translation of *amthāl* as "parabolas" and not "similitudines" is found in his translation of a passage from Maimonides's *Guide of the Perplexed* (*Dalālat al-Ḥā'irīn*, text established by S. Munk, ed. Issachar Joel [Jerusalem, 5691/1930–1931]); trans. Schlomo Pines [Chicago, 1963]). He quotes the passage from the prologue affirming that the "key" to the meaning of prophecy is "faḥṣ al-amthāli wa-ma'nahā wa-ta'wīl alfāẓihā" ["an understanding of the parables, of their import, and of the meaning of the words occurring in them"] (*Dalālat*, p. 6; *Guide*, p. 10, all emphasis mine). Martini translates this passage in the *Pugio* as "intelligere parabolas, atque metaphoras, similitudines atque aenigmata" ["to understand parables and metaphors, likenesses and enigmas"] (p. 427, emphasis mine). Here Martini first renders *amthāl* as "parabolas" and only thirdly associates it with "similitudines." Moreover, he immediately follows this with a translation of Ezek. 17:2, translating the biblical word *mašal* (the exact equivalent of the Arabic *mathal*) as "parabola." Elsewhere in the *Pugio* (e.g., pp. 485, 505, 549, 552, etc.) he employs "similitudo" to refer to God's "likeness," in which man was created, according to Gen. 1:26.

[17] Martini's reference to Augustine in the *Explanatio* comes from his *Sermones ad Scripturam* 117, Patrologia Latina 38, ed. Jacques-Paul Migne (Paris, 1844), cols 666–7.

known in Latin translation as the *Contrarietas Alfolica* and *Liber denudationis*.[18] More importantly, although relatively minor changes in themselves, these details reflect a flexible approach to translation in Martini's early works that contrasts sharply with his punctilious approach in his later anti-Jewish writing.

Despite the similarities and repetitions in the *Explanatio* and the *De Seta* with regard to their sometimes loose approach to translation, there are important differences between the two works that also hint at more significant tendencies that develop in Martini's later writing and, because of this, might suggest that the *De Seta* was composed after the *Explanatio*. Because the *De Seta* is explicitly polemical, whereas the *Explanatio* blends its polemical attack with apologetic explanations of Christian belief, *De Seta* cites much more material from non-Christian sources (more than twice as many citations as the *Explanatio*), including more references to *ḥadīth* as well as citations from Ibn Isḥāq's biographical work on Muḥammad, preserved in the rendition of Ibn Hishām, the *Sīrat Rasūl Allāh*. Although Martini implicitly characterizes Islamic sources as *auctoritates* in the *Explanatio*, this characterization becomes explicit in the *De Seta*. In the former, he claims that the incorrupt nature of both biblical Testaments can be proven "per auctoritates" [by authorities],[19] among which he includes the citations from the Qur'ān, and this implicit characterization is also found in the *De Seta* when Martini repeats this passage (52). In the *De Seta*, however, he goes one step further and specifically names one citation from the Qur'ān as an *auctoritas* (40). This characterization is significant because in his later works he does not hesitate to designate his non-Christian sources as *auctoritates*, a clear departure from the less explicit language of the *Explanatio*. Along with this move to characterize non-Christian sources as *auctoritates*, Martini demonstrates an increasing need to show his mastery of those sources by citing more widely from them and representing their language more carefully.

This shift is evident in the way Martini gives the titles of his sources in the *Explanatio* as compared with the *De Seta*. When a book of Qur'ān or *ḥadīth* is named in the former, there is no explanation of its translation. In the *De Seta*, by contrast, Martini regularly follows the title with a brief, explanatory translation. For example, in the passage shared by both texts, the book titles are sometimes translated and sometimes just transliterated, but no translation is given for the transliteration.[20]

---

[18] We can find another example of his subtle changes to the Qur'ānic text in his translations in his citation of 93:6–7, "Did [God] not … find you [Muḥammad] astray and direct you?" In the *De Seta*, Martini makes an important addition to the text, stating, "Deus invenit Machometum erroneum, id est in errore legis Dei et direxit eum" ["God found Muḥammad errant, that is, in error (concerning) the law of God, and directed him"] (p. 20). Here, Martini not only turns a question into a statement but also adds in the commentary explaining "errant" as in error over God's law, placing extra emphasis on Muḥammad's alleged "error." Thomas Burman, *Reading the Qur'ān in Latin Christendom, 1140–1560* (Philadelphia, 2007), has noted that both the *Explanatio* and the *De Seta* show the influence of the *Liber denudationis*, possibly in its original Arabic form (pp. 47–9).

[19] March, p. 452.

[20] March, p. 454; and Martini, *De Seta*, pp. 54–6.

In various other citations from Arabic sources in the *De Seta*, by contrast, names are transliterated and then translated. For example, the text introduces its citations with statements such as, "Secundum quod legitur in libro qui vocatur *Ciar*, id est, *Actus Machometi* ..." ["According to what is read in the book called *Siyār*, that is, *The Acts of Muḥammad* ..."] (18); or "Dixit in *Alcorano*, in tractatu *Raharim* [*sic*], id est, *Prohibitionis* ... item ... in tractatu *Zaf* ... id est, *Ordinis* ..." ["It says in the Qur'ān, in the tract *al-Taḥrīm*, that is, *The Prohibition* ... also ... in the tract *al-Ṣaff* (The Row/Rank), that is, *The Order* ..."] (26, and see also 30).[21]

Although these added details of transliteration within the translation also seem trivial, they intimate the first glimpse of what will become a much more common practice in Martini's subsequent polemical works. Understood as part of a trajectory of development toward more precise use of original language sources, these differences point to an increased need to supplement his translations with more untranslated material and also suggest that the *De Seta* was composed later than the *Explanatio*. Between the two texts, Martini begins to focus on what will be a central concern of his later writing: how to characterize the authority of his sources and, more importantly, how to represent that authority in the most "authentic" form. As we have already seen through his burgeoning use of transliteration, the keynote of that evocation of authenticity is the representation of language.

The *Explanatio* and the *De Seta*, and possibly the *Vocabulista* lexicon, represent the output of an early stage in Martini's career. A second stage begins in 1267 with the anti-Jewish *Capistrum Iudaeorum* [*Muzzle for the Jews*][22] and culminates 11 years later with Martini's largest and best-known work, the *Pugio Fidei* [*The Dagger of Faith*],[23] an enormous polemical tome, amounting to more than 700 pages in the two seventeenth-century editions.[24] In both works, Martini virtually abandons his former polemic with Islam and devotes himself to a refutation of

---

21 Burman has observed the importance of these translations of the titles of Qur'ānic books, noting that Martini, like his contemporary Dominican Riccoldo da Monte Croce, did not follow the idiosyncratic reorganization of the books found in the Qur'ān translation of Robert of Ketton (p. 97).

22 *Capistrum Iudaeorum*, ed. and trans. Adolfo Robles Sierra (2 vols, Würzburg, 1990).

23 *Pugio fidei adversus Mauros et Iudaeos* (Paris, 1651; Leipzig, 1687; Leipzig ed. repr. Farnborough, 1967). References here are to the 1687 edition.

24 A succinct analysis of the *Capistrum* can be found in Jeremy Cohen, "The *Capistrum Iudeorum* of Raymundus Martini [Hebrew]," in Ezra Fleischer et al. (eds), *Me'ah Še'arim: Studies in Medieval Jewish Spiritual Life in Memory of Isadore Twersky* (Jerusalem, 2001), pp. 279–96; and Jeremy Cohen, *Living Letters of the Law. Ideas of the Jew in Medieval Christianity* (Berkeley, 1999), pp. 342–58. A fuller analysis can be found in Ursula Ragacs, *"Mit Zaum und Zügel muss man ihr Ungestüm bändigen." Ps 32, 9: Ein Beitrag zur christlichen Hebraistik und antijüdischen Polemik im Mittelalter* (Frankfurt am Main and New York, 1997). On the *Pugio*, see Jeremy Cohen, *The Friars and the Jews: The Evolution of Medieval Anti-Judaism* (Ithaca, 1982), pp. 136–69; and Robert Chazan, *Daggers of Faith: Thirteenth-Century Missionizing and Jewish Response* (Berkeley, 1989), pp. 115–37. For an overview of the manuscripts and editions of the *Pugio*, see Ryan Szpiech, "Citas árabes en

Judaism on the basis of biblical, post-biblical, Talmudic, and midrashic sources. Insofar as we can associate Raymond Martini with Raymond of Peñafort, we can date the beginning of this turn to Judaism around the time of the Disputation of Barcelona in 1263. We can situate Martini's focus on Judaism among other Dominican efforts in the decade after the Disputation, such as the harangue of Friar Paul Christiani, the Christian protagonist at Barcelona, in Paris in 1272.[25] As Martini states in the opening lines to the *Pugio fidei*, "Nulla pestis sit efficacior ad nocendum quam familiaris inimicus. Nullus autem inimicus Christianae fidei magis sit familiaris, magisque nobis inevitabilis, quam Iudaeus" ["No plague may be more effective at harming than a familiar enemy. No enemy, moreover, may be more familiar to the Christian faith, or more ineluctable for us, than the Jew"] (2).

In Martini's turn to anti-Jewish writing, his engagement with primary source materials intensifies dramatically, and with it, the task of translation becomes more than just a window into the sources of his adversaries—it becomes the weapon of his own rhetorical self-justification and his primary tool in polemical assault. As language became a more central issue in his argumentation, his attention to the details of the original text increased and his efforts to show his understanding and mastery of such details became more patent. The focusing of his attention on the original language of his sources is especially clear if we compare his citation of the same text in different works. Although the *Capistrum* is an anti-Jewish work, Martini cites a number of primary Arabic sources in translation and repeats a few of the same Qur'ān passages previously cited in the *Explanatio* and *De Seta*. For example, we can compare his citation of Qur'ān 4:171 in the *De Seta* and the *Capistrum*. The original text in Arabic can be translated, "The Messiah Jesus, son of Mary, is the messenger of God and [is] his word, which he put into Mary, and [is] a spirit from Him." In the *De Seta*, the citation reads, "Christus est verbum Dei quod Deus posuit in Mariam et est Spiritus ex eo" ["Christ is the word of God which God put in Mary and which is a Spirit from him"] (24). The *Capistrum*, by contrast, reads, "Messias est Ijce ibnu Maryam, id est Iesus filius Mariae, nuntius Dei, et verbum eius quod deposuit apud Maryam, et spiritus de ipso" ["The Messiah is ʿĪsā ibn Maryam, that is Jesus son of Mary, messenger of God, and is his word which he put into Mary, and a spirit from him"] (1:254). This rendering is more accurate, changing "posuit," "he put," as in the *De Seta*, into "deposuit," "he deposited or gave to," thus more accurately rendering the Arabic "alqāhā," "He put or said it forth." It is also more complete, adding back the detail that the Messiah is "rasūl Allāh," God's messenger. Perhaps most importantly, Martini makes an attempt in the *Capistrum*, albeit a feeble one, at transliteration by giving the name of Jesus phonetically as it is in the Qur'ānic text, "ʿĪsā ibnu Maryama."

---

caracteres hebreos en el *Pugio fidei* del dominico Ramón Martí: entre la autenticidad y la autoridad," in *Al-Qanṭara: Revista de estudios árabes* 32.1 (2011): 71–107.

[25] For the Hebrew account of this debate, see Joseph Shatzmiller (ed.), *La deuxième controverse de Paris: un chapitre dans la polémique entre chrétiens et juifs au Moyen Âge* (Paris, 1994).

This difference is indicative of a larger shift in the *Capistrum* in which Martini cites widely from the Babylonian Talmud and major exegetical midrashim, and in many passages intersperses transliteration of Hebrew and Aramaic with Latin translation. In one example found within his calculations concerning the prophecy within the book of Daniel, he cites a Talmudic passage to support his understanding of the Hebrew words for day and year: "Legitur in Massekhta Ros hasanah in principio ... Wyom ehad hassanah id est dies unus in anno asah snah, id es computatur annus" ["It reads in the beginning of the Tractate *Rosh Ha-Shanah ... we-yom eḥad ha-šanah*, that is, the first day of the year, *ʿasah šanah*, that is, is calculated as a year"] (1:172).[26] In this very simple example, we see that he has moved from a transliteration of the title only to a transliteration of both title and text within his translation. While some of his attempts at transliteration in the *Capistrum* are simple and alternate coherently between original and translation, others involve a dense and sometimes confusing combination of transliteration, translation, and commentary, such as his citation of the gloss of French exegete Solomon ben Isaac (Rashi), on Isaiah 5:15, in which Rashi cites the Aramaic translation *Targum Jonathan* (2:264). In this and numerous other passages, Martini's text ends up being a garbled combination of transliteration of Hebrew texts and of Aramaic translations from the *Targumim* found within those, all layered on top of his own translations, within which he inserts his own polemical remarks. Among the hundred-odd citations of Talmud and midrash in the *Capistrum*, not to mention the hundreds more from the Hebrew Bible itself, there are dozens of passages that go beyond translation and attempt to evoke the original in this clumsy way by means of interspersed and ever more abundant transliteration. Although the results most often muddle rather than clarify the meaning of the original text, they point to his increasing attention to the language of his citations and his growing dissatisfaction with mere translation into Latin.

This tendency toward increasing use of original languages in Martini's work reaches its most developed form in his magnum opus, the *Pugio Fidei*. On the basis of more than 2,000 citations from the Hebrew Bible, as well as hundreds of post-biblical textual *auctoritates* drawn from a dizzying plethora of sources including both Talmuds, most major halakhic and aggadic midrashim, and dozens of works of commentary and philosophy from Jewish tradition, Martini concludes that rabbinical traditions themselves support the notion of Christianity as the New Israel in history.[27] (For the cover page and frontispiece of the 1687 Leipzig edition,

---

[26] The original Talmudic passage from BT Rosh ha-Shanah 2b reads: "we-yom eḥad *ba*-šanah *ḥašuv* šanah" (my emphasis). In citing from the edition of Robles Sierra, I have not copied his additions of diacritical marks into the edited text, but have added my own transliteration in the English translation.

[27] For an index of Martini's citations from Hebrew texts, see Ch. Merchavia, "Pugio Fidei—An Index of Citations" [Hebrew], in *Galut aḥar Golah* (Jerusalem, 1988), pp. 203–34. On Martini's other sources, see Görge Hasselhoff, "Some Remarks on Raymond Martini's (c. 1215/30–c. 1284/85) Use of Maimonides," *Trumah* 12 (2002): 133–48; and Philippe Bobichon, "La 'bibliothèque' de Raymond Martin au couvent Sainte-Catherine de Barcelone: sources antiques et chrétiennes du *Pugio fidei* (ca. 1278)" (forthcoming).

RAYMUNDI MARTINI
ORDINIS PRÆDICATORUM
PUGIO FIDEI
ADVERSUS
MAUROS
ET
JUDÆOS,
CUM
OBSERVATIONIBUS
JOSEPHI DE VOISIN,
ET INTRODUCTIONE
JO. BENEDICTI CARPZOVI,
Qui simul appendicis loco
HERMANNI JUDÆI OPUSCULUM
DE SUA CONVERSIONE
ex MSCto Bibliothecæ Paulinæ Academiæ
Lipsiensis recensuit.
LIPSIÆ,

Fig. 13.1 *Pugio Fidei*, Leipzig, 1687, cover page and frontispiece.

see Figure 13.1.) While the *Pugio* multiplies the amount of sources at least fourfold compared with the *Capistrum*, it also moves ever closer to the original authorities of its adversaries by replacing interspersed transliteration with actual citation in original scripts. Thus, we can compare the relatively tangled transliterations in the *Capistrum* given above with the same citations as given in the *Pugio* (275, reproduced in Figures 13.2, and 954, respectively). In these and numerous other passages found in both the *Capistrum* and the *Pugio*, Martini dispenses with the clumsy recourse to transliteration and simply transcribes the original verse in full in its original script, and then follows this with his translation into Latin. By placing the *Pugio* alongside his other writing, we can see it as the culmination of this trend of representing non-Christian sources more and more accurately in what he understood to be their most "original" form.

We can also explain Martini's practices of transcription and transliteration with the help of his own comments about language within the *Capistrum* and *Pugio*, which suggest that the central motivation of Martini's increasingly frequent and precise engagement with original source material from Arabic and Hebrew is defensive, a way to forestall any claims by potential adversaries charging him with a lack of real knowledge of the original texts being cited. Martini in fact explicitly addresses such counter-claims of Jewish interlocutors in the opening of the *Capistrum*:

SECVNDA PARS. CAP. III. 275

ipse annus est decimus nonus Regis Nebucadrezar, id est Nebucadnezar) *regis Babylonis, venit Nebusar-Adan princeps cocorum, stetitque coram rege Babel in Jerusalem, & combussit domum Domini, & domum regis, & omnes domos Jerusalem, & omnem domum magnam combussit igne.* Cum itaque in anno decimo nono Nabuchodonosoris destructum sit templum, ut hic expressum est, & ipse regnaverit XLV. annis, ut paulò ante * ostensum est sacræ Scripturæ testimoniis; ipsum scilicet Nabuchodonosorem à destructione templi XXVII. annis regnasse manifestum est. Fol. 220. * M. & D. §. *Judæi verò*

Nec obstat quod primus annus imperfectus est; moris etenim Scripturæ sacræ docet Talmud fuisse, non solùm septem menses, absque decem diebus, quos annus iste habuit, sed etiam diem unum pro anno quandoque ponere, ut in massechet *Rosch haschanah* in capite *Arba rasche Schanim* מר אמר יום אחד בשנה חשוב שנה *Mar dixit, Dies unus in anno computatur quandoque pro anno.*

Adde itaque istis XXVII. annis, quibus Nabuchodonosor post destructionē templi regnasse probatum est viginti tres, quibus regnavit Evilmerodach filius ejus, ut supra * per authenticam traditionem ostensum est; & habebis L. annos: Hoc quoq; modo persequere reliquos prædictæ traditionis annos, videlicet III. quibus regnavit Baltasar, duos Darii, & tres * Cyri, quem ipsi Cores vocant, & XIV. Asveri, & VI. Darii annos, sub quo secundum templum consummatum est; & habebis cum prædictis quinquaginta à primi templi destructione usque ad secundi consummationem annos LXXVIII. Ergo cum ibi ipsi non ponant nisi solum LXX. annos, ut supra ostensum est, * etiam secundum computum suum, eos VIII. annos nobis furari manifestum est, ita quod nulla tergiversatione valet inficiari. * M. & D. *in propinquiori* §. * *secundum; cos.* * §. *sciendum*

VIII Cæterum satis videtur quod Judæi, ut vulgò dicitur, si orbum invenirent, fraudulenter comederent cum ipso ficus: quemadmodum enim præfatos VIII. annos in oculis hominum insensibiliter surripere nituntur; ita quoque de XXX. annis quibus regnavit Cyrus, furtim nobis XXVII. subtrahere moliuntur: *a* sed cum Josephus Judæus eorum historiographus, quem ipsi יוסף בן גוריון *Joseph ben Gorion* vocant: & Græcus quoque *Cæsariensis Eusebius*; necnon & Latinus *Paulus Orosius* in Historiis suis; *Hieronymus etiam super Zachariam*; & *Beda super Esdra cap. 4.* Cum omnes, inquam, isti Cyrum sive Cores, ut ipsi vocant, triginta annis, ut prætactum est, regnasse posuerint: historia quoque Scholastica in fine historiæ Danielis, Capitulo *Porro*: & Glossa primo Esdræ quinto, & in aliis locis quàm plurimis plurimi idem hoc fecerint, patet Judæos esse falsiloquos, fures, atque latrones, & frustra ante pennatorum, & videntium oculos suæ retiacula jacere falsitatis. *a* Vide Observationes nostras.

Quod vero Cyrus regnaverit XXX. annis, ut ab omnibus his dictum est, patet ex eo, quod dicit *Josephon abbreviator Josephi* in hunc modum.

ויהי בלילה ההיא בשכב המלך בלשצר על מטתו ויקם הסריס ויך את המלך וימיתהו * In edit. Basil.
וישא את ראשו מעליו וישאהו ויברח עמו אל מחנה כורש ודריוש * ויתן להם את מלכי מדי
ראש בלשצר ויספר להם את כל אשר עשה בלשצר לכל כלי בית האלהים וכו׳ ופרס
β אז נדר כורש לבנות את היכל יהוה בירושלים ולשלוח את הגולה סבבל לירושלים
ולהשיב את כלי המקדש וכו׳ γ ויחלה דריוש מלך מדי למות ויהי כי קרבו ימיו וישלח β Vide Observationes nostras.
ויקרא לכורש δ קרובו ובעל בתו ויבא למדי וימליכהו תחתיו ותהי הממלכה אחרי
למדי ולפרס ודריוש נאסף אל עמיו וימלך תחתיו כורש מלך פרס על מלכות מדי γ. Cap. 16. δ
ופרס וכו׳ וילחם כורש במזרח וילכוד את כל [* העברות] הודו והרוכבים ε כל ארץ
כוש וכל היושבים [באפסי] הדרום ובמערב ועד אפסי ארץ ספרד ובצפן כל ארץ * [מעברות] ε
מקדון וכל ארץ כפתור ויארוע וכל ארץ אלאן ואלאסר והרי אלתהוגא והשר
ועד הרי השלג אשר אין לעברם ומלך על כל ממלכות הארץ ויתר דבריו הלא הם
כתובים על ספר מלכי מדי ופרס ועל ספר יוסף בן גוריון היא יוסיפון אשר הגלה
אותו מירושלים טיטוס בן אספסיאנוס ועל ספר מלכי רומיים וכו׳ ζ וילחם עוד כורש ζ Cap. 18.

Mm ij במלך

Fig. 13.2 *Pugio Fidei*, Leipzig, 1687, p. 275.

Duobus autem modis Iudaei circa textum veritatem impugnant, vel subterfugiunt, vel suam contra eum ingerunt falsitatem, scilicet, vel dicendo non sic haberi in Hebraeo … vel si forte textum concesserint, dicendo non sic debere intelligi, vel exponi. Auctoritates igitur istas, cum Dei auxilio, verbum ex verbo transferam, et concordias quandoque atque verborum expositionem rabinorum suorum ponam interius, vel exterius, in margine contra primum. Contra secundum vero, collegi in Talmud, et ex aliis libris authenticis apud eos, quaedam dicta magistrorum suorum antiquorum inducentium vel exponentium auctoritates huiusmodi … quae quidem, vel interseram, vel in margine ponam, eadem similiter verbum ex verbo sicut expressius fieri poterit transferendo.

> [There are two ways that the Jews impugn the accuracy of a text, either by using subterfuge or by introducing their own false ideas against it, namely, by saying that it is not thus in Hebrew ... or if they concede the text (is thus), by saying that it should not be understood or explained thus. With the help of God, therefore, I will translate these authorities word for word, and, against the first (point), I will sometimes put the commentary on the words of their Rabbis within (my text) or outside it in the margin. Against the second (point), I have collected from the Talmud and from other books held to be authentic among them certain sayings of their ancient teachers who adduce or expound authorities of this type ... like these which I will intersperse (in the body of the text) or put in the margin, translating them, word for word to the degree possible, in like manner ...] (1:54)

It is striking that Martini explicitly addresses his use not only of translation and placement of the citations (and transliterated passages) but also of the original, transcribed language of his sources. As he says, the language itself, not the understanding of the polemicist who cites it, is an effective response to the counter-arguments of Jews in debate. To counter such alleged Jewish "tricks" ("dolos"), "optimum erit si istud opusculum non solum in Latino, sed etiam in Hebraeo, et scientia legendi, etsi non intelligendi Hebraicum habeatur" ["It will be best if this treatise (be written) not only in Latin, but also in Hebrew, and that one have the knowledge of reading Hebrew, even if he cannot understand it"] (1:56). Martini thus specifically addresses the role of original language in his polemical argumentation, noting that it is a specific technique for responding to Jewish ripostes to Christian arguments. He here not only names his post-biblical sources as *auctoritates* and specifies that they come *ex libris authenticis apud eos*; he also specifically addresses the problem posed by their "authentic" perspective of doubt by advocating for both careful, literal ("word-for-word") translations and he recognizes for the first time in his writing the importance of original languages. His distinction between the ability to "read" and "understand" Hebrew—that is, between knowing how to read a citation out loud and knowing what that citation actually says—points to his increasing belief that the cited authorities themselves—and their authentic form as transcribed by him in the original languages—are more important for a polemical argument than the interpretation or commentary of the polemicist. Just as the evolution of his own textual practice suggests, Martini understood polemical conflict to be as much a war of words—including their sounds and shapes—as one of arguments and ideas.

The *Capistrum* is not, however, written in Hebrew, but in Latin, and shows that Martini clearly felt the need to continue developing his approach in the *Pugio* by supplanting transliteration with full transcription of original texts. In the prologue to the work, he specifically addresses the need for even more precise translations:

> Caeterum inducendo authoritatem textus ubicumque ab Hebraico fuerit desumptum, non septuaginta sequar, nec interpretem alium; et quod maioris praesumptionis videbitur, non ipsum etiam in hoc reverebor Hieronymum, nec tolerabilem linguae Latinae vitabo improprietatem, ut eorum quae apud Hebraeos

> sunt, ex verbo in verbum, quotiescumque servari hoc poterit,[28] transferam veritatem. Per hoc enim Iudaeis falsiloquis lata valde spatiosaque subterfugiendi praecludetur via; et minime poterunt dicere, non sic haberi apud eos.
> [Furthermore, in bringing forth the authority of the text, whenever the Hebrew text will be taken up, I will not follow the Septuagint or any other (translation). What will seem even more presumptuous, I will not revere Jerome in this, nor will I avoid the improper use, within tolerable limits, of the Latin language, so that, as often as possible, I will translate the truth, word for word, of those (passages) found in the Hebrew. In this way, the wide and spacious way of subterfuge is precluded to the false-speaking Jews. Hardly will they be able to say that (the text) is not thus among them.] (4)

Although his biblical citations in Latin do show constant intersection with the Latin Vulgate, they do not, as the text itself implies, adhere only to it. In fact, it regularly deviates in syntax and word order, seemingly in an effort to better render the original Hebrew text.[29] As Martini's remarks in both the *Capistrum* and the *Pugio* make manifest, Martini came to see the original language of his proof texts as the most effective response to dissenting arguments in polemical debates with Jews. Although his statements do not prove that Martini's primary focus was, as Chazan and others have affirmed, on "missionizing" rather than a kind of inward-looking apologetic writing that posits an imaginary Jewish reader or listener in purely formulaic terms,[30] nevertheless, his focus is increasingly on what he describes as "apud eos authenticus," "authentic among them" (*Pugio* 2, and see also 510, 808, and 859), a virtue interpreted not only in terms of content but also in terms of form.[31] This focus is in line with the trajectory of use of his source

---

[28] Consultation with the earliest manuscripts and consideration of the sense of this passage has led me to emend the Leipzig edition to read "poterit" not "potuit." See also the abbreviation in Adriano Cappelli, *Lexicon abbreviaturarum: Dizionario di abbreviature latine ed italiane* (Milan, 1979), p. 283, and the marginal note in *Pugio*, p. 4.

[29] To get an accurate sense of Martini's use of the Vulgate, one must avoid comparison with the seventeenth-century editions, which seem to insert changes back into the text, and instead compare directly with the Sainte-Geneviève manuscript. To give just one example of a change by Martini, we can quote Martini's citation of Proverbs 23:29, which begins, "Who has woe? Who has sorrow?" [*Le-mi ʿoi, le-mi ʿavoi*, which might be freely translated as "Who has 'alas'? Who has 'alack'?"]. Many medieval Latin versions interpret *ʿavoi* as a conflation of *ʿav* [father] and *ʿoi*, and thus mistranslate this verse as "cui vae cuius patri vae" ["To whom woe? To whose father woe?"]. Martini avoids this distorted reading, translating the text more carefully as "Cui vae cui heu" ["Who has 'woe'? Who has 'oh'?"]. See Sainte-Geneviève MS 1405, f. 8r and cf. Leipzig ed. *Pugio*, p. 199.

[30] Chazan, p. 115.

[31] On the question of Martini's commitment to "missionizing," see Harvey Hames, "Reason and Faith: Inter-Religious Polemic and Christian Identity in the Thirteenth Century," in Yossef Schwartz and Volkhard Krec (eds), *Religious Apologetics—Philosophical Argumentation* (Tübingen, 2004), pp. 267–84; and the recent critique of Vose. For a discussion of the passages cited above, see Cohen, *Living Letters*, pp. 343–4.

material over the course of his career, and his increasing use of transliteration as a supplement to mere translation, and then of transcription as a supplement to transliteration, can be understood within this context.

Martini's evolution from rough translation to translation interspersed with transliteration to full transcription led him to make a number of difficult choices about the meaning of "authentic" language in the *Pugio.* For example, although the bulk of Martini's citations in the *Pugio* are from Hebrew sources—considering the Bible alone, Martini cites the New Testament around 150 times, but cites the Hebrew Bible more than 2,300 times—nevertheless, he includes a few citations from the New Testament in which he includes both the Latin Vulgate and a Hebrew translation.[32] Even more curious are Martini's Arabic citations of the Qur'ān in the *Pugio.* In the anti-Muslim polemics of the twelfth and thirteenth centuries, including Martini's own *Explanatio* and *De Seta,* it was commonplace to point to Muslim beliefs concerning Jesus and Mary in arguments against Islam. In the growth of anti-Jewish writing starting at the end of the thirteenth century, this attack on Muslim ideas took a strange turn and became, for a short period, part of an appeal to Islamic sources as support for Christian arguments made against Jews. The result is that in Martini's *Pugio,* there appear in parts 2 and 3—the anti-Jewish sections of the text—a handful of citations of the Qur'ān and *ḥadīth* traditions concerning Jesus and Mary. Although these had been previously cited in the *De Seta* against Islam, they are here given as pro-Christian authorities against the Jews.[33] In the citations in part 2 (*Pugio*, pp. 365–6; cf. Sainte-Geneviève MS 1405, f. 65v), he gives only the Latin translation. In the citations in part 3 of the text, however, he gives both the Latin translations and the Arabic original. Even more curiously, in part 3 he does not give these Arabic citations—the only Arabic citations, apart from a single Judeo-Arabic citation from Maimonides (*Pugio* 565), in his entire corpus of writing—in Arabic script, but transliterates them into

[32] The examples I have found in the Leipzig edition of the *Pugio* include pp. 772, 776, 818, and 825 (also in the manuscript sources), two more examples in the Paris edition, and I have found three other examples in the manuscripts not in either print edition, e.g., Sainte-Geneviève MS 1405, ff. 281r, 282v, and 300r, Coimbra MS 720, ff. 230r (seen in Figure 13.3), 231r, and 242v, and Salamanca, Biblioteca Universitaria MS 2352, ff. 216v, 217v, 231r (partly corresponding to Latin passages on 749 and 751 of the print edition). For a full study of these Hebrew citations, see Ryan Szpiech, "The Aura of an Alphabet: Interpreting the Hebrew Gospels in Ramon Martí's *Dagger of Faith* (1278)" (forthcoming). On the differences between the Sainte-Geneviève manuscript and the Leipzig print edition, see Ch. Merchavia, "The Hebrew Version of the 'Pugio Fidei' in the Sainte-Geneviève Manuscript," [Hebrew] *Kiryat Sefer* 51 (1976): 283–8.

[33] Martini repeats a citation used in the *De Seta* from Qur'ān 3:42: "Item quod dixit in Alcorano, in tractatu Abram, quod Deus preelegit et sanctificavit et preelegit beatam mariam super mulieres seculorum" ["Also it says in the Qur'ān, in the book Abraham, that God chose and sanctified and chose the blessed Mary above the women of the world"] (*De Seta*, 24 and cf. *Pugio*, 750).

Hebrew characters with Tiberian vocalization.[34] Folio 230r from Coimbra, Biblioteca Geral da Universidade, MS 720, one of three medieval manuscripts containing an example of both the Hebrew translation of the New Testament (Lk. 1:47–8) as well as the transliteration of the Qur'ān into Hebrew characters (but lacking the vocalization), is reproduced in Figure 13.3 (p. 186).

What sense can we make of these two final examples of translation and transliteration, especially in light of our argument that Martini's language use reflects his polemical strategy of establishing the authority of his text through his appeal to authenticity? From a literal perspective, neither the Hebrew translations of the New Testament nor the Arabic passages from the Qur'ān transliterated into Hebrew characters represents the most "original" or "authentic" forms of these texts. Nevertheless, both examples do provide examples of Martini's philosophy of language in the context of his polemical project. In marshaling Arabic authorities against Jews, he chose to give them not in the form most authentic to Muslims, but in that form in which an Arabic-speaking Jew might approach the Qur'ān. Similarly, in offering citations of the New Testament, he conceded more authority to his citations as *auctoritates* by putting them on par with those Hebrew proof texts "authentic among them." At the same time, the transliteration of the Qur'ān into Hebrew characters might represent an attempt to approximate (in legible, Hebrew letters) a phonetic rendering of the text as it might sound when read aloud. The presence of what look like pronunciation marks in the Sainte-Geneviève manuscript (the *atnaḥ*, *meteg*, and the *sof pasuq*, for example) in both the Hebrew Gospels passages and in the Qur'ān in Hebrew characters offers further support to this interpretation. Equally notable is that Martini even includes some of the original Arabic text—the same text already given in Hebrew characters on the right side of the folio—in *transliterated* form within the Latin translation on the left side, further suggesting the importance of representing the sound of the original text, even within the translation itself.[35]

[34] The vocalization is not present in Coimbra MS 720, but is only present in Sainte-Geneviève MS 1405 and in the initial lines of Salamanca, Biblioteca Universitaria MS 2352. Despite the fact that the Arabic text in Hebrew characters is found in these three manuscript sources as well as the print edition, it has gone virtually undetected by scholars of Martini's work. It should be noted that these passages do not constitute an example of what is commonly termed "Judeo-Arabic"—a Middle Arabic register or dialect, usually written in Hebrew characters, particular to Jews—but rather represent a case of Classical (Qur'ānic) Arabic transliterated into Hebrew letters. For an edition, translation, and study of both the Arabic citations and the Latin translation, as well as the Latin citations given in part 2 of the *Pugio*, see Szpiech, "Citas árabes."

[35] The transliterated section, not reproduced in the printed editions but present in various manuscripts, reads "erat ipsa *min alqanitín* id est de illis quae amant silencium" ["She (i.e., Mary) was *min al-qānitīn*, that is, from among those who love silence"]. See Sainte-Geneviève MS 1405, f. 281v, Coimbra MS 720, f. 230v, and Salamanca, Biblioteca Universitaria MS 2352, f. 217r.

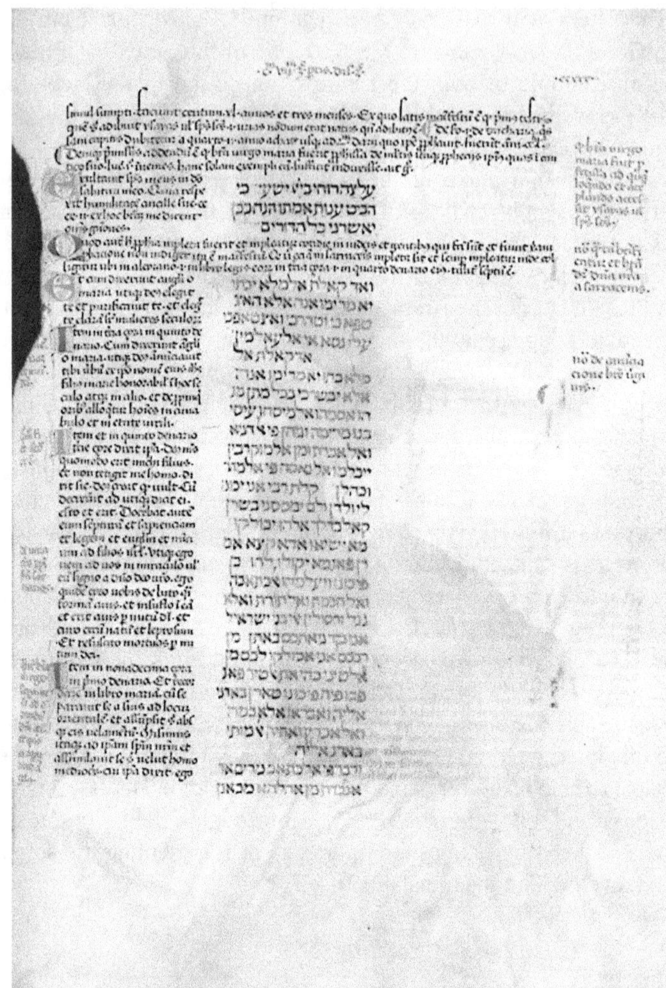

Fig. 13.3 Coimbra, Biblioteca Geral da Universidade, MS 720, f. 230r. (Reproduced by permission of the Biblioteca Geral de Universidade, Coimbra.)

As with these peculiar citations of the Qur'ān in Hebrew characters and the New Testament in Hebrew translation, so his citations throughout the *Pugio* are guided by a conception of authenticity that is represented not as an abstract linguistic display, but as an *experience* of an imagined Jewish interlocutor of original Scriptures in seemingly "original" scripts. In his translations, he displays his mastery of the original text. In his transliterations into Latin script, he tries to make the sounds of the original available to Christian readers who might read them aloud to Jews, even if they do not understand them. In his transcriptions, he puts the text itself on display as a proof in service of his Christian polemical argument. In his translation of Latin into Hebrew and his transliteration of Arabic text into Hebrew characters, he does not only proffer the imagined knowledge of his polemical enemy. By giving these non-Jewish authorities a Hebrew garb, a form that is implicitly non-Christian but still comprehensible, he also aims to approximate the imagined perspective of the imagined Jewish enemy by simulating the authority of an "original" (in this case, non-Latin) text.

These examples offer, on the one hand, an additional way to think about David Damrosch's concept of "Scriptworlds," which he defines as "the power of scripts to cross the boundaries of time, space, and language itself."[36] In this case, script also has the power to evoke identity, and in the context of supersessionist polemic, the invocation of a script constitutes the means for the hijacking of a whole Scripture, and the alphabet itself begins to take the place of the imagined Hermeneutical Jew (or Muslim) as a new theological witness to the historical triumph of Christianity. On the other hand, these two examples evince Martini's response to a dilemma plaguing his own work and in essence troubling that of the entire Christian movement of appropriation and exploitation of original language sources in the twelfth to the fourteenth centuries: within the medieval Jewish-Christian logomachy over *auctoritas*, the quest for the polemical authority in authenticity required interpretive choices about what authenticity meant, about whether it was to be seen as an absolute, objective rule of translation or a phenomenal, subjective effect of presentation. By making his evocation of authenticity dependent on the ambiguities of translation, Martini begins to ground his entire polemical edifice on a perpetually unsteady foundation, one that makes language, like religious identity premised on abrogative supersession, seem unstable and ultimately untranslatable. Over the trajectory of the evolution of his use of language and translation, transliteration, and transcription, Martini became increasingly aware that, in the zero-sum game of religious polemic, "no plague is more effective at damaging" than a failure to marshal the necessary *auctoritas* and control its potentially undermining ambiguity.

[36] David Damrosch, "Scriptworlds: Writing Systems and the Formation of World Literature," *MLQ* 68 (2007): 196–219 at 218–19.

Bibliography

Abbattouny, Mohammed, Jürgen Renn, and Paul Weinig, "Transmission and Transformation: The Translation Movements in the Medieval East and West in Comparative Perspective," *Science in Context* 14.1 (2001): 1–12.

Ahern, John, "Singing the Book: Orality in the Reception of Dante's *Comedy*," in Amilcare A. Iannucci (ed.), *Dante: Contemporary Perspectives* (Toronto: University of Toronto Press, 1997), pp. 214–39.

Al-As ma'ī, Abū Sa'īd 'Abd al-Malik, *Kitāb al-nabāt wa 'l-shajar,* in Louis Cheikho and August Haffner (eds), *Dix traités de philologie arabe* (Beirut: Imprimerie Catholique, 1914), pp. 17–62.

Alexakis, A., *Codex Parisinus Graecus 1115 and Its Archetype*, Dumbarton Oaks Studies 34 (Washington, DC: Dumbarton Oaks Research Library and Collection, 1996).

Al-Idrīsī, Muhammad, *Compendium of the Properties of Diverse Plants and Various Kinds of Simple Drugs* (Mörlenbach: Institute for the History of Arabic-Islamic Science at the Johann Wolfgang Goethe University, 1995).

———, *The Entertainment of Hearts and Meadows of Contemplation* (Stuttgart: Institute for the History of Arabic-Islamic Science at the Johann Wolfgang Goethe University, 1984).

Alighieri, Dante, *La Commedia secondo l'antica vulgata*, ed. Giorgio Petrocchi, Società Dantesca Italiana, Edizione Nazionale (4 vols, Milan: Arnoldo Mondadori Editore, 1966–1967).

———, *Convivio*, ed. Maria Simonelli (Bologna: R. Pàtron, 1966).

———, *Dante's* "Il Convivio" ("The Banquet"), trans. Richard H. Lansing (New York: Garland, 1990).

———, *Dante's Inferno*, trans. Tom Phillips (New York: Thames and Hudson, 1985).

———, *The Divine Comedy: Inferno, Purgatorio, Paradiso: Italian Text and Translation, Commentary*, trans. Charles S. Singleton (6 vols, Princeton: Princeton University Press, 1970, 1973, 1975).

———, *The Inferno of Dante: A New Verse Translation*, trans. Robert Pinsky (New York: Farrar, Straus and Giroux, 1994).

———, *L'Ottimo Commento della Divina Commedia*, ed. Alessandro Torri (3 vols, Pisa: N Capurro, 1827–1829).

———, *Purgatorio: A New Verse Translation* by W.S. Merwin (New York: Knopf, 2000).

——— (attrib.), *The Fiore and the Detto d'Amore: A Late 13th-Century Italian Translation of the Roman de la Rose, Attributable to Dante Alighieri*, trans. Christopher Kleinhenz and Santa Casciani (Notre Dame: University of Notre Dame Press, 2000).

Al-Shaka', Mustafā, Al-Maghrib wa –'l-andalus: afāq islāmiyya, wa hadāra insāniyya, wa mabāh ith adabiyya (Beirut: Dar Al-Kutub al-Islamiyya, 1407/1987).

The Anglo-Norman Dictionary, Aberstwyth University and Swansea University, August 14, 2012, <http://www.anglo-norman/net/>.

Die Apokalypse des Pseudo-Methodius. Die ältesten griechischen und lateinischen Übersetzungen, ed. W.J. Aerts and G.A.A. Kortekaas, Corpus scriptorium Christianorum Orientalium 569–70, Corpus scriptorium Christianorum Orientalium. Subsidia 97–8 (2 vols, Leuven: Peeters, 1998).

Ascoli, Albert, *Dante and the Making of a Modern Author* (Cambridge: Cambridge University Press, 2008).

Augustine of Hippo, *Sermones ad Scripturam* 117, Patrologia cursus completus ... series Latina [Patrologia Latina] 38, ed. Jacques-Paul Migne (Paris: Migne, 1844), cols. 666–7.

Avril, François and Jean Lafaurie (eds), *La Librairie de Charles V* (Paris: Bibliothèque nationale, 1968).

Baldini, Rossella, "Zucchero Bencivenni, 'La santà del corpo.' Volgarizzamento del 'Régime du corps' di Aldobrandino da Siena (a. 1310) nella copia coeva di Lapo di Neri Corsini (Laur. Pl. LXXIII 47)," *Studi di lessicografia italiana* 15 (1998): 21–300.

Barblan, Giovanni (ed.), *Dante e la bibbia* (Florence: Olschki, 1988).

Barrett, Robert W., "Leeks for Livery: Consuming Welsh Difference in the Chester *Shepherds' Play*," in Catherine A.M. Clarke (ed.), *Mapping the Medieval City: Space, Place, and Identity in Chester, c. 1200–1600* (Cardiff: University of Wales Press, 2011), pp. 184–200.

Batt, Catherine, "'De celle mordure vient la mort dure': Perspectives on Puns and their Translation in Henry, Duke of Lancaster's *Le Livre de Seyntz Medicines*," in Jacqueline Jenkins and Olivier Bertrand (eds), [*8th International Conference on the Theory and Practice of Translation in the Middle Ages*], The Medieval Translator/Traduire au Moyen Âge 10 (Turnhout: Brepols, 2007), pp. 405–17.

Beaune, Colette, *The Birth of an Ideology: Myths and Symbols of Nation in Late-Medieval France*, trans. Susan Ross Huston (Berkeley: University of California Press, 1991).

Beckwith, Sarah, *Signifying God: Social Relation and Symbolic Act in the York Corpus Christi Plays* (Chicago: University of Chicago Press, 2001).

Bedos-Rezak, Brigitte Miriam, "Les juifs et l'écrit dans la mentalité eschatologique du Moyen Âge chrétien occidental (France 1000–1200)," *Annales. Histoire, Sciences Sociales* 49 (1994): 1049–63.

Beer, Jeanette, *A Medieval Caesar* (Geneva: Librairie Droz, 1976).

——— (ed.), *Medieval Translators and their Craft* (Kalamazoo: Western Michigan University Medieval Institute Publications, 1989).

——— (ed.), *Translation Theory and Practice in the Middle Ages* (Kalamazoo: Western Michigan University Medieval Institute Publications, 1997).

——— and Kenneth Lloyd-Jones (eds), *Translation and the Transmission of Culture between 1300 and 1600* (Kalamazoo: Western Michigan University Medieval Institute Publications, 1995).

Bénéteau, David P., "Per un'edizione critica dei 'Fatti dei Romani,'" *Italianistica* 26 (1997): 401–11.

Beowulf: A New Verse Translation, trans. R.M. Liuzza (Peterborough, Ontario: Broadview Press, 2000).

Berschin, Walter, *Greek Letters and the Latin Middle Ages. From Jerome to Nicholas of Cusa,* rev. and expanded edition, trans. Jerold C. Frakes (Washington, DC: Catholic University of America Press, 1988).

Bibliothèque nationale de France, Gallica, Paris, BnF, MS naf 4338, *Recueil de traités de dévotion en prose et en vers: Legiloque* ..., August 14, 2012, <http://gallica.bnf.fr/ark:/12148/btv1b84557917>.

Billanovich, Giuseppe, "Il Boccaccio, il Petrarca e le più antiche traduzioni in italiano delle decadi di Tito Livio," *Giornale storico della letteratura italiana* 130 (1953): 311–37.

Binski, Paul, *Medieval Death: Ritual and Representation* (Ithaca: Cornell University Press, 1996).

Bischoff, Bernhard, *Manuscripts and Libraries in the Age of Charlemagne*, trans. M. Gorman (Cambridge: Cambridge University Press, 1994).

Blaise, Albert, *Dictionnaire latin-français des auteurs chrétiens* (Turnhout, Belgium: Brepols, 1954).

———, *Dictionnaire latin-français des auteurs du moyen-âge*, Corpus Christianorum: Continuatio mediaevalis (Turnhout, Belgium: Brepols, 1975).

Bobichon, Philippe, "La 'bibliothèque' de Raymond Martin au couvent Sainte-Catherine de Barcelone: sources antiques et chrétiennes du *Pugio fidei* (ca. 1278)" (forthcoming).

Boccaccio, Giovanni, *De Casibus virorum illustrium*, in *Tutte le opere di Giovanni Boccaccio*, ed. Vittore Branca (9 vols, Milan: Mandadori, 1964–1998), vol. 9.

———, *Genealogie deorum gentilium libri*, ed. Vincenzo Romano (2 vols, Bari: G. Laterza, 1951).

St. Bonaventure of Bagnoregio, *Opera Omnia S. Bonaventurae*, vol. 1 Commentaria in Quatuor Libros Sententiarum Magistri Petri Lombardi (Ad Claras Aquas [Quaracchi]: Collegium, 1882).

Bresc, Henri and Annliese Nef, *Idrîsî: la première géographie de l'Occident* (Paris: Groupe Flammarion, 1999).

Brieger, Peter, "Pictorial Commentaries to the *Commedia*," in Peter Brieger, Millard Meiss, and Charles S. Singleton (eds), *Illuminated Manuscripts of the Divine Comedy* (2 vols, Princeton: Princeton University Press, 1969).

Buridant, Claude, "*Translatio medievalis*: Théorie et pratique de la traduction médiévale," in *Travaux de linguistique et de littérature XXI* (Strasbourg: le Centre de Philologie et de Littératures Romanes de l'Université de Strasbourg, 1983), pp. 81–136.

Burman, Thomas, *Reading the Qur'ān in Latin Christendom, 1140–1560* (Philadelphia: University of Pennsylvania Press, 2007).

Burnley, J.D., "Late medieval English translation: types and reflections," in Roger Ellis (ed.), assisted by Jocelyn Price [Wogan-Browne], Stephen Medcalf, and Peter Meredith, *The Medieval Translator: The Theory and Practice of Translation in the Middle Ages*, papers read at a conference held 20–23 August 1987 at the University of Wales Conference Centre, Gregynog Hall (Cambridge: D.S. Brewer, 1989), pp. 37–53.

Butterfield, Ardis, *The Familiar Enemy: Chaucer, Language and Nation in the Hundred Years War* (Oxford: University Press, 2009).

Cappelli, Adriano, *Lexicon abbreviaturarum: Dizionario di abbreviature latine ed italiane*, 6th ed. (1967; repr. Milan: Ulrico Hoepli Editore, 1979).

Cassell, Anthony K., *Dante's Fearful Art of Justice* (Toronto: University of Toronto Press, 1984).

Casella, Maria Teresa, *Tra Boccaccio e Petrarca. I volgarizzamenti di Tito Livio e di Valerio Massimo* (Padua: Antenore, 1982).

Cavedoni, Celestino, *Raffronti tra gli autori biblici e sacri e la Divina commedia* (Città di Castello: S. Lapi Tipografo-Editore, 1896).

Caviness, Madeleine, "Anchoress, Abbess, and Queen: Donors and Patrons or Intercessors and Matrons?" in June Hall McCash (ed.), *The Cultural Patronage of Medieval Women* (Athens: University of Georgia Press, 1996).

Center for Medieval Studies, Fordham University, *The French of England*, August 14, 2012, <http://www.fordham.edu/french_of_england/>.

———, *The French of Italy*, August 14, 2012, <http://www.fordham.edu/frenchofitaly/>.

Chamberlain, Lori, "Gender and the Metaphorics of Translation," *Signs* 13.3 (1988): 454–72.

Chaucer, Geoffrey, *The Legend of Good Women*, in Larry D. Benson (gen. ed.), *The Riverside Chaucer*, 3rd ed. (Oxford: Oxford University Press, 2008), pp. 587–630.

———, *Lenvoy de Chaucer a Bukton*, in Larry D. Benson (gen. ed.), *The Riverside Chaucer*, 3rd ed. (Oxford: Oxford University Press, 2008), pp. 655–6.

Chazan, Robert, *Daggers of Faith: Thirteenth-Century Missionizing and Jewish Response* (Berkeley: University of California Press, 1989).

Chenu, M.-D., "Auctor, Actor, Autor," *Bulletin du Cange: Archivum Latinitatis Medii Aevi* 2 (1927): 81–6.

———, *Toward Understanding St. Thomas*, trans. A.-M. Landry and D. Hugues (Chicago: Regnery, 1964).

Cheshire including Chester, Records of Early English Drama, ed. Elizabeth Baldwin, Lawrence M. Clopper, and David Mills (2 vols, Toronto: British Library and University of Toronto Press, 2007).

The Chester Mystery Cycle, ed. R.M. Lumiansky and David Mills, Early English Text Society s.s. 3 and 6 (2 vols, London: Oxford University Press, 1974, 1986).

Chiamenti, Massimiliano, *Dante Alighieri traduttore* (Florence: Le Lettere, 1995).

Chiesa, Paolo, "Traduzioni e traduttori a Roma nell'alto medioevo," in *Roma fra Oriente e Occidente*, Settimane di Studi del Centro Italiano di Studi sull'Alto Medioevo 49 (Spoleto: Centro italiano di studi sull'alto medioevo, 2002), pp. 455–92.

Chung-Apley, Jane Geein, "The Illustrated 'Vie et Miracles de Saint Louis' of Guillaume de Saint-Pathus (Paris, B.N., Ms. fr. 5716)," PhD dissertation, University of Michigan, 1998.

Ćirković, Sima M., *The Serbs* (Malden, MA: Wiley-Blackwell, 2004).

Clemence of Barking, *The Life of St. Catherine*, ed. William MacBain, Anglo-Norman Text Society18 (Oxford: B. Blackwell, 1964).

Clopper, Lawrence, "History and Development of the Chester Cycle," *Modern Philology* 75 (1978): 219–46.

Clopper, Lawrence M., *Drama, Play, and Game: English Festive Culture in the Medieval and Early Modern Period* (Chicago: University of Chicago Press, 2001).

———, "Lay and Clerical Impact on Civic Religious Drama and Ceremony," in Marianne G. Briscoe and John C. Coldewey (eds), *Contexts for Early English Drama* (Bloomington: Indiana University Press, 1989), pp. 102–36.

———, "The Principle of Selection of the Chester Old Testament Plays," *Chaucer Review* 13 (1979): 272–83.

Cohen, Jeremy, "The *Capistrum Iudeorum* of Raymundus Martini [Hebrew]," in Ezra Fleischer et al. (eds), *Me'ah Še'arim: Studies in Medieval Jewish Spiritual Life in Memory of Isadore Twersky* (Jerusalem: The Hebrew University Magnes Press, 2001), pp. 279–96.

———, *The Friars and the Jews: The Evolution of Medieval Anti-Judaism* (Ithaca: Cornell University Press, 1982).

———, *Living Letters of the Law. Ideas of the Jew in Medieval Christianity* (Berkeley: University of California Press, 1999).

Coletti, Theresa, "The Chester Cycle in Sixteenth-Century Religious Culture," *Journal of Medieval and Early Modern Studies* 37 (2007): 531–47.

Coll, José María, "Escuelas de Lenguas Orientales en los siglos XIII y XIV," *Analecta Sacra Tarraconensia* 17 (1944): 115–38; 18 (1945): 59–89; 19 (1946): 217–40.

Cornish, Alison, *Vernacular Translation in Dante's Italy: Illiterate Literature* (Cambridge: Cambridge University Press, 2011).

Corriente, Federico, *El léxico árabe andalusí según el "Vocabulista in Arabico"* (Madrid: Universidad Complutense, 1989).

———, "Notas de lexicología hispanoárabe. I. Nuevos romancismos en Aben Quzmán y crítica de los propuestos. II. Los romancismos del 'Vocabulista in Arabico': addenda et corrigenda," *Vox Romanica* 39 (1980): 183–210.

———, "Notas de lexicología hispanoárabe. III. Los romancismos del Vocabulista. IV. Nuevos berberismos del hispanoárabe," *Awrāq* 4 (1981): 5–30.

Cressy, David, "God's Time, Rome's Time, and the English Protestant Regime," *Viator* 34 (2003): 392–406.

———, “The Protestant Calendar and the Vocabulary of Celebration in Early Modern England,” *Journal of British Studies* 29 (1990): 31–52.

Cunningham, Gilbert F., *The Divine Comedy in English: A Critical Bibliography*, 2 vols, 1: *1782–1900*; 2: *1901–1966* (New York: Barnes and Noble, 1965–1967).

Curtius, Ernst Robert, *Europäische Literatur und lateinisches Mittelalter* (Bern: Francke, 1948).

———, *European Literature and the Latin Middle Ages*, trans. Willard R. Trask (1953; repr. Princeton: Princeton University Press, 1990, with new Afterword by Peter Godman).

Da Imola, Benvenuto, *Comentum super Dantis Aldhigerij Comoediam*, ed. W.W. Vernon and G.F. Lacaita (5 vols, Florence: Barbera, 1887).

Dahan, Gilbert, *Les intellectuels chrétiens et les juifs au Moyen Âge* (Paris: Cerf, 1990).

Damrosch, David, “Scriptworlds: Writing Systems and the Formation of World Literature,” *MLQ* 68 (2007): 195–219.

Dartmouth Dante Project, August 14, 2012, <http://dante.dartmouth.edu>.

Database of Latin Dictionaries, August 14, 2012, <http://www.brepolis.net> (Turnhout, Belgium: Brepols, 2005–).

Davidson, Clifford, *Festivals and Plays in Late Medieval Britain* (Aldershot: Ashgate, 2007).

Delisle, Léopold, “Notice sur un recueil de traités de dévotion ayant appartenu à Charles V,” *Bibliothèque de l’École des Chartes* 6ème sér. 5 (1869): 532–42.

Derrida, Jacques, *On Hospitality*, trans. Rachel Bowlby (Stanford: Stanford University Press, 2000).

Deyermond, Alan D., “*La historia de la linda Melosina*: Two Spanish Versions of a French Romance,” in Alan D. Deyermond (ed.), *Medieval Hispanic Studies Presented to Rita Hamilton* (London: Tamesis, 1976): pp. 57–65.

Dictionnaire du moyen français (1350–1500), DMF2012, August 14, 2012, <http://www.atilf.fr/dmf/>.

Dondaine, A., “Contra Errores Graecorum: Premiers écrits polémiques des dominicains d’Orient,” *Archivium Fratrum Praedicatorum* 21 (1951): 320–446.

Dronke, Peter, “The Return of Eurydice,” *Classica et Mediaevalia* 23 (1962): 198–215.

Du Cange, Charles du Fresne, *Glossarium mediae et infimae latinitatis* (10 vols, Niort: L. Favre, 1883–1887).

Dubler, César, “Los Nombres Arabes de Matéria Medica en la Obra del Doctor Laguna,” *Al-Andalus* 16 (1951): 142–8.

Duffy, Eamon, *The Stripping of the Altars: Traditional Religion in England 1400–1580* (New Haven: Yale University Press, 1992).

Dujčev, I. and M.A. Salmina, *Srednebolgarskii perevod khroniki Konstantina Manassii v slavianskikh literaturakh* (Sofia: Bolgarskoi Akademii Nauk, 1988).

Dwyer, Richard A., “Arthur’s Stellification in the *Fall of Princes*,” *Philological Quarterly* 57 (1978): 155–71.

Ebin, Lois A., *John Lydgate*, Twayne's English Authors Series 407 (Boston: Twayne, 1985).

Eco, Umberto, *Experiences in Translation*, trans. Alistair McEwen (Toronto: University of Toronto Press, 2001).

Edwards, William and Brian Merrilees (eds), *Dictionarius familiaris et compendiosus: le dictionnaire latin-français de Guillaume Le Talleur*, Corpus Christianorum: Continuatio mediaevalis, Lexica Latina Medii Aevii: Nouveau Recueil des lexiques latins-français du moyen âge 3 (Turnhout: Brepols, 2002).

——— (eds), *Dictionarius Firminis Verris: Dictionnaire latin-français de Firmin Le Ver*, Corpus Christianorum: Continuatio mediaevalis, Lexica Latina Medii Aevii: Nouveau Recueil des lexiques latins-français du moyen âge 1 (Turnhout, Belgium: Brepols, 1994).

Ellis, Roger (ed.), *The Oxford History of Literary Translation in English*, vol. 1: *To 1550* (Oxford: Oxford University Press, 2008).

——— (ed.), assisted by Jocelyn Price [Wogan-Browne], Stephen Medcalf, and Peter Meredith, *The Medieval Translator: The Theory and Practice of Translation in the Middle Ages*, papers read at a conference held 20–23 August 1987 at the University of Wales Conference Centre, Gregynog Hall (Cambridge: D.S. Brewer, 1989).

Emmerson, Richard K., "Contextualizing Performance: The Reception of the Chester *Antichrist*," *Journal of Medieval and Early Modern Studies* 29 (1999): 89–119.

Enciclopedia dantesca, 2nd ed. (6 vols, Rome: Istituto dell'Enciclopedia Italiana, 1984).

The Encyclopedia of Islam, ed. H.A.R. Gibb et al. (12 vols, Leiden: Brill, 1986–2004).

English Historical Documents, gen. ed. David C. Douglas, vol. 4: *1327–1485*, ed. A.R. Myers (London: Eyre and Spottiswood, 1969).

Entwistle, William J., *The Arthurian Legend in the Literatures of the Spanish Peninsula* (New York: Kraus Reprint Co., 1975).

Evans, Ruth, "Translating Past Cultures?" in Roger Ellis and Ruth Evans (eds), *The Medieval Translator* 4 (Exeter: University of Exeter Press, 1994), pp. 20–45.

Les Fastes du gothique: Le siècle de Charles V: Galeries nationales du Grand Palais, 9 octobre 1981–1er février 1982 ([Paris]: Ministère de la culture; Éditions de la Réunion des musées nationaux, 1981).

I Fatti di Cesare, ed. Luciano Banchi (Bologna: G. Romagnoli, 1863).

Li Fet des Romains, ed. L.-F. Flutre and K. Sneyders de Vogel (2 vols, Paris: Droz, 1938).

Fitzgerald, Christina M., *The Drama of Masculinity and Medieval English Guild Culture* (New York: Palgrave, 2007).

Fleming, John V., "The Pentecosts of Four Poets," in Robert F. Yeager and Charlotte C. Morse (eds), *Speaking Images: Essays in Honor of V.A. Kolve* (Asheville: Pegasus, 2001), pp. 111–41.

Flutre, Louis-Fernand, *Li Fait des Romains dans les littératures française et italienne du XIIIe au XVIe siècle* (Paris: Hachette, 1932).

Folena, Gianfranco, "*Volgarizzare* e *tradurre*," in *La traduzione: saggi e studi* (Trieste: Edizioni Lint, 1973), pp. 59–120.

Friedman, John Block, "Eurydice, Heurodis and the Noon-Day Demon," *Speculum* 41 (1966): 22–9.

———, *Orpheus in the Middle Ages* (Syracuse: Syracuse University Press, 2000).

Frontón Simón, Miguel Ángel, "*La historia de la Linda Melosina*: edición y estudio de los textos españoles," PhD dissertation, Universidad Complutense de Madrid, 2002.

Gadamer, Hans Georg, *Truth and Method*, 2nd rev. ed., trans. Joel Weinsheimer and Donald G. Marshall (New York: Continuum Publishing Company, 2000).

Gagliardi, Donatella, "*La historia de la linda Melosina*: una o due versioni castigliane del romanzo di Jean d'Arras?" *Medioevo romanzo* 22.1 (1998): 116–41.

Garcías Palou, Sebastián, *El Miramar de Ramon Llull* (Palma de Mallorca: Diputacion Provincial de Baleares, 1977).

Gathercole, Patricia May, "Lydgate's *Fall of Princes* and the French Version of Boccaccio's *De casibus*," in F. Simone (ed.), *Miscellanea di studi e recherche sul Quattrocentro francese* (Turin: Giappichelli, 1967), pp. 165–78.

Geary, Patrick J., *Living with the Dead in the Middle Ages* (Ithaca: Cornell University Press, 1994).

Georgius Monachus, *Georgii Monachi Chronicon*, ed. Carolus de Boor (2 vols, Leipzig: B.G. Teubneri, 1904).

Gerbert of Aurillac, *The Letters of Gerbert, with His Papal Privileges as Sylvester II*, trans. H.P. Lattin (New York: Columbia University Press, 1961).

Giamboni, Bono, *Fiore di Rettorica*, ed. Giambattista Speroni (Pavia: Dipartimento di Scienza della Letteratura e dell'Arte medioevale e moderna, 1994).

Gjuzelev, Vassil, *Bulgarien zwischen Orient und Okzident: Die Grundlagen seiner geistigen Kultur vom 13. bis 15. Jahrhundert* (Vienna: Böhlau, 1993).

Gmelin, Hermann, *Die Göttliche Komödie, Kommentar* (3 vols, Stuttgart: Klett-Cotta, 1954–).

Godefroy, Frédéric, *Dictionnaire de l'ancienne langue française et de tous ses dialectes du IXe au XVe siècle* (10 vols, Paris: F. Vieweg, libraire-éditeur, 1881–1902).

Goldhill, Simon, *Who Needs Greek? Contests in the Cultural History of Hellenism* (Cambridge: Cambridge University Press, 2002).

González de León, Fernando, "Soldados Pláticos and Caballeros: The Social Dimensions of Ethics in the Early Modern Spanish Army," in David J.B. Trim (ed.), *The Chivalric Ethos and the Development of Military Professionalism* (Leiden: Brill, 2003), pp. 235–68.

Gorni, Guglielmo, *Dante prima della Commedia* (Florence: Cadmo, 2001).

Gousset, Marie-Thérèse, "Libraires d'origine normande à Paris au XIVe siècle," in Pierre Bouet and Monique Dosdat (eds), *Manuscrits et enluminures dans le monde normand (Xe–XVe siècles): Colloque de Cerisy-la-Salle (octobre 1995): actes* (Caen: Presses universitaires de Caen, 1999), pp. 169–80.

Gray, Thomas, *Scalacronica 1272–1363*, ed. and trans. Andy King (Woodbridge: Surtees Society, 2005).

Gregory, Stewart, William Rothwell, and David Trotter (eds), *Anglo-Norman Dictionary*, 2nd ed. (2 vols, London: Modern Humanities Research Association, 2005).

Griffin, Clive, *The Crombergers of Seville: The History of a Printing and Merchant Dynasty* (Oxford: Clarendon Press, 1988).

Griffin, David, "Los Mozarabismos del 'Vocabulista' atribuído a Ramón Martí," *Al-Andalus* 23 (1958): 251–338; 24 (1959): 85–124, 333–80; 25 (1960): 93–170.

Groppi, Felicina, *Dante traduttore* (Rome: Herder, 1962).

Gros-Louis, Kenneth R., "Robert Henryson's *Orpheus and Eurydice* and the Orpheus Tradition of the Middle Ages," *Speculum* 41 (1966): 643–55.

Guenée, Bernard, "La culture historique des nobles: Le succès des *Faits des Romains* (xive–xve siècles)," in Philippe Contamine (ed.), *La noblesse au moyen âge, xie–xve siècles: Essais à la mémoire de Robert Boutruche* (Paris: Presses universitaires de France, 1976), pp. 265–7.

Guido de Columnis, *Guido de Columnis'* Historia destructionis Troiae, ed. Nathaniel Edward Griffin, Mediaeval Academy of America Publications 26 (Cambridge, MA: Mediaeval Academy of America, 1936).

Hadj Sadok, Muhammad, *Al-Idrīsī: le maġrib au 6e siècle de l'hégire (12e siècle après J.-C.)* (Paris: Publisud, 1983).

Haigh, Christopher, "The Church of England, Catholics, and the People," in Peter Marshall (ed.), *The Impact of the English Reformation 1500–1640* (London: Arnold, 1997), pp. 235–56.

Hamburger, Jeffrey, "Body vs. Book: The Trope of Visibility in Images of Christian-Jewish Polemic," in David Ganz, Thomas Lentes, and Georg Henkel (eds), *Ästhetik des Unsichtbaren: Bildtheorie und Bildgebrauch in der Vormoderne*, KultBild 1 ([Berlin]: Reimer, 2004), pp. 113–45.

Hames, Harvey, "Reason and Faith: Inter-Religious Polemic and Christian Identity in the Thirteenth Century," in Yossef Schwartz and Volkhard Krec (eds), *Religious Apologetics—Philosophical Argumentation* (Tübingen: Mohr Siebeck e.K., 2004), pp. 267–84.

Harf-Lancner, Laurence, "La serpente et le sanglier: les manuscrits enluminés des deux romans français de Mélusine," *Le Moyen Âge* 101 (1995): 65–87.

———, "L'illustration du *Roman de Mélusine* de Jean d'Arras dans les éditions du XVe et du XVIe siècle," *Le livre et l'image en France au XVIe siècle*, special issue of *Cahiers V.L. Saulnier* 6 (1989): 29–55.

Harty, Kevin J., "The Unity and Structure of *The Chester Mystery Cycle*," in Kevin J. Harty (ed.) *The Chester Mystery Cycle: A Casebook* (New York: Garland Publishing, 1993), pp. 69–88.

Hasselhoff, Görge, "Some Remarks on Raymond Martini's (c. 1215/30–c. 1284/85) Use of Maimonides," *Trumah* 12 (2002): 133–48.

Hawkins, Peter S., *Dante's Testaments: Essays in Scriptural Imagination* (Stanford: Stanford University Press, 1999).

Hedeman, Anne D., "Constructing Memories: Scenes of Conversation and Presentation in Pierre Salmon's *Dialogues*," *Journal of the Walters Art Gallery* 54 (1996): 119–34.

———, "Pierre Salmon's Advice for a King," *Gesta* 32.2 (1993): 113–23.

———, *Translating the Past: Laurent de Premierfait and Boccaccio's De casibus* (Los Angeles: J. Paul Getty, 2008).

Heinzelmann, Martin, *Translationsberichte und andere Quellen des Reliquienkultes*, Typologie des sources du Moyen Age occidental 33 (Turnhout: Brepols, 1979).

Henry, Duke of Lancaster, *Le Livre de Seyntz Medicines*, ed. É.A. Arnould, Anglo-Norman Text Society 2 (Oxford: Blackwell, 1940).

Henryson, Robert, *The Poems of Robert Henryson*, ed. Denton Fox (Oxford: Clarendon Press, 1981).

Hexter, Ralph, "Medieval Articulations of Ovid's Metamorphoses: From Lactantian Segmentation to Arnulfian Allegory," *Mediaevalia* 13 (1987): 63–82.

Higgins, David, *Dante and the Bible: An Introduction* (Bristol: University of Bristol Press, 1992).

Historia de la Linda Melosina: Edition, Study, and Notes, ed. Ivy A. Corfis (Madison: *Hispanic Seminary* of Medieval Studies, 1986).

Hollander, Robert, *Allegory in Dante's "Commedia"* (Princeton: Princeton University Press, 1969).

Hollywood, Amy, "'Beautiful as a Wasp': Angela of Foligno and Georges Bataille," *Harvard Theological Review* 92.2 (1999): 219–36.

Holsinger, Bruce, *Music, Body, and Desire in Medieval Culture: Hildegard of Bingen to Chaucer* (Stanford: Stanford University Press, 2001).

The Holy Bible: Douay Rheims Version, trans. Bishop Richard Challoner (Rockford: Tan Books and Publishers, 2000; repr., rev. ed).

Houven, Herbert, *Roger II of Sicily: A Ruler Between East and West* (Cambridge: Cambridge University Press, 2002).

Humbert of Romans, *Opera de Vita Regulari*, ed. J.J. Berthier (2 vols, Rome: Befani, 1888–1889).

Huot, Sylvia, "A Book Made for a Queen: The Shaping of a Late Medieval Anthology Manuscript (B.N. fr. 24429)," in Siegfried Wenzel (ed.), *The Whole Book: Cultural Perspectives on the Medieval Miscellany*, Recentiores (Ann Arbor: University of Michigan Press, 1996).

———, "Polytextual Reading: The Meditative Reading of Real and Metaphorical Books," in Mark Chinca and Christopher Young (eds), *Orality and Literacy in the Middle Ages: Essays on a Conjunction and its Consequences in Honour of D.H. Green*, Utrecht Studies in Medieval Literacy 12 (Turnhout: Brepols, 2005), pp. 203–22.

———, "The Writer's Mirror: Watriquet de Couvin and the Development of the Author-Centred Book," in Bill Bell, Jonquil Bevan, and Philip Bennet (eds), *Across Boundaries: The Book in Culture & Commerce* (Winchester, Hampshire, UK; New Castle, DE: St. Paul's Bibliographies; Oak Knoll Press, 2000), pp. 29–46.

Ingham, Richard, "Bilingualism and Syntactic Change in Medieval England," *Reading Working Papers in Linguistics* 8 (2005): 1–25.

Jacobs, Angelica (ed.), *Die byzantinische Geschichte bei Joannes Zonaras in slavischer Übersetzung* (Munich: W. Fink, 1970).

Jacobus Mediolanensis, *Stimulus amoris fr. Jacobi Mediolanensis*, Bibliotheca franciscana ascetica medii aevi 4 (Quaracchi: ex typographia Collegii s. Bonaventurae, 1905).

James, Mervyn, "Ritual, Drama, and Social Body in the Late Medieval English Town," *Past and Present* 98 (1983): 3–29.

Jean d'Arras, *L'Histoire de la Belle Mélusine de Jean d'Arras: Reproduction en fac-similé de l'édition de Genève imprimée par A. Steinschaber en 1478*, ed. Wilhelm-Joseph Meyer (Paris: E. Champion, 1924).

———, *Melusine. Nouvelle édition conforme à celle de 1478*, ed. Charles D. Brunet (Paris: P. Jannet, 1854).

———, *Mélusine ou La Noble Histoire de Lusignan*, ed. Jean-Jacques Vincensini (Paris: Librairie générale française, 2003).

Jones, Peter Murray, "Image, Word, and Medicine in the Middle Ages," in Jean A. Givens, Karen M. Reeds, Alain Touwaide (eds), *Visualizing Medieval Medicine and Natural History, 1200–1550* (Aldershot: Ashgate, 2006), pp. 1–24.

Jongkees, A.G., "Translatio Studii: les avatars d'un thème médiéval," in D.P. Blok (ed.), *Miscellanea Mediaevalia in Memoriam Jan Frederik Niermeyer* (Groningen: J.B. Wolters, 1967), pp. 41–51.

Jordan of Saxony, *Acta Capitulorum Generalium Ordinis Praedicatorum ab anno 1220 usque ad annum [1844]*, ed. Benedictus Maria Reichert (Rome: In Domo Generalitia, 1898–1904).

Jullien de Pommerol, M.-H., "La bibliothèque de Boniface VIII," in Giuseppe Lombardi and Donatella Nebbiai dalla Guarda (eds), *Libri, lettori e biblioteche dell'Italia medievale (secoli ix–xv). Fonti, testi, utilizzazione del libro* (Roma: *ICCU/CNRD* Editions, 2000), pp. 487–505.

Julius Caesar, *Bellum Gallicum*, ed. Otto Seel (Leipzig: Teubner, 1968).

Kačanovskij, Vladimir, "Iz srbsko-slovjenskoga prievoda bizantinskoga ljetopisa Joanna Zonare," *Starine* 14 (1882): 125–72.

Kay, Sarah, "Translating Theory," *New Medieval Literatures* 9 (2007): 199–202.

Kennedy, Elspeth, "The Scribe as Editor," in *Mélanges de langue et de littérature du Moyen Age et de la Renaissance offerts à Jean Frappier*, Publications romanes et françaises CXII (Geneva: Droz, 1970), pp. 523–31.

Kennedy, Kevin, "The Permanence of an Idea: Three Ninth-Century Frankish Ecclesiastics and the Authority of the Roman See," in H. Mordek (ed.), *Aus Kirche und Reich: Studien zu Theologie, Politik und Recht im Mittelalter. Festschrift für Friedrich Kempf zu seinem 75. Geburtstag und fünfzigjährigen Doktorjubiläum* (Sigmaringen: Jan Thorbecke Verlag, 1983), pp. 105–16.

King, Pamela, *The York Mystery Cycle and the Worship of the City* (Cambridge: D.S. Brewer, 2006).

Kleinhenz, Christopher, "Dante's Towering Giants: *Inferno* XXXI," *Romance Philology* 27 (1974): 269–85.

———, "The Land of the Living and the Land of the Dead: Burial, Entombment, and Cemeteries in Dante's *Divine Comedy*," *Religion & Literature* 31.1 (1999): 49–59.

———, "On Dante and the Visual Arts," in Teodolinda Barolini and H. Wayne Storey (eds), *Dante and the New Millennium* (New York: Fordham University Press, 2003), pp. 274–92.

———, "The Poetics of Citation: Dante's *Divina Commedia* and the Bible," in Albert N. Mancini, Paolo A. Giordano, and Anthony J. Tamburri (eds), *Italiana 1988: Selected Papers from the Proceedings of the Fifth Annual Conference of the American Association of Teachers of Italian, November 18–20, 1988, Monterey, CA*, Rosary College Italian Studies 4 (River Forest, IL: Rosary College, 1990), pp. 1–21.

Kniga vremennyia i obraznyia Georgiia mnikha: Khronika Georgiia Amartola v drevnem slavianorusskom perevode. Tekst, issledovanie, slovar', ed. Vasilii I. Istrin (3 vols, Petrograd: Izd. otd-niia russkago iazyka i slovesnosti Rossiiskoi Akademii nauk, 1920–1930).

Krämer, Ulrike, *Translatio imperii et studii: zum Geschichts- und Kulturverständnis in der französischen Literatur des Mittelalters und der frühen Neuzeit*, Abhandlungen zur Sprache und Literatur 98 (Bonn: Romanistischer Verlag, 1996).

Krochalis, Jeanne and Ruth J. Dean, "Henry of Lancaster's *Livre de Seyntz Medicines*: New Fragments of an Anglo-Norman Work," *National Library of Wales Journal* 18 (1973–1974): 87–94.

Kumler, Aden, *Translating Truth: Ambitious Images and Religious Knowledge in Late Medieval France and England* (New Haven; London: Yale University Press, 2011).

Lancashire, Ian, "Moses, Elijah and the Back Parts of God: Satiric Scatology in Chaucer's *Summoner's Tale*," *Mosaic* 14 (1981): 17–30.

Laurent de Premierfait, *Laurent de Premierfait's Des Cas des Nobles Hommes et Femmes, Book 1, translated from Boccaccio*, ed. Patricia May Gathercole, Studies in the Romance Languages and Literatures 74 (Chapel Hill: University of North Carolina Press, 1968).

Lavrov, Piotr A., "Iugoslavianskaia peredelka Zonary," *Vizantiiskii vremennik* 3.4 (1897): 452–60.

Legaré, Anne-Marie, "L'Image du livre comme adjuvant mémoriel dans le *Conte des trois chevaliers et des trois livres*," in Frank Willaert, Herman Braet, Thom Mertens, and Theo Venckeleer (eds), *Medieval Memory: Image and Text*, Textes et études du moyen âge 27 (Turnhout: Brepols, 2004), pp. 129–43.

Lerud, Theodore K., *Memory, Images, and the English Corpus Christi Drama* (New York: Palgrave Macmillan, 2008).

Letopista na Konstantin Manasi. Fototipno izdanie na Vatikanskiia prepis na srednobulgarskiia prevod, ed. Ivan Dujčev (Sofia: Bŭlgarska akademiiâ na naukite, 1963).

Levin, Bernard, "Die griechisch-arabische Evangelien-Übersetzung: Vat. Borg. ar. 95 und Ber. orient. oct. 1108," PhD dissertation, University of Uppsala, 1938.

Lewis, Charlton and Charles Short, *A Latin Dictionary*, 1st ed. (Oxford: Clarendon Press, 1879).

Liber de vita Christi ac omnium pontificum, ed. Giacinto Gaida, Rerum italicarum scriptores 3/1 (Città di Castello: S. Lapi, 1932).

Lindemann, Margarete, *Die französischen Wörterbücher von den Anfängen bis 1600: Entstehung und typologische Beschreibung* (Tübingen: Verlag Max Niemeyer, 1994).

———, *Zum Suffixwechsel von "-eresse" zu "-euse" und "-trice" im Französischen* (Tübingen: TBL-Verlag Narr, 1977).

Lucan, *De bello civili*, ed. J.D. Duff, Loeb Classical Library (1928; repr. London: W. Heinemann, 1969).

Lumiansky, R.M. and David Mills (eds), *The Chester Mystery Cycle: Essays and Documents* (Chapel Hill: University of North Carolina Press, 1983).

Lusignan, Serge, *Parler vulgairement: Les intellectuels et la langue française au XIIIe et XIVe siècles*, ed. Pierre Boglioni, 2nd ed., Études médiévales (Montréal: Les Presses de l'Université de Montréal, 1987).

Lydgate, John, *Fall of Princes*, ed. Henry Bergen (4 vols, Washington, DC: Carnegie Institution of Washington, 1923–1927).

———, *Lydgate's Troy Book*, ed. Henry Bergen, Early English Text Society, e.s. 97, 103, 106, 126 (4 vols, London: K. Paul, Trench, Trübner & Co., 1906–1935).

———, *John Lydgate, Troy Book: Selections*, ed. Robert R. Edwards (Kalamazoo: Published for TEAMS in association with the University of Rochester by Medieval Institute Publications, Western Michigan University, 1998).

Macrides, Ruth and Paul Magdalino, "The Fourth Kingdom and the Rhetoric of Hellenism," in Paul Magdalino (ed.), *The Perception of the Past in Twelfth-Century Europe* (London: Hambledon Press, 1992), pp. 117–56.

Maggini, Francesco, *I primi volgarizzamenti dei classici latini* (Florence: Le Monnier, 1952).

Mahoney, Dhira B., "Courtly Presentation and Authorial Self-fashioning: Frontispiece Miniatures in Late Medieval French and English Manuscripts," *Mediaevalia* 21 (1996): 97–160.

Maimonides, Moses, *Dalālat al-Ḥā'irīn*, text established by S. Munk, ed. Issachar Joel (Jerusalem: Magnes, 5691/1930–1931).

———, *Guide of the Perplexed*, trans. Schlomo Pines (Chicago: University of Chicago Press, 1963).

Manasses, Constantine, *Constantini Manassis Breviarium chronicum*, ed. Odysseus Lampsidis (2 vols, Athens: Corpus fontium historiae Byzantinae, 1996).

———, *Die slavische Manasses-Chronik* [1922], ed. Joan Bogdan, German intro. J. Schröpfer (Munich: Fink, 1966).

March, J., "Ramon Martí y la seva *Explanatio simboli Apostolorum*," *Annuari de l'Institut d'Estudis Catalans* (1908): 443–96.

Marchesi, Concetto, "Di alcuni volgarizzamenti toscani in codici fiorentini," *Studi romanzi* 5 (1907): 123–236; repr. in his *Scritti minori di filologia e di letteratura* (3 vols, Florence: Olschki, 1978), vol. 1, pp. 343–432.

Mariani, Andrea, "Traslatare," in *Enciclopedia dantesca*, 2nd ed. (6 vols, Rome: Istituto dell' Enciclopedia Italiana, 1984), vol. 5, p. 699.

Markopoulos, Athanasios, "Sumvolē stē chronologēsē tou Geōrgiou Monachou," *Summeikta* 6 (1985): 223–31.

Marroni, Sergio, *I fatti dei Romani. Saggio di edizione critica di un volgarizzamento fiorentino del Duecento* (Rome: Viella, 2004).

Marshall, Peter, *The Catholic Priesthood and the English Reformation* (Oxford: Clarendon Press, 1994).

Marti, Berthe, "Arnulfus and the *Fets des Romains*," *Modern Language Quarterly* 2 (1941): 3–23.

Martin, Robert, "Le préfixe A-/AD- en moyen français," *Romania* 119 (2001): 289–322.

Martini, Raymond, "De Seta Machometi o De origine, progressu, et fine Machometi et quadruplici reprobatione prophetiae eius," ed. and trans. Josep Hernando i Delgado, *Acta historica et archaeologica medievalia* 4 (1983): 9–51.

———, *Pugio fidei adversus Mauros et Iudaeos* (Paris, 1651; Leipzig: Lenckisch, 1687; Leipzig ed. repr. Farnborough, UK, 1967).

———, *Raimundi Martini Capistrum Iudaeorum*, ed. and trans. Adolfo Robles Sierra (2 vols, Würzburg: Echter Verlag, 1990).

———, *Vocabulista in Arabico, pubblicato per la prima volta supra uno codice de la Biblioteca Riccardiana di Firenze*, ed. Celestino Schiaparelli (Florence: Tip. dei Successori Le Monnier con I carat. Arabi della Stam. Medicea, 1871).

Marzot, Giulio, *Il linguaggio biblico nella Divina Commedia* (Pisa: Nistri-Lischi, 1956).

Massimo, Valerio, *De' fatti e detti degni di memoria della città di Roma e delle stranie genti*, ed. Roberto De Visiani (Bologna: G. Romagnoli, 1867–1868).

Matthew, Donald, *The Norman Kingdom of Sicily* (Cambridge: Cambridge University Press, 1992).

McCracken, Peggy, *The Curse of Eve, the Wound of the Hero* (Philadelphia: University of Pennsylvania Press, 2003).

Medcalf, Stephen, "On Reading Books from a Half-Alien Culture," in Stephen Medcalf (ed.), *The Later Middle Ages* (London: Methuen, 1981), pp. 1–55.

Merchavia, Ch., "The Hebrew Version of the 'Pugio Fidei' in the Sainte-Geneviève Manuscript," *Kiryat Sefer* 51 (1976): 283–8.

———, "Pugio Fidei—An Index of Citations," in *Galut aḥar Golah* (Jerusalem: Mekhon Ben-Tsevi le-ḥeḳer ḳehilot Yiśra'el ba-Mizraḥ, Yad Yitsḥaḳ Ben-Tsevi yeha-Universiṭah ha-'Ivrit bi-Yerushalayim, 1988), pp. 203–34.

Merrilees, Brian, "L'apport des lexiques bilingues à l'étude de la créativité lexicale en latin médiéval," *Bulletin Du Cange: Archivum Latinitatis Medii Aevi* 63 (2005): 109–17.

———, “Le Mirouer des nouveaulx escoliers: l’*Aalma* du manuscrit Paris, BnF lat. 14748,” in Yvan Lepage and Christian Milat (eds), *Por s’onor croistre. Mélanges de langue et de littérature médiévales offerts à Pierre Kunstmann* (Ottawa: Éditions David, 2008), pp. 131–40.

———, “Translation and Definition in the Medieval Bilingual Dictionary,” in Jeanette Beer (ed.), *Translation Theory and Practice in the Middle Ages* (Kalamazoo: Western Michigan University, Medieval Institute Publications, 1997), pp. 199–214.

Merrilees, Brian and Jacques Monfrin (eds), *Glossarium Gallico-Latinum: le Glossaire français-latin du ms. Paris lat. 7684*, Corpus Christianorum: Continuatio mediaevalis, Lexica Latina Medii Aevii: Nouveau Recueil des lexiques latins-français du moyen âge 2 (Turnhout: Brepols, 1998), pp. 141–269.

Meyer-Lee, Robert, “Lydgate’s Laureate Pose,” in Larry Scanlon and James Simpson (eds), *John Lydgate: Poetry, Culture and Lancastrian England* (Notre Dame: University of Notre Dame Press, 2006), pp. 36–60.

Meyerhof, Max, “Esquisse d’histoire de la pharmacologie et botanique chez les Musulmans d’Espagne,” *Al-Andalus* 3 (1935), 1–41.

The Middle English Dictionary, August 14, 2012, <http://quod.lib.umich.edu/m/med>.

Mills, David, *Recycling the Cycle: The City of Chester and Its Whitsun Plays* (Toronto: University of Toronto Press), 1998.

———, “Some Theological Issues in Chester’s Plays,” in David N. Klausner and Karen Sawyer Marsalek (eds), *“Bring furth the pagants”: Essays in Early English Drama Presented to Alexandra F. Johnston* (Toronto: University of Toronto Press, 2007), pp. 212–29.

Minnis, Alastair J., *Medieval Theory of Authorship*, 2nd ed. (Philadelphia: University of Pennsylvania Press, 1988).

——— (ed.), *Late-Medieval Religious Texts and Their Transmission: Essays in Honour of A.I. Doyle* (Cambridge: D.S. Brewer, 1994).

Mirour de Seinte Eglyse, ed. A.D. Wilshere, Anglo-Norman Text Society 40 (London: Anglo-Norman Text Society, 1982).

Moore, Edward, *Studies in Dante, First Series: Scripture and Classical Authors in Dante* (Oxford: Clarendon Press, 1896).

Mortimer, Nigel, *John Lydgate’s Fall of Princes: Narrative Tragedy in Its Literary and Political Contexts* (Oxford: Oxford University Press, 2005).

Niccoli, Alessandro, “Trasmutare (Transmutare, Tramutare),” *Enciclopedia dantesca*, 2nd ed. (6 vols, Rome: Istituto dell’ Enciclopedia Italiana, 1984), vol. 5, pp. 699–700.

Noble, Thomas F.X., “The Declining Knowledge of Greek in Eighth- and Ninth-Century Papal Rome,” *Byzantinische Zeitschrift* 78 (1985): 56–62.

———, “The Intellectual Culture of the Early Medieval Papacy,” in *Roma nel’alto Medioevo*, Settimane di Studi del Centro Italiano di Studi sull’ Alto Medioevo 48 (2 vols, Spoleto: Centro italiano di studi sull’alto medioevo, 2001), vol. 1, pp. 179–213.

Nolan, Maura, "'Now wo, now gladnesse': Ovidianism in the *Fall of Princes*," *ELH* 71.3 (2004): 531–58.

Okubo, Masami, "Le rossignol et le mystère de Jésus-Christ. A propos d'un poème inédit: Le livret du rossignolet," *Reinardus: Yearbook of the International Reynard Society/Annuaire de la Société internationale renardienne* 4 (1991): 137–46.

———, "Le rossignol sur la croix: une figure du rossignol-Christ dans la poésie médiévale," *Reinardus: Yearbook of the International Reynard Society/ Annuaire de la Société internationale renardienne* 6 (1993): 81–93.

Olson, Glending, "The End of *The Summoner's Tale* and the Uses of Pentecost," *Studies in the Age of Chaucer* 21 (1999): 209–45.

Omont, Henri, *Bibliothèque Nationale: Catalogue général des manuscrits français*, vol. 2 (Paris, E. Leroux, 1900).

Ormrod, Mark, "The Use of English: Language, Law, and Political Culture in Fourteenth-Century England," *Speculum* 78 (2003): 750–87.

Ovid, *Ovid's Metamorphoses, Books 1–5*, ed. William S. Anderson (Norman: University of Oklahoma Press, 1997).

Papi, A. Benvenuti, "Corsini, Neri," in Alberto M. Ghisalberti (ed.), *Dizionario biografico degli italiani*, vol. 29 (Rome: Istituto della Enciclopedia Italiana, 1983), pp. 647–9.

Papini, Gianni A., "I Fatti dei Romani," *Studi di filologia italiana* 31 (1973): 97–155.

Pappano, Margaret, and Nicole Rice, "'Beginning and Beginning-Again': Processions, Plays, and Civic Politics in York and Chester," *Studies in the Age of Chaucer* 30 (2008): 269–301.

Paravicini Bagliani, A., "Le bibliotheche curiali duecentesche," in Giuseppe Lombardi and Donatella Nebbiai dalla Guarda (eds), *Libri, lettori e biblioteche dell'Italia medievale (secoli ix–xv). Fonti, testi, utilizzazione del libro* (Roma: *ICCU/CNRD* Editions, 2000), pp. 263–75.

———, *Medicina e scienze della natura alla corte dei Papi nel Duecento* (Spoleto: Centro Italiano di Studi sull'Alto Medioevo, 1991).

Parodi, Ernesto G., "Le storie di Cesare nella letteratura italiana dei primi secoli," *Studi di Filologia Romanza* 4 (1889): 237–501.

Passerini, Luigi, *Genealogia e storia della famiglia Corsini* (Florence: Tipi di M. Cellini e c., 1858).

Patterson, Lee, "The Logic of Textual Criticism and the Way of Genius: The Kane-Donaldson Piers Plowman in Historical Perspective," in Jerome J. McGann (ed.), *Textual Criticism and Literary Interpretation* (Chicago: University of Chicago Press, 1985), pp. 55–91; repr. in Lee Patterson, *Negotiating the Past: The Historical Understanding of Medieval Literature* (Madison: University of Wisconsin Press, 1987), pp. 77–113.

Pearsall, Derek, "Authorial Revision in Some Late-Medieval English Texts," in A.J. Minnis and Charlotte Brewer (eds), *Crux and Controversy in Middle English Textual Criticism* (Cambridge: Boydell and Brewer, 1992), pp. 39–48.

———, *John Lydgate* (Charlottesville: University Press of Virginia, 1970).

———, *John Lydgate (1371–1449): A Bio-Bibliography* (Victoria, BC, Canada: University of Victoria, 1997).

Perkinson, Stephen, *The Likeness of the King: A Prehistory of Portraiture in Late Medieval France* (Chicago: University of Chicago Press, 2009).

Petrucci, Armando, "Reading and Writing *Volgare* in Medieval Italy," in Armando Petrucci, *Writers and Readers in Medieval Italy. Studies in the History of Written Culture*, ed. and trans. Charles M. Radding (New Haven: Yale University Press, 1995), pp. 169–235.

Pietrobono, Luigi, *Il Poema sacro* (2 vols, Bologna: University of Michigan Library, 1915).

Podskalsky, Gerhard, *Byzantinische Reichseschatologie. Die Periodisierung der Weltgeschichte in den vier Grossreichen (Daniel 2 und 7) und dem Tausendjährigen Friedensreiche (Apok. 20). Eine Motivgeschichtliche Untersuchung* (Munich: de Gruyter, 1972).

Polain, M.-Louis, *Catalogue des livres imprimés au quinzième siècle des Bibliothèques de Belgique* (4 vols, Brussels: Société des Bibliophiles et Iconophiles de Belgique, 1932).

Pollock, Sheldon, "Cosmopolitan and Vernacular in History," *Public Culture* 12.3 (2000): 591–625.

Pound, Ezra, *Make It New* (London: Faber and Faber, 1934).

Price, B.B., "Patronage of Science," in Thomas F. Glick, Steven J. Livesey, and Faith Wallis (eds), *Medieval Science, Technology and Medicine: An Encyclopedia* (London: Routledge, 2005), p. 386.

Ragacs, Ursula, "Mit Zaum und Zügel muss man irh Ungestürm bändigen." Ps 32, 9: Ein Beitrag zur christlichen Hebraistik und antijüdischen Polemik im Mittelalter (Frankfurt am Main; New York: P. Lang, 1997).

Rashed, Marwan, "Nicolas d'Otrante, Guillaume de Moerbeke et la 'Collection Philosophique,'" *Studi medievali* 43 (2002): 693–717.

Raymond of Peñafort, *Summa de Paenitentia*, ed. Xaverio Ochoa and Aloisio Diez (Rome: Commentarium pro religiosis, 1976).

Renevey, Denis and Christiania Whitehead (eds), *Lost in Translation?*, The Medieval Translator / Traduire au Moyen Âge 12 (Turnhout: Brepols, 2009).

Renoir, Alain, *The Poetry of John Lydgate* (Cambridge, MA: Harvard University Press, 1967).

Ricoeur, Paul, *On Translation*, trans. Eileen Brennan, intro. Richard Kearney (London: Taylor and Francis, 2006).

———, *Sur la traduction* (Paris: Bayard, 2004).

Rigo, Paola, *Memoria classica e memoria biblica in Dante* (Florence: Olschki, 1994).

Rivera, Isidro J., "*The Historia de la linda Melosina* and the Construction of Romance in Late Medieval Castile," *MLN* 112.2 (1997): 131–46.

Rizzo, Silvia, *Ricerche sul latino umanistico* (Rome: Edizioni di storia e letteratura, 2002).

Rodríguez Velasco, Jesús D., *El Debate sobre la caballería en el siglo XV: la tractadística caballeresca en su marco europeo* (Salamanca: Junta de Castilla y León, Consejería de Educación y Cultura, 1996).

Rogers, William Elford, *Interpretation in Piers Plowman* (Washington, DC: Catholic University of America Press, 2002).

Roglieri, Maria Ann, *Dante and Music: Musical Adaptations of the "Commedia" from the Sixteenth Century to the Present* (Aldershot: Ashgate, 2001).

Romero Tobar, Leonardo, "Ediciones en castellano de la *Melusina* de Jean d'Arras," in *Homenaje a Justo García Morales: miscellánea de estudios con motivo de su jubilación*, ed. Francisco Javier Aguirre González De Durana (Madrid: Anabad, 1987), pp. 1005–20.

Roques, Mario, *Recueil général des lexiques français du Moyen Age (XIIe–XVe siècle) I: Lexiques alphabétiques*, Tome I (Paris: Honoré Champion, 1936).

Rosendale, Timothy, "'Fiery toungues': Language, Liturgy, and the Paradox of the English Reformation," *Renaissance Quarterly* 54 (2001): 1142–64.

Rothwell, William, "Henry of Lancaster and Geoffrey Chaucer: Anglo-French and Middle English in Fourteenth-Century England," *Modern Language Review* 99 (2004): 313–27.

Roubaud-Bénichou, Sylvia, *Le roman de chevalerie en Espagne: entre Arthur et Don Quichotte* (Paris: Champion, 2000).

Rouse, Mary and Richard Rouse, "French Literature and the Counts of Saint-Pol ca. 1178–1377," *Viator* 41.1 (2010): 101–40.

Rouse, Richard, "Mahiet, the Illuminator of Cambridge University Library, MS Dd.5.5," in Stella Panayotova (ed.), *The Cambridge Illuminations: The Conference Papers* (London: Harvey Miller Publishers, 2007), pp. 173–86.

Rouse, Richard H. and Mary A. Rouse, *Manuscripts and Their Makers: Commercial Book Producers in Medieval Paris, 1200–1500*: *Illiterati et uxorati* (2 vols, Turnhout: Harvey Miller, 2000).

———, "*Ordinatio* and *Compilatio* Revisited," in Mark D. Jordan and Kent Emery, Jr. (eds), *Ad Litteram: Authoritative Texts and Their Medieval Readers* (Notre Dame: Notre Dame University Press, 1992), pp. 113–34.

Rufinus of Aquileia, *Tyrannii Rufini Opera*, ed. Manlio Simonetti, Corpus Christianorum Series Latina 20 (Turnhout: Brepols, 1961).

Rydén, Lennart, "The Andreas Salo Apocalypse: Greek Text, Translation, and Commentary," *Dumbarton Oaks Papers* 28 (1974): 197–261.

Rytting, Jenny Rebecca, "*Pearl* and the Translation of Scriptural Paraphrase," in Rosalynn Voaden, René Tixier, Teresa Sanchez Roura, and Jenny Rebecca Rytting (eds), *The Theory and Practice of Translation in the Middle Ages*, The Medieval Translator / Traduire au Moyen Age 8 (Turnhout: Brepols, 2003), pp. 281–93.

Sacchetti, Franco, *Il Trecentonovelle*, ed. Antonio Lanza (Florence: Sansoni, 1984).

Salter, Elizabeth and Derek Pearsall, "Pictorial illustration of late medieval poetic texts: the role of the frontispiece or prefatory picture," in Flemming Gotthelf Andersen (ed.), *Medieval Iconography and Narrative: A Symposium* (Odense: Odense University Press, 1980), pp. 100–123.

Sandler, Lucy Freeman, "The Image of the Book-Owner in the Fourteenth Century: Three Cases of Self-definition," in Nicholas Rogers (ed.), *England in the Fourteenth Century: Proceedings of the 1991 Harlaxton Symposium*, Harlaxton Medieval Studies 3 (Stamford, UK: Paul Watkins, 1993).

———, "The Images of Words in English Gothic Psalters," in Brendan Cassidy and Rosemary Muir Wright (eds), *Studies in the Illustration of the Psalter* (Stamford, UK: Shaun Tyas, 2000), pp. 67–86.

Schirmer, Walter F., *John Lydgate: A Study in the Culture of the XVth Century*, trans. Ann E. Keep (London: Methuen & Co., 1961).

Schneider, Jakob Hans Josef, "Das Wort idiota im mittelalterlichen Latein," in Elisabeth Charlotte Welskopf (ed.), *Untersuchungen ausgewählter altgriechischer sozialer Typenbegriffe und ihr Fortleben in Antike und Mittelalter* (Berlin: Akademie-Verlag, 1981), pp. 132–57.

The Seven Psalms: A Commentary on the Penitential Psalms, translated from the French into English by Dame Eleanor Hull, ed. Alexandra Barratt, Early English Text Society, o.s. 307 (Oxford: Published for the Early English Text Society by the Oxford University Press, 1995).

Shakespeare, William, *King Lear*, ed. Jay H. Halio (Cambridge: Cambridge University Press, 1992).

Shapiro, Alan, "Translation as Hospitality," *Literary Imagination* 12 (2010): 140–50.

Sharrer, Harvey L., *A Critical Bibliography of Spanish Arthurian Material* (London: Grant and Cutler, 1977).

Shatzmiller, Joseph (ed.), *La deuxième controverse de Paris: un chapitre dans la polémique entre chrétiens et juifs au Moyen Âge* (Paris: E. Peeters, 1994).

Short, Ian, *Manual of Anglo-Norman* (London: Anglo-Norman Text Society, 2007).

Singleton, Charles S., *Dante's Commedia: Elements of Structure*, Dante Studies 1 (Cambridge, MA: Harvard University Press, 1954).

———, *Journey to Beatrice*, Dante Studies 2 (Cambridge, MA: Harvard University Press, 1958).

———, "In Exitu Israel de Aegypto," *Seventy-Eighth Annual Report of the Dante Society* (1960): pp. 1–24.

Sir Gowther, in *The Middle English Breton Lays*, ed. Anne Laskaya and Eve Salisbury (Kalamazoo: Medieval Institute Publications, 1995), pp. 274–307.

Sir Orfeo, in *Middle English Romances: Authoritative Texts, Sources and Backgrounds, Criticism*, ed. Stephen H.A. Shepherd (New York: W.W. Norton, 1995).

Slavianskii perevod Khroniki Simeona Logofeta [1905], ed. V.I. Sreznevskii (London: Variorum Reprints, 1971).

Smith, Kathryn A., "Book, Body, and the Construction of the Self in the Taymouth Hours," in Katherine Allen Smith and Scott Wells (eds), *Negotiating Community and Difference in Medieval Europe: Gender, Power, Patronage, and the Authority of Religion in Latin Christendom*, Studies in the History of Christian Traditions 142 (Leiden: Brill, 2009).

Sneyders de Vogel, K., "Les Vers dans *Les Faits des Romains*," *Mélanges de philologie offerts à Jean-Jacques Salverda de Grave* (Groningen: Société Anonyme d'Éditions J.B. Wolters, 1933).

Sponsler, Claire, *Drama and Resistance: Bodies, Goods, and Theatricality in Late Medieval England* (Minneapolis: University of Minnesota Press, 1997).

Staccioli, Giuliano, "Sul ms. Hamilton 67 di Berlino e sul volgarizzamento della 'IVa Catilinaria' in esso contenuto," *Studi di filologia italiana* 42 (1984): 27–58.

Staley, Lynn, *Languages of Power in the Age of Richard II* (University Park: Pennsylvania State University Press, 2005).

———, *Margery Kempe's Dissenting Fictions* (University Park: Pennsylvania State University Press, 1994).

Stanton, Robert, "Linguistic Fragmentation and Redemption before King Alfred," *Yearbook of English Studies* 36 (2006): 12–26.

Steel, Carlos, "Guillaume de Moerbeke et Saint Thomas," in J. Brams and W. Vanhamel (eds), *Guillaume de Moerbeke: recueil d'études à l'occasion du 700e anniversaire de sa mort (1286)* (Leuven: Leuven University Press, 1989), pp. 57–82.

Stein, Robert, "Multilingualism," in Paul Strohm (ed.), *Oxford Twenty-First Century Approaches to Literature: Middle English* (Oxford: Oxford University Press, 2007).

Stevenson, Jill, "Sensual Bodies and Devotional Encounters: The Influence of Performance on Lay Visual Piety in Late Medieval York," PhD dissertation, City University of New York, 2006.

Sticca, Sandro, "Traduttore/Traditore: Convertere, Vertere, Transferre, Interpretari and Leonardo Bruni's De Interpretatione Recta," *Mediaevalia* 26.2 (2005): 7–36.

Stone, Louise and William Rothwell (eds), *Anglo-Norman Dictionary*, 1st ed. (London: Modern Humanities Research Association, 1977–1992).

Strohm, Paul (ed.), *Oxford Twenty-First Century Approaches to Literature: Middle English* (Oxford: Oxford University Press, 2007).

Suetonius, *De Vita Caesarum Libri VIII*, I.45, ed. M. Ihm (2 vols, 1908; repr. Stuttgart: Teubner, 1978), vol. 1, p. 23.

Summit, Jennifer, *Memory's Library: Medieval Books in Early Modern England* (Chicago: University of Chicago Press, 2008).

Symeon the Logothete, *Symeonis Magistri et Logothetae Chronicon*, ed. Staffan Wahlgren (2 vols, Berlin: Walter de Gruyter, 2006).

Szittya, Penn R., "The Friar as False Apostle: Antifraternal Exegesis and the *Summoner's Tale*," *Studies in Philology* 71 (1974): 19–46.

Szpiech, Ryan, "The Aura of an Alphabet: Interpreting the Hebrew Gospels in Ramon Martí's *Dagger of Faith* (1278)" (forthcoming).

———, "Citas árabes en caracteres hebreos en el *Pugio fidei* del dominico Ramón Martí: entre la autenticidad y la autoridad," *Al-Qanṭara: Revista de Estudios Árabes* 32.1 (2011): 71–107.

———, *Conversion and Narrative: Reading and Religious Authority in Medieval Polemic* (Philadelphia: University of Pennsylvania Press, 2013).

Tanturli, Giuliano, "Volgarizzamenti e ricostruzione dell'antico. I casi della terza e quarta Deca di Livio e di Valerio Massimo, la parte del Boccaccio (a proposito di un'attribuzione)," *Studi medievali* 27 (1986): 811–88.

Tavormina, M. Teresa, "Henry of Lancaster: *The Book of Holy Medicines*," in Anne Clark Bartlett and Thomas H. Bestul (eds), *Cultures of Piety: Medieval English Devotional Literature in Translation* (Ithaca: Cornell University Press, 1999), pp. 19–40.

Taylor, Andrew, "Reading the Body in *Le Livre de Seyntz Medecines*," *Essays in Medieval Studies* 11 (1994): 103–18.

Tobler, Adolf, Erhard Lommatzsch and Hans Helmut Christmann (eds), *Altfranzösisches Wörterbuch: Adolf Toblers Nachgelassene Materialen* (12 vols, Berlin: Weidmannsche; Wiesbaden: F. Steiner, 1925–2002).

Travis, Peter W., *Dramatic Design in the Chester Cycle* (Chicago: University of Chicago Press, 1982).

———, "The Social Body of the Dramatic Christ in Medieval England," in Albert H. Tricomi (ed.), *Early Drama to 1600*, Acta 13 (Binghamton: Center for Medieval and Early Renaissance Studies, 1985), pp. 17–36.

A Tretis of Discrescyon of Spirites, in *The Cloud of Unknowing and Related Treatises*, ed. Phyllis Hodgson (Salzburg: Catholic Records Press, 1982), pp. 147–53.

Uguccinone da Pisa, *Derivationes / Uguccione da Pisa: Edizione Critica Princeps*, ed. Enzo Cecchini and Arbizzoni Guido et al., Edizione nazionale dei testi mediolatini 11, Edizione nazionale dei testi mediolatini serie I 6 (Tavarnuzze, Florence: SISMEL edizioni del Galuzzo, 2004).

Van der Velden, Hugo, *The Donor's Image: Gerard Loyet and the Votive Portraits of Charles the Bold*, Burgundica 2 (Turnhout: Brepols, 2000).

Venuti, Lawrence, *The Translator's Invisibility: A History of Translation* (London: Routledge, 2008).

Vircillo-Franklin, Carmela, *The Latin Dossier of Anastasius the Persian: Hagiographic Translations and Transformations* (Toronto: Pontifical Institute of Medieval Studies, 2004).

Virgil, *Aeneid*, trans. H. Rushton Fairclough (Cambridge, MA: Harvard University Press, 1967).

Virgin Lives and Holy Deaths: Two Exemplary Biographies for Anglo-Norman Women, ed. and trans. Jocelyn Wogan-Browne and Glyn S. Burgess (London: Phoenix, 1996).

Un volgarizzamento inedito di Valerio Massimo, ed. Vanna Lippi Bigazzi (Florence: Accademia della Crusca, 1996).

Vose, Robin, *Dominicans, Muslims, and Jews in the Medieval Crown of Aragon* (Cambridge: Cambridge University Press, 2009).

Vossler, Karl, *Mediaeval Culture: An Introduction to Dante and His Times* (2 vols, New York: Ungar, 1958).

Wallace, David, "Problematics of European Literary History, 1348–1400," in Indira Ghose and Denis Renevey (eds), *The Construction of Textual Identity in Medieval and Early Modern Literature* (Tübingen: Gunter Narr, 2009), pp. 38–109.

——— (ed.), *Europe: A Literary History, 1348-1418*, August 14, 2012, <http://www.english.upenn.edu/~dwallace/regeneration/>.

Warren, Michelle R., "Translating in the Zone," *New Medieval Literatures* 9 (2007): 191–8.

Wartburg, Walther von, *Französisches Etymologisches Wörterbuch: Eine Darstellung des galloromanischen Sprachschatzes* (Bonn: Klopp, 1928–).

Watson, Nicholas, "Censorship and Cultural Change in Late Medieval England: Vernacular Theology, the Oxford Translation Debate, and Arundel's Constitutions of 1409," *Speculum* 70 (1995): 822–64.

———, "Outdoing Chaucer: Lydgate's *Troy Book* and Henryson's *Testament of Cresseid* as Competitive Imitations of *Troilus and Criseyde*," in Karen Pratt (ed.), *Shifts and Transpositions in Medieval Narrative: A Festschrift for Dr. Elspeth Kennedy* (Woodbridge: Boydell and Brewer, 1994), pp. 89–108.

Weinberger, Eliot, *Anonymous Sources: A Talk on Translators and Translation*, Encuentros 39 (Washington, DC: Inter-American Development Bank, 2000).

Weiss, Robert, *Medieval and Humanist Greek* (Padova: Editrice Antenore, 1977).

Wenzel, Siegfried, *Macaronic Sermons: Bilingualism and Preaching in Late-Medieval England* (Ann Arbor: University of Michigan Press, 1994).

Wilkins, Ernest Hatch, "Dante and the Mosaics in His Bel San Giovanni," in *The Invention of the Sonnet and Other Studies in Italian Literature* (Rome: Edizioni di Storia e Letteratura, 1959), pp. 51–60.

Williams, Deanne, *The French Fetish from Chaucer to Shakespeare* (Cambridge: Cambridge University Press, 2004).

Wogan-Browne, Jocelyn (ed.), with Carolyn Collette, Maryanne Kowaleski, Linne Mooney, Ad Putter, and David Trotter, *Language and Culture in Medieval Britain: The French of England c.1100–c.1500* (Woodbridge: Boydell and Brewer, 2009).

Woolf, Rosemary, *The English Mystery Plays* (Berkeley: University of California Press, 1972).

Yeager, Robert F., *John Gower's Poetic: The Search for a New Arion*, Publications of the John Gower Society 2 (Cambridge: Brewer, 1990).

Zampieri, Adriana, "Una primitiva redazione del volgarizzamento di Valerio Massimo," *Studi sul Boccaccio* 10 (1977–1978): 21–41.

Zetzel, James E.G., *Marginal Scholarship and Textual Deviance: The Commentum Cornuti and the Early Scholia on Persius* (London: Institute of Classical Studies, 2005).

Zieman, Katherine, *Singing the New Song: Literacy and Liturgy in Late Medieval England* (Philadelphia: University of Pennsylvania Press, 2008).

Zonaras, John, *Ioannis Zonarae epitome historiarum*, ed. Ludwig August Dindorf (3 vols, Leipzig, 1868–1875).

———, *Ioannis Zonarae epitomae historiarum libri XVIII*, ed. Moritz Pinder and Theodor Büttner-Wobst (3 vols, Bonn: Weber, 1841–1897).

———, *Paralipomen Zonarin*, ed. Osip Bodianskii (Moscow: Izd. Imp. ob-va Istorīi i Drevnosteĭ Rossīĭskikh, 1847).

Zumthor, Paul, *Essai de poétique médiévale* (Paris: Editions du Seuil, 1972).

Index

For Product Safety Concerns and Information please contact our EU representative GPSR@taylorandfrancis.com
Taylor & Francis Verlag GmbH, Kaufingerstraße 24, 80331 München, Germany

www.ingramcontent.com/pod-product-compliance
Lightning Source LLC
Chambersburg PA
CBHW071523110726
47908CB00003B/935

* 9 7 8 1 1 3 8 1 0 8 1 3 4 *